Rev. James R. Dalele
Mount Mary College
Milwaukee, Wisc.

b. May 17/78

RUDOLF BULTMANN
IN CATHOLIC THOUGHT

RUDOLF BULTMANN
IN
CATHOLIC THOUGHT

Edited by Thomas F. O'Meara, O.P.
and Donald M. Weisser, O.P.

HERDER AND HERDER

1968
HERDER AND HERDER NEW YORK
232 Madison Avenue, New York 10016

Imprimi Potest: Gilbert J. Graham, O.P., Provincial
Nihil obstat: Leo J. Steady, Censor Librorum
Imprimatur: ✠ Robert F. Joyce, Bishop of Burlington
July 19, 1968

CONTENTS

6

A PREFATORY LETTER
FROM RUDOLF BULTMANN

I was most interested to learn about your collection of essays treating my theology.

It greatly pleases me that my theological work has contributed to an authentic fraternal discussion, animating a fruitful exchange of views between Catholic and Protestant theologians. I greet the publication of this collection of essays as a sign that a deep and true community exists between Catholic and Protestant theologians. This community looks beyond every difference and beyond reciprocal criticism, and it forms the necessary foundation for genuine dialogue.

Please accept my best wishes for your work.

Very sincerely yours,
Rudolf Bultmann

ABBREVIATIONS

The Writings of Rudolf Bultmann:

EF	*Existence and Faith.* Translated by S. Ogden. New York, Meridian, 1960.
EPT	*Essays, Philosophical and Theological.* Translated by J. C. Greig. New York, Macmillan, 1955.
FC	*Form Criticism.* Translated by F. C. Grant. New York, Harper and Row, 1962.
GV, I II III	*Glauben und Verstehen.* Tübingen, Mohr, 1933, 1952, 1960.
HE	*History and Eschatology.* New York, Harper Torchbooks, 1962.
HST	*The History of the Synoptic Tradition.* Translated by John Marsh. New York, Harper and Row, 1963.
J	*Das Evangelium des Johannes.* Göttingen, Vandenhoeck und Ruprecht, 1950.
JCM	*Jesus Christ and Mythology.* New York, Charles Scribner's Sons, 1958 (Scribner Library paperback).
JW	*Jesus and the Word.* Translated by Louise Pettibone Smith and Erminie Huntress Lan-

	tero. New York, Charles Scribner's Sons, 1958 (Scribner Library paperback).
NTM	"New Testament and Mythology," in *Kerygma and Myth* (*KM,* I). Edited by Hans Werner Bartsch. New York, Harper Torchbooks, 1961.
PC	*Primitive Christianity in its Contemporary Setting.* Translated by R. H. Fuller. New York, Meridian Books, 1956.
TNT, I II	*Theology of the New Testament.* Translated by Kendrick Grobel. New York, Charles Scribner's Sons, 1951, 1955.
TWB	*This World and the Beyond.* Translated by J. Knight. New York, Charles Scribner's Sons, 1960.

Other Abbreviations Used in this Book:

BT	*Being and Time.* By Martin Heidegger. Translated by John Macquarrie and Edward Robinson. New York, Harper and Row, 1962.
BZ (NF)	*Biblische Zeitschrift* (Neue Folge).
CBQ	*Catholic Biblical Quarterly.*
DBS	*Dictionnaire de la Bible, Supplément.* Paris, Letouzey, 1928 ff.
KM, I II	*Kerygma and Myth.* Edited by Hans Werner Bartsch. Translation and revised edition by R. H. Fuller. Volume I: New York, Harper Torchbooks, 1961; Volume II: London, SPCK, 1962.
KuM, I–VI, 2	*Kerygma und Mythos.* Edited by Hans Werner Bartsch. Hamburg, Herbert Reich, Evangelischer Verlag, 1948–1964.

10

LThK   *Lexikon für Theologie und Kirche* (2nd ed.).
            Edited by Josef Hofer and Karl Rahner. Frei-
            burg, Herder, 1957 ff.

RB   *Revue Biblique.*

RGG   *Religion in Geschichte und Gegenwart* (3rd
            ed.). Edited by H. von Campenhausen, *et al.*
            Tübingen, J. C. B. Mohr (Paul Siebeck),
            1957 ff.

RSR   *Recherches de sciences religieuses.*

TS   *Theological Studies.*

TWNT   *Theologisches Wörterbuch zum Neuen Testa-
            ment.* Edited by G. Kittel. Stuttgart, Kohlham-
            mer, 1932 ff.

ZThK   *Zeitschrift für Theologie und Kirche.*

A complete bibliography of Rudolf Bultmann's writings from
1903–1965 may be found in Charles Kegley, ed., *The Theology
of Rudolf Bultmann* (New York, Harper and Row, 1966), pp.
289–310. The best bibliography of books and articles on Bultmann, together with analytic comment, is found in Günther
Bornkamm, "Die Theologie Rudolf Bultmanns in der neueren
Diskussion," *Theologische Rundschau* (NF), 28 (1963), pp.
33–141.

CONTRIBUTORS AND
ACKNOWLEDGMENTS

JOSEF BLANK is a member of the Seminar for New Testament Studies at the University of Würzburg, Germany, and author of *Krisis,* a study in Johannine theology (1964).

JEAN DANIÉLOU, S.J., is professor at the Institut Catholique in Paris and the author of many studies in biblical and patristic theology. His essay is translated from *KuM,* VI, 1, pp. 39–44.

HEINRICH FRIES, for many years a leader in German ecumenism, is professor at the University of Munich and director of the Ecumenical Institute there. His books in English include *Aspects of the Church* and *Bultmann, Barth and Catholic Theology.* "Entmythologisierung und theologische Wahrheit" is translated and adapted from *Gott in Welt: Festgabe für Karl Rahner,* ed. J. B. Metz, *et al.* (Freiburg, Herder, 1964), I, pp. 366–391.

CLAUDE GEFFRÉ, O.P., is regent of studies for the Dominicans of the Paris province and professor of theology at Le Saulchoir.

GOTTHOLD HASENHÜTTL is associated with Professor Hans Küng in the Ecumenical Institute of the University of Tübingen.

JOHN L. MCKENZIE, S.J., author of numerous studies on the Bible, *Authority in the Church* (1966) and *Dictionary of the*

Bible (1965), is professor of New Testament at the University of Notre Dame.

RENÉ MARLÉ, S.J., author of the important *Introduction to Hermeneutics* (1967), is professor at the Institut Catholique in Paris. "Bultmann et l'Ancien Testament" is translated from *Nouvelle revue théologique*, 78 (1956), pp. 473–486.

THOMAS F. O'MEARA, O.P., author of *Mary in Protestant and Catholic Theology* (1966), is professor at the Aquinas Institute, Association of Theological Faculties, in Iowa.

HELMUT PEUKERT is preparing to qualify for a chair of theology at a German university. His doctoral thesis was on Martin Heidegger.

RUDOLF SCHNACKENBERG is professor of New Testament exegesis at the University of Würzburg. "Zur formgeschichtlichen Methode in der Evangelienforschung" is translated from *Zeitschrift für katholische Theologie*, 85 (1963), 16–32.

DONALD M. WEISSER, O.P., is a member of the Center for Studies in Religious Education, Oak Park, Illinois.

14

INTRODUCTION

By the Editors

It has become commonplace to say that the Roman Catholic Church rediscovered history at the Second Vatican Council. We can go further and say that it also perceived a new man, man-in-history. It saw that God had entered history with his word to Israel and with his Word, Jesus Christ, and that this Word was for men and their assemblies, their *ecclesias,* realized again and again in changing history.

Keryma and theology, preaching and liturgy, Church and man, are within history. There must be a constant correlation of the message given to the Church with today's hearers of this word. Without compromising the fact that Jesus Christ has come, but listening more carefully to the Spirit, and in open and free exchange with society and culture, the Church finds itself recognizing history and historicity again and again.

Part of a new appreciation of time and space, history and culture, is dialogue with important theologians, among whom Rudolf Bultmann is an eminent figure. No doubt, there are Roman Catholic theologians who question some of Bultmann's principles in interpreting the existence of Jesus of Nazareth on earth and the proclamation of those events in the Gospels. Still, Catholicism's acceptance of the movement towards unity, of the ecclesial nature and authentic traditions of other Christian communities, of the valued role of their observers at the Council—

15

these are the foundation for a positive study by Catholic theologians of this important exegete and theologian. Significantly, Paul Tillich in one of his last discussions linked Bultmann with Catholic theology after Vatican II.

The center of [theological] interest is now Bultmann and the whole problem of historical criticism, which in itself is a widening of the religious point of view. Allow me to add a much greater and more important example, namely, the Catholic Church. The Catholic Church up to the Reform was wide open . . . but with the coming of the Reform, the Roman Catholic Church lost this openness and in many respects narrowed down. That is what Pope John felt so deeply.[1]

Tillich does not wish to identify these two open movements, but his designation of each in its own sphere is justification enough for the following pages.

Rudolf Bultmann was born on August 20, 1884, in the small town of Wiefelstede in what was then the Grand Duchy of Oldenburg in northwest Germany.[2] His father, the son of a Lutheran missionary in Sierra Leone, was himself a Lutheran pastor. From 1903 until 1912 young Bultmann studied theology in Tübingen, Berlin, and Marburg under such teachers as the Church historian Karl Müller, the Old Testament scholar Hermann Gunkel, the historian of dogma Adolph Harnack, the systematic theologian Wilhelm Herrmann, the New Testament scholars Adolf Jülicher and Johannes Weiss. The last named,

---

[1] Paul Tillich in *Ultimate Concern,* ed. D. Mackenzie Brown (New York, 1965), p. 63.
[2] For biographical material see R. Bultmann, "Autobiographical Reflections," in *The Theology of Rudolf Bultmann,* ed. C. W. Kegley (New York, 1966), pp. xix–xxv—also printed in R. Bultmann, *EF,* pp. 283–288; Heinrich Fries, *Barth, Bultmann and Catholic Theology* (Pittsburg, 1968); E. Fuchs, "Rudolf Bultmann," *RGG,* I, pp. 1511–1512; Paul Leo, "Kerygma and Mythos: The Theology of Rudolf Bultmann," *The Lutheran Quarterly,* 5 (1953), pp. 359–370; W. Philip, *Der Protestantismus im 19. and 20. Jh.* (Bremen, 1965), pp. 359–361; H. Schlier, "Rudolf Bultmann," *LThK,* II, pp. 768–769; E. Wolf, "Rudolf Bultmann," *Theologians for Our Time* (Notre Dame, 1965).

16

who had brilliantly reopened the question of Jesus's claim to Messiahship and who was one of the leading modern textual critics of the New Testament, urged Bultmann to become a lecturer in New Testament. Bultmann's thesis for the licentiate in theology at Marburg was published in 1910: *Der Stil der paulinischen Predigt und die kynisch-stoische Diatribe* ("The Style of the Pauline Preaching and the Diatribe of the Cynics and Stoics"). Weiss had proposed this theme, and for Bultmann's *Habilitationsarbeit* (a research work qualifying the author for a university-level professorship) Adolf Jülicher proposed *Die Exegese des Theodor von Mopsuestia*. Upon its completion in 1912, Bultmann was called as *Privatdozent* (instructor) in the field of New Testament to the University of Marburg. Four years later he accepted an assistant-professorship in Breslau. In 1920 he became full professor at the University of Giessen, and in the following year he returned to Marburg in the same position.

As student and teacher Bultmann entered a climate of New Testament exegesis and Protestant theology which was emerging from the dominance of nineteenth century liberalism. A theologian who once was one of his students recalls:

> The starting point of Bultmann was historical criticism in its most radical form. To those who studied under the young teacher in Marburg some thirty years ago, as this writer did, he gave the impression of being a faithful heir to the ideals of the Marburg school. . . . Bultmann's first important book, *The History of the Synoptic Tradition,* on the one hand pushed historical criticism to the limits of radicalism. He emphasized very strongly the formative influence of the Church upon the sayings of Jesus, as well as upon the stories of his actions. . . . But, on the other hand, this book introduced an approach to New Testament criticism which was a step beyond the literary criticism of the preceding generation.[3]

Bultmann was opposed on general theological principles to the liberal theology of immanence: God as a world-principle, Christ

[3] Paul Leo, *art. cit.,* p. 359.

as religious genius and leader of the founders of religions, the Bible as unusual among historical and poetic literature, faith as a religious experience, dogmatics as a system, the Christian life as a reasonable ethics. In 1924 in an essay on "Liberal Theology and a Recent Theological Movement," he showed that he had other views of the past and other plans for the future. Looking back some decades later, Bultmann wrote:

> It seemed to me that in this new theological movement it was rightly recognized, as over against the "liberal" theology out of which I had come, that the Christian faith is not a phenomenon of the history of religion, that it does not rest on a "religious a priori" (Troeltsch), and that therefore theology does not have to look upon it as a phenomenon of religious or cultural history. It seemed to me that . . . the new theology had correctly seen that Christian faith is the answer to the word of the transcendent God that encounters man and that theology has to deal with this word and the man who is encountered by it. This judgment, however, has never led me to a simple condemnation of "liberal" theology; on the contrary, I have endeavored throughout my entire work to carry further the tradition of historical-critical research as it was practiced by the "liberal" theology and to make our more recent theological knowledge fruitful for it.[4]

Bultmann's forward impetus in exegesis was twofold; he employed the latest research into the religious milieu of the New Testament times and writers, and applied the new method of form-criticism.

The critical school of Old Testament exegesis of Gunkel and Herrmann had developed the study of the individual forms in the Old Testament—for example hymns or royal psalms. The study of the possible sources and analogies for the New Testament had led to a quest for the pre-literary building process in traditions and elements underlying the Gospels. Schmidt and Dibelius began the study of form-criticism in the New Testament in 1919 and Bultmann soon joined them. The Gospels should have literary forms as other literature does. Through

[4] Rudolf Bultmann, in Kegley, *op. cit.,* p. xxiv

18

the examination of these forms the origins of the New Testament, its layers of development and interpretation, and the work of individual and communal authors in verses, chapters, and books could be discovered. The forms of the discourses, miracles, and narratives could distinguish the work of the evangelist, or that of a redactor, or the tradition of a liturgy or community from what was of Jesus. Not only would we then have a more accurate understanding of the New Testament, but we might better be able to solve the problem of the interplay of faith and history in the New Testament, and around Jesus.

Bultmann's post-liberal theological principals were part of the movement called "dialectical theology." Bultmann, Paul Tillich, Karl Barth, Friedrich Gogarten, Emil Brunner, E. Thurneysen—these men followed each their own way often with extensive differences. What this group had in common, however, was to make the act of faith free from the props of history or social philosophy, to make theology basically the explanation of a kerygma for the individual person, to make the event (if not the Gospel narration) of Christ central. For Barth, Christ was the center of theology to be accepted by sinful man in faith, and thereby to reach the fullness of the personal Christian message. For Tillich, theology would be the correlation of a message of the transcendent and immanent God and the presence of New Being to man's concrete existence. For Bultmann, it would be the interpretation of the New Testament message in terms free of unreal thought-forms (myth, spirits), for man in terms of existential analysis. For all, there was a demand for a new theological view with the same bipolar emphasis: the kerygma in Christ and man's belief were to be commitments without metaphysical or historical guarantees, but at the same time this message and event was to be brought to man in terms which would make an impact on his life.

Tillich describes Marburg:

In Marburg, in 1925, I began work on my *Systematic Theology*, the first volume of which appeared in 1951. At the same time that Heidegger was in Marburg as professor of philosophy, influencing

19

some of the best students, existentialism in its twentieth-century form crossed my path. It took years before I became fully aware of the impact of this encounter on my own thinking. I resisted, I tried to learn, I accepted the new way of thinking more than the answer it gave.[5]

Bultmann was a professor then, as was Martin Heidegger who was lecturing in philosophy on topics such as Aristotle and Kant. Heidegger's *Sein und Zeit* would be published in 1927; and the work of Rudolf Otto on the idea of the holy (with which Bultmann disagreed) was prominent. Tillich was beginning to write his *Systematic Theology* which would not be published until a quarter of a century later. Bultmann thus adds to Tillich's description of Marburg:

> The theological faculty in those days was by no means of one mind, and the various divisions within it, especially the tension between myself and Rudolf Otto . . . , stirred even the students and led to lively discussions. These became especially animated whenever theologians from other universities, such as Karl Barth and Friedrich Gogarten, were invited to Marburg to lecture. These years were also enriched by the fact that the interchange between theologians and philosophers was very lively . . . This was particularly the case when Martin Heidegger taught in Marburg from 1922 to 1928. I soon engaged in an exchange with him, as I had done previously with Nicolai Hartmann and was to do subsequently with Erich Frank and Julius Ebbinghaus. There was also fruitful work with the instructors in philosophy who were interested in theology—Hans-Georg Gadamer, Gerhard Kruger, and Karl Löwith —in which the New Testament instructors Heinrich Schlier and Günther Bornkamm also participated.[6]

[5] Paul Tillich, "Autobiographical Reflections," in *The Theology of Paul Tillich,* ed. C. W. Kegley and R. W. Bretall (New York, 1952), p. 14.

[6] Rudolf Bultmann, in Kegley, *op. cit.,* pp. xxii–xxiii. On Bultmann's beginnings as a dialectical theologian, see J. D. Smart, *The Divided Mind of Modern Theology* (Philadelphia, 1967); J. Moltmann, *Die Anfänge der dialektischen Theologie* (Munich, 1966), 2 vols.

Bultmann returns to Heidegger and Barth again:

The work of my existential philosophy, which I came to know through my discussions with Martin Heidegger, became of decisive significance for me. I found here the concept through which it became possible to speak adequately of human existence and therefore also of the existence of the believer. In my efforts to make philosophy fruitful for theology, however, I have come more and more into opposition to Karl Barth, I remain grateful to him, however, for the decisive things I have learned from him. I do not believe that a final clarification of our relationship—to which Heinrich Ott has made a good beginning in his book *Geschichte und Heilsgeschichte in der Theologie Rudolf Bultmanns* (1955)—has as yet been reached. On the other hand, a unity in theological intentions between Gogarten and myself has become more and more apparent.[7]

In contacts with Heidegger further theological perspectives were fashioned. Bultmann accepted Heidegger's analysis of human existence (which occupied the greater part of the unfinished *Sein und Zeit*). It is also clear that in the area of hermeneutics Heidegger and Bultmann are related. Yet as Heinrich Ott has shown, Bultmann's theology is in dialogue with only some aspects of Heidegger's philosophy—a philosophy which is in scope more ontological than Bultmann's use of it would imply.

Bultmann's *History of the Synoptic Tradition* (1921) was the first of several monumental works. From the beginning, however, he was writing not only studies on New Testament exegesis, but on general theological topics, such as the theology of God, natural theology, faith. Bultmann's exegetical prowess was supported by complimentary essays in classical thought and comparative religion. *Jesus* in 1926 examined the central figure of Christianity under the principles of Bultmann's own exegesis and the problem these historical forms raised: where did the Jesus of history enter the New Testament and early Christianity, and where did the Christ of faith dominate? The first of several

---

[7] *Ibid.*, p. xxiv.

21

volumes of collected essays (entitled *Glauben und Verstehen*) appeared in 1933, and the coming decade saw works devoted to Pauline thought.

In 1927 an essay on the Gospel of John began Bultmann's work in that area which culminated in 1941 under the title *New Testament and Mythology,* with the subtitle "The Problem of Demythologizing and New Testament Preaching." For those who were acquainted with Bultmann's manifold writing, this work was not the surprise it caused in wider circles. But it did present his views in an impressive and forceful condensation which equalled Barth's *Commentary on the Epistle to the Romans* as a theological trumpet blast. The essay posed a conflict between the mythological world-view and mentality of the New Testament and the scientific one of modern man; the solution lay in a demythologizing of the Scriptures and the interpretation of the myth-shrouded message in the terms of existential analysis (Heidegger).

Essays on classical, theological, synoptic, philological, exegetical, and hermeneutical topics continued to appear. In 1948 the two volume *Theology of the New Testament* presented the particular theological milieu, viewpoint, and purpose of the synoptic, Johannine, and Pauline traditions. *Primitive Christianity in its Contemporary Setting* followed in 1949. Bultmann's lectures to the University of Edinburgh were published as *History and Eschatology* (1957). In 1951 he visited the United States, and a lecture series given at that time was published in *Jesus Christ and Mythology*. A second visit took place in 1959.

Although Professor Bultmann was eighty in 1964, he is still very much an active force in theology. He has frequently commented on the vast discussion of his program of demythologizing, and he has recently responded to a large collection of essays by Protestant theologians on his theology. One of the finest essays commenting on Bishop J. A. T. Robinson's *Honest to God* was Bultmann's essay in the *Journal for Theology and*

22

the Church.[8] and it is hoped that his commentary on the letters of John will appear in the coming few years.

These books and articles have had an enormous influence on Protestant and Catholic theology alike as has Bultmann's teaching at Marburg. Ernst Käsemann, Ernst Fuchs, Günther Bornkamm, Hans Conzelmann, Gerhard Ebeling, Heinrich Schlier, are all students of Bultmann, and important figures in their own right in exegesis and theology. Despite their differences and development beyond Bultmann, they are another witness to his influence.

 The following book is a collection of essays. Catholic theologians and exegetes from Germany, France, and the United States turn their attention to one or more aspects of Bultmann's thought. In today's era of specialization when the presentation of a problem to a computer consumes more time than the machine's response, universal systems seem prohibited. Textbooks are replaced by bibliographies and another *Summa theologiae* is practically inconceivable. Bultmann is a theologian who transcends specialization. It is a sign of the depth and breadth of his work that theologians from many fields are asked to consider his work. The present essays are arranged to correspond to the main areas of his work: his program of interpreting the New Testament through demythologizing and subsequent existential hermeneutic; his exegesis of the New Testament; and his views on various theological topics.

An encounter with Bultmann is more than an acceptance or rejection of a particular exegetical school, more than an interest in his hermeneutics or demythologizing. As Karl Barth has pointed out, an encounter with Bultmann is basically an encounter with the foundations of a theology of human existence, the Christian message, and man's response in faith. The very structure and nature of theology is involved, for form-criticism is basically a theological method, as is demythologizing.

[8] "The Idea of God and Modern Man," *Translating Theology into the Modern Age,* vol. II of *Journal for Theology and the Church* (New York, 1965), pp. 83–95.

Bultmann's existential view of John, his theological interpretation of Mark or Paul, always leads the reader to the
basic presupposition of theology. Thus the call for demythologizing is already present in Bultmann's theological outlook in
the 1920's, and the subsequent theology of the kerygma in
terms of Heidegger's analysis of *Dasein* has its roots in early
essays on man, God, and faith, and in his work on John. It is
important to realize the distinction between Bultmann's exegetical results and his theological principles, between the
unity of his thought and its diversity, and the ultimate role
of Bultmannian interpretation that we have here in a distinct
theology, a new Christian theology. The new Christian theology
is a challenge and possible aide to every theologian today.

It is a mistake to see Bultmann only in terms of the past
leading to the present, or only through "demythologizing,"
which is a practical theological program for people today. What
is surprising is that most of the questions discussed in today's
theology recall Bultmann's work and ideas. Bultmann's over-all
endeavor "constitutes a kind of program for theologians and
philosophers of religion in the second half of the twentieth
century."[9] The exegetical method of form-criticism, the study
of the religious milieu at the time of Jesus, gnosticism, the
relationship of faith to history and existence, the use of contemporary philosophy to explain the kerygma—all of these
are well known. But beyond them, Bultmann has written
significantly on the encounter of Christianity with secularism,
the problem of natural religion, Lutheran justification, talking
about God, different theological perspectives in the New Testament, the origin of the theological names given to Jesus by early
Christian communities. His analysis of secularism and atheism
(its roots lie in essays written between 1925 and 1935) perceives the real source of the problem, a problem which French
and American Catholics insisted in locating in conflicts between

[9] C. W. Kegley, "Preface," *The Theology of Rudolf Bultmann, ed.
cit.,* p. ix.

24

science and religion rather than in the more profound and widespread encounter of faith with the secular city.

Bultmann remains important even for theology tomorrow because what is central for him is theological method—the theological reinterpretation and communication of the Gospel to people now. In all his work, whether it is a lengthy exposition on Johannine theology or lectures on Jesus Christ and faith, he is really asking what is the human response to the New Testament message—the method in the writings themselves, the contemporary hermeneutic needed to vivify them, the method for understanding and preaching the kerygma.

Theology is in a post-Bultmannian era, but it is a mistake to see the present period as one limited to a discussion of his writings, or, even more unsatisfactory, to see it limited to dialogue with his disciples. The importance of theologians such as Karl Rahner, J. B. Metz, Harvey Cox, Jürgen Moltmann, W. Pannenberg, who are not descendents of Bultmann, shows this attitude as insufficient. "Post-Bultmannian" means that central theological issues have often been raised by his thought explicitly or implicitly. Now, and in coming decades, we will go beyond them (retrieving them in the Heideggerian sense), helped by American sociology, linguistic analysis, ecumenical theology, theologies of hope and future and future revolution, and by young theologians, young ideas, new cultural situations.

The following essays are not just descriptions of Bultmann's thought, but studies and critiques of it from viewpoints within the Catholic traditions. Any ecumenical collection of this sort has to be seen as a dialogue rather than as a clear definitive series of positive and negative evaluations. The essays have been written and selected to give a sufficient view of Bultmann's work. As with our earlier volume, *Paul Tillich in Catholic Thought,* the purpose of these essays is not, ultimately, criticism, but dialogue in order to reflect, to learn how the Christian message might be better brought to man today. Actually it was a pastoral concern which motivated Bultmann to develop and publish his program of demythologizing. He

25

believed that man today could not accept the message of the New Testament because the world of the Scriptures was so different from today's milieu. One of theology's perennial problems is not to forget what Heidegger and Bultmann have recalled: the historicity of man the believer.

In a troubled, open letter on Bultmann's theology, the Protestant faculty of theology at Tübingen said that his theology was not the cause but rather the symptom of a crisis. Bultmann's thought is a sign of the problematical relationship between Christian theology and secular culture. Vatican II is Catholicism's initial recognition of the problem of theological hermeneutic for today. And Catholicism has learned to say with Barth that we may be in need of listening to quite unexpected voices in order to be true to the demands of our own theology. Karl Rahner in an address at the end of the Vatican Council (the final essay, we might say, of the great amount of work he did for that Council) says:

There are many questions which present themselves today in the post-Vatican II world. They are the old questions, which always remain pertinent and always present themselves in epochal new ways: how theology can speak of God, and his existence in the midst of mankind, in such a way that the words can be understood by the men of today and tomorrow; how it can so proclaim Christ in the midst of an evolving universe that the word of the God-man and the incarnation of the eternal Logos in Jesus of Nazareth do not sound like myths which men cannot any longer take seriously.[10]

The following dialogues aspire to the deepest form of ecumenism where Protestants and Catholics not only learn to see each other positively and accurately, but work together to fashion a theology which is truth before the event of Jesus Christ, and an invitation to the world.

[10] Karl Rahner, S.J., *The Church After the Council* (New York, 1966), pp. 24 f.

26

RUDOLF BULTMANN
IN CATHOLIC THOUGHT

I. DEMYTHOLOGIZING AND THEOLOGICAL TRUTH

By Heinrich Fries

The relation between demythologizing and Christian truth some time ago broke out of the confines of professional circles and became a subject of wider discussion. Through the communications media (with their well-known tendency to oversimplify), the question is becoming accessible to an ever-increasing audience. Demythologizing in its various ramifications —the problem of what Jesus said and did historically, the role of theology, myth, and interpretation in the New Testament, the rediscovery of Jesus Christ as man as well as God—these questions have far more than academic interest. They touch the heart, the content, the practice of the Christian faith and of its preaching.[1] This problematic raised by the theologians is slowly permeating through the American scene, into college theology classes, popular magazine articles, and even the difficult arena which is that of adolescent religious education. Often individual theologians have protested that the theological question of demythologizing, unfolded and developed by Bultmann with astonishing results, was only of academic interest, or that it was being taken too seriously by Catholic or Protestant theology, or that it was too erroneous to be considered by the orthodox theologian at all. None of these positions is correct.

[1] See *NTM*, 1–44; G. Hasenhüttl, *Der Glaubensvollzug* (Essen, 1963).

What is demythologizing? What is this word which has made Rudolf Bultmann, the serious exegete, the erudite scholar of the history of religions, so widely known? Bultmann's initial, pithy essay on this topic appeared in 1941; it began a discussion which has lasted through several decades. His position was quite simple: the New Testament is permeated with myth; this myth-framework must not be eliminated but must be interpreted; this interpretation is done in terms of my own personal existence. Bultmann begins by pointing out that the cosmology of the New Testament is essentially mythical in character. The world is described in levels: earth, heaven, and hell. There are angels, devils, and a God, all acting upon our earth. This mythical view of the world which the New Testament presupposes for presenting the events of redemption, is impossible for modern man to accept: it is obsolete. But it is not just the cosmology of the New Testament which is mythological. Bultmann says that ideas such as a preëxistent divine being, a redeemer on the cross, a savior for men's sins, resurrection, the Son, the Logos, a church joined to Christ by baptism and the Eucharist—all of this is mythical. Christian preaching cannot expect modern man to accept these dimensions of which he has no experience. Man's knowledge and mastery of the world have advanced to such an extent through science and technology that the New Testament position is no longer tenable. This drastic criticism of the New Testament does not mean elimination of the kerygma. Bultmann realizes that, unlike with nineteenth-century criticism, we cannot accept one part of the New Testament and reject the others. The entire New Testament proclamation must be demythologized. His motive is not to make the New Testament relative to the modern world at all costs, although he repeats this need over and over again. His concern is simply whether the New Testament message consists only of mythical aspects or whether it has a deeper meaning. He concludes that it does have a deeper meaning, that the existentialist interpretation of the New Testament produces a basic message about God's accept-

30

ance of my human existence. Because of my hope and
confidence in God, who has witnessed to himself in Jesus the
man from Nazareth dying on the cross, I now believe that I
have been accepted with my needs and sins by God. The
basic kerygma of the New Testament is not Christology, not
soteriology, but rather anthropology. By invoking a single
religious truth, God's acceptance of man, the New Testament
bears witness to my own positive, existential, human understanding.

The question of demythologizing is by no means a purely
contemporary problem. It appeared in Plato in almost the
same terms, demythologizing and theology, theology as the
practice of demythologizing. According to Plato, theology had
the duty of freeing the myths, the narratives of the deeds and
sayings of the Greek gods, from their shortcomings and diffi-
culties. Theology was to interpret the myths critically, keeping
an eye to the standards of proper political culture and education (Plato's criticism of the myths appears in his *Politics*).[2]
Plato's undertaking is not a demythologizing in the radical
sense of the term, that is, the abolition of myth; it is, rather
(and this is exactly what is contemporary about it), an interpretation of myth. It is "mythology," if by that term we understand the effort to draw the *logos*, the sense, the meaning, the
original saying from the myths and so to travel the "way
from *mythos* to *logos*" (W. Nestle). For that reason it can be
said that the truth hidden in *mythos*, in the myths about the
gods, comes to light in the sense of *alētheia*, unconcealment,
revelation.

How little Plato intended demythologizing in the sense of an
abolition of myths becomes clear in the way he himself sought
to express through old and new myths the insights which
occurred to him as a philosopher and which exceeded the
expressive capacity of words, concepts, and ideas. This was
developed especially in a dialectic about divine things and about

[2] Plato, *Politics*, II, 379a.

the totality of being at the summit of philosophical thought.[3]

Aristotle, in contrast to Plato, banned *mythos* and the myths from philosophy and relegated them to the poets.

This essay will not consider what Plato and Aristotle had to say on the matter of demythologizing. Rather, it is the contemporary discussion which is the point at issue. Moreover, here we are concerned with *Christian* theology and theological truth, that is, with the scientific reflection connected with the encounter and response of faith before God's historical self-disclosure and self-communication culminating in Christ. Demythologizing asks what theological truth is. Are they enemies, or the same thing? Demythologizing, the interpretation of the myths, lays claim to be a way (even *the* way) to theological truth. The opposite view is that mythology, interpreted or not, is no way to theological truth, because it stands in contradiction to it. If the latter is right, then *mythos* and mythological elements, regardless of their form or dimension can only falsify, obscure, or obstruct theological truth. Consequently, the Christian message, theological truth, will indeed need demythologizing.

I

Theological truth is the truth which is at stake in Christian theology. It involves the *logos* about the Christian event and faith. *Logos* implies word, proposition, communication, meaning. Demythologizing raises the question of God-talk, but speaking not about God in general, nor about God as he appears in the philosophy of Plato and Aristotle. For Christian theology, God's *Logos* has opened up, disclosed, revealed, and communicated himself to men in his life, in the historical events of calling individuals, choosing a *single* people, preach-

[3] Plato, *Timaeus* 29c–d; on this subject see G. Söhngen, "Philosophie und Theologie," *Handbuch theologischer Grundbegriffe* (Munich, 1963), II, pp. 317 ff.

32

ing his word, his will, his love, his justice, his promise, living his mission in the concrete language of history, event, and word. God's self-disclosure, the revelation of his plan, took place through his coming in the person of Jesus of Nazareth. In him God's word, will, justice, and love became an empirical event in the unique, concrete, historical form of a man. God could not have disclosed himself in a more intensive way than in becoming man. In Jesus revelation is unique and definitive; yet, it awaits the future unfolding and completion of the Christ-event.

Theology is concerned with communicating the word of this God, the God who, in Pascal's phrase, is not the God of philosophy but the God of Abraham, Isaac, and Jacob, the God who lived among us in Jesus of Nazareth. We must add that the God of Christian revelation does have a relation to the God of the philosophers. But this is not to say that the philosophers could have conceived this Christian God themselves, for the revelation of God on the cross is foolishness to the Greeks (see 1 Cor. 1:23). Nevertheless, the God who discloses himself for men in Christ says "yes" to every authentic aspect in philosophy and the world religions, for the God of Christian revelation is to be the God of all men and for all men, and this is precisely what he claims to be.[4]

The problem of theology can be approached from another position. We have treated theology from the point of view of the phenomenon and reality of revelation. God's Word as historical fact, as incarnate person, came for our salvation. Man must respond. We call his response faith, the personal and existential bestowal of oneself to the living God, a total submission to him who discloses and surrenders himself to me for my salvation. Faith implies "I believe you." In a total commitment of faith, I accept all coming to me from him to whom I yield myself in faith. Faith receives and articulates

[4] See J. Ratzinger, *Der Gott des Glaubens und der Gott der Philosophen* (Munich, 1960).

33

"the other" by whom it lives. This is precisely the historical, personal, and divine fullness of him who is revelation.[5]

Since faith is a personal act, it achieves its unique realization where man meets God personally, in the man Jesus Christ. Faith is the way in which the person of Jesus Christ becomes accessible to me; but it is also the act which enables me "to be in Christ," to follow him, to have the mind, the spirit, the mission of Christ (see 1 Cor. 2:16; Phil. 2:5).

Here in man's faith in man hearing God's articulated yet mysterious self-disclosure, the theme of theology becomes present. Theology is faith, but it comes from it, expresses it, striving for an articulated, reflective understanding of it. Theology is *logos,* disclosure of meaning, a reflective historical effort searching faith and its content, its meaning, its interrelations, its coordination with man. Theological truth is the truth at issue in our theology of revelation and faith, an opening up, uncovering, manifesting, articulating the matter of revelation and faith. With St. Thomas we define truth as "that which manifests and proclaims existence"[6]; it is a way in which what exists comes to light. With Heidegger we see truth as beings seen in their *alētheia,* their disclosedness, their unconcealment, their enlightenment, their revealedness, their intelligibility.[7] Truth so understood is applicable also to revelation and faith. Theological truth, then, presents the given in revelation and faith and brings it to light and speech.

How can the data given in revelation and faith be recognized to such an extent that it "attests" that truth is possible in theological apprehension and judgment? Our considerations here are only a small contribution to solving this difficulty. The special difficulty of theological truth is how to give human articulation to the reality of God's free Word and act, although this self-disclosure appears in the world. We have no

[5] See H. Fries, *Glauben – Wissen* (Berlin, 1960).

[6] Thomas Aquinas, *De Veritate,* q. 1, a. 1; Aquinas cites Hilary of Poitier, *De Veritate, V; PL* 10, 131.

[7] See Martin Heidegger, *Vom Wesen der Wahrheit* (Frankfurt, 1954).

34

especially adequate categories for it. So, God's Word and deeds must be understood and expressed in a human way.

In theological truth, we have the tension of the finite spirit falling short before the divine infinity. Theological truth struggles under the sign of the analogous and the inadequate. Theology does not exist in timeless ideas or in detached, self-existing facts and objects. The truth which theology expresses takes place in the form of history, event; it occurs in the shape of persons, above all in Jesus of Nazareth. Theology's truth is grounded in John's gospel that the "truth came through Jesus Christ" (1:17). Not only does Jesus speak the truth, but Jesus is the truth: "I am the truth" (John 14:6). Jesus is saying that the reality, the disclosedness, the revelation of God takes place in me and is present in me—exclusively in me.

This uniqueness of theology stressing the universality of truth and at the same time seeing this truth present in an individual person in history, Jesus Christ, has been expressed by Thomas Aquinas with the term "*universale concretum.*" The concrete individual is not here deduced from the universal; rather, it is the principle of the universal. Theological truth is radically different.

Revelation and faith, "beginning in fullness," is historically represented and mediated through the servant Church in history. But the Church is a human mediator. Therefore, the reality of revelation and faith is proposed anew to each historical age. It must sustain itself. It must verify its new expression by questioning life, society, and itself anew. The listening, believing, praying, and learning Church penetrates through the promised Spirit ever deeper into Christ's truth.

Theological truth, Christian truth, is not some thing or statement in revelation which we believe in lieu of knowledge. It is not a personal or secular world-view; it is not information. Theological truth affects me, in a twofold manner: first, my life and existence encounter it, because this truth approaches me, touching the meaning and salvation of my human existence.

35

Theol. truth is not information.

Jesus Christ and the theology of him is an existential truth, a "truth for me." Secondly, man is encountered as he understands and expresses himself in theological truth. Theological truth is truth about man; theology is anthropology. In this sense Bultmann's famous principle, to speak of God is to speak of man, is correct.[8]

II

How is demythologizing related to Christian truth, to theology? This can only be answered by explaining what *mythos* and mythology are. Myth is used today in different, often confusing ways. *Mythos* originally meant word, story, legend. It also meant an authoritative word, a holy word, a word of the tradition. From the beginning and of its nature, *mythos* is already distinguished from *logos,* the word provided apart from authority or tradition by insight into content and meaning. Myths are tales and stories about the gods, their deeds, their history, their fate. In a myth the activities and accomplishments of the gods are closely connected with the world and with man. Theogony is cosmogony; cosmogony is theogony. The fate of the gods is the fate of the world; an event for the world is an event from the gods. The choices of the gods determine the actions, the future and the destiny, the life and death of man, and conversely. This mystical dialogue between gods and men becomes especially manifest in the critical life situations: birth, misfortune, guilt, longing for salvation, love, death. These experiences of human existence, with their radical questions, find their authentic significance, the true meaning and the possibility of an answer, in recourse to the divine.[9]

Mythology is *mython legein,* the recitation of a holy,

[8] See *GV,* I, pp. 26–37.
[9] See G. Lanczkowski and H. Fries, "Mythos," *LThK,* VII, pp. 746–751.

36

authoritative word proclaiming the narrative of the deeds and choices of the gods. From this festive proclamation of the holy word, worship arises as a representation, recalling, and making real of the deeds of the gods in words, pictures, and dramatic history.

Mythology has a definitive form of language. Mythological speaking is speaking in pictures. The world becomes the locale for the appearance of divine things, that is, hierophany. Mythology is graphic speech. It especially makes use of the schema of space and spatial presentation; above and below, within and without, here and beyond. The events of divine and human destiny are played out in a single drama on the levels of heaven, earth, and the underworld.

What does this analysis of myth have to do with Christian theology? If Christian (theological) corresponds to how it was then the mythological bears no resemblance to it whatsoever. We must conclude: demythologizing is necessary for meeting Christian theological truth. We should not be shocked by this strong statement. What is to be demythologized? The Bible itself, the authentic witness of revelation and faith, when it comes into contact with the word or matter of myth, clearly repudiates it. This attitude appears in the biblical account of creation, which is concerned with going beyond the contemporary myths of cosmogony. For the New Testament, the famous passage of 2 Peter must be cited: although it is one of the latest texts of the Bible, it sums up, for that very reason, the whole of revelation: "For we did not follow cleverly devised myths when we made known to you the power and coming of our Lord Jesus Christ, but we were eye-witnesses of his majesty"(1:16).

The fundamental thesis of Bultmann's theology of demythologizing is that we can find in the books of the Old and New Testaments expressions and representations which make use of mythological categories, and which express what they have to say in mythological language. According to this thesis, the biblical testimony to revelation is set forth in mythical and

37

mythological elements which must be demythologized in order to obtain their theological truth. A key text in Bultmann says:

> The cosmology of the New Testament is essentially mythical in character. The world is viewed as a three-storied structure, with the earth in the centre, the heaven above, and the underworld beneath. Heaven is the abode of God and of celestial beings—the angels. The underworld is hell, the place of torment. Even the earth is more than the scene of natural, everyday events, of the trivial round and common task. It is the scene of the supernatural activity of God and his angels on the one hand, and of Satan and his demons on the other. These supernatural forces intervene in the course of nature and in all that men think and will and do. Miracles are by no means rare. Man is not in control of his own life. Evil spirits may take possession of him. Satan may inspire him with evil thoughts. Alternatively, God may inspire his thought and guide his purposes. He may grant him heavenly visions. He may allow him to hear his word of succour or demand. He may give him the supernatural power of his Spirit. History does not follow a smooth unbroken course; it is set in motion and controlled by the supernatural powers.[10]

For Bultmann, theology must demythologize these mythological elements of the Bible. Mythical cosmology has been banished by the scientific view of the world which admits neither levels nor divine interventions. This world has recognizable laws and structures which can be mastered by man and will be increasingly controlled by him. The world of man is becoming an increasingly humanized, de-divinized world. Mythological thought is abolished by the critical understanding of causality as natural and empirical rather than divine. Today's thought is not pictorial but conceptual; it is found in existential philosophy and (in a rather different way) in the non-representational thinking of modern science and physics.

Demythologizing responds to the fact that modern man does not see himself as a theater for other-worldly influences, but as

[10] *NTM*, p. 1.

38

a person capable of deciding for himself. How should we preach the message of revelation and faith? The New Testament presents the message to contemporary man in an unacceptable manner, making it unbelievable. What results is the misunderstanding of the Christian message and the rejection of belief. Today's way to truth in theology and to the man for whom this truth has been given lies only in demythologizing.

In addition to these reasons for demythologizing the Bible, Bultmann finds a theological reason. The Bible contains as its critical message the truth of the "non-worldliness," the hiddenness of God, the truth that God is the wholly-other, qualitatively distinguished from everything the "world" can imply. But this transcendence of God cannot be expressed in myth logically. In mythical expression the critical difference between God and the world cannot be seen, instead, God and world coalesce.

Theology demands demythologizing, a twofold "critical destruction" (that is, "reduction") of biblical mythology. This reduction operates concretely in each case so that a group of biblical expressions is interpreted beyond its link with myth. Belief in spirits and demons, miracles (especially those of healing), statements about the end of the world, sacraments, the understanding of death as punishment for sin, vicarious satisfaction through Jesus Christ's death, the resurrection and ascension of Christ as historical events—all of the mythological expressions attributed in the New Testament to the person, life, and experience of the historical Jesus are unacceptable in their literal, objective meaning because they are intrinsically impossible. God does not enter our world; he does not reveal himself in and beyond nature and history. *HOW DO YOU KNOW?*

Here Bultmann grounds demythologizing on hermeneutics and existential analysis. But demythologizing has only begun. Demythologizing is not concerned with the removal of mythological elements or with the abolition of myth. Its concern is with myth's correct *interpretation*. This interpretation ultimately centers on one unequivocal area: questions of our existence. Bultmann sees the interest of every text, especially every biblical

39

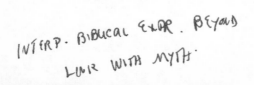
INTERP. BIBLICAL ERROR. BEYOND LINK WITH MYTH.

text, not in information or teaching but in the question of man, the possibility and reality of his existence as it appears in the text. Interpretation is existential interpretation; interpretation is hermeneutic. The myths and what is said in them are to be questioned about the understanding of our existence implied in their statement. The New Testament, which is formally an address, a preaching, treats expressly of man's existence. It describes human existence in its degraded and inauthentic states. This disclosure takes place according to the fashion of mythological talk, but the reality is the same as that encountered in existential philosophy. However—and this is the special point of the New Testament kerygma—the transfer of existence from its degraded and inauthentic state (from sin and death) to authenticity (grace and life), the deliverance "from oneself to oneself," does *not* take place through man's knowledge or activity. This is what philosophy believed and what constitutes the error and *hubris* of philosophy according to theology. Instead it takes place exclusively through the loving actions of God as revealed in Jesus Christ on the cross and constantly made present to man in preaching; this is theological truth. The New Testament proclaims the act of God "which makes possible man's authentic life."[11] Revelation and kerygma not only give a comprehensive understanding of existence, they present an authentic realization of existence. Everything which the New Testament attests to happens, becomes meaningful for our existence.

The challenge of the demythologizing process is a noble and positive task; the existential interpretation of the Bible grounds existential theology. As existential interpretation and theology, demythologizing in Bultmann's view not only eliminates the unnecessary conflict between faith and knowledge but frees the inner meaning of the New Testament kerygma from the stumbling blocks connected with it. God has acted decisively in Christ, and all this has happened for me. Demythologizing is at the service of faith, it is an enabler of faith. It calls faith back

[11] *Ibid.*, p. 33.

40

to its radical and real significance, especially as faith is seen in the Lutheran tradition; faith alone, word alone, grace alone. Bultmann conceives his program as the accomplishment of the desire of the Reformation. It is worked out on the level of knowledge of the theological principles of the Reformation. (It frees knowledge, as Luther freed faith, justification from works.) "The man who wishes to believe in God as his God must realize that he has nothing in his hand on which to base his faith. He is suspended in mid-air, and cannot demand a proof of the Word which addresses him. For the ground and object of faith are identical."[12] It is precisely through this incapacity for proof that Christian preaching is safeguarded from being a mythology.

III   DEMY. "FREES" KNOWLEDGE.

In Bultmann's thinking we meet the impressive tension today between demythologizing and Christian theological truth. There are other forms of demythologizing, varied according to whether they focus on existentialism, secularism, communism, capitalism. The basic question of demythologizing is whether or not myth is bound up with the Christian message and truth. Myth is, first of all, a prelude, a temporal presupposition of Christian revelation. This means simply that the message of revelation and faith encountered men who lived in the horizon and world of myth. These men used myth to express their thoughts about God and his activity, about the divine causality in the beginning, development, and end of all things. Likewise, they used myth to express their experience, their existential perplexity, about gods and events. Basically, this was the situation of all men who stood outside the explicit revelation of the Old Testament.

The classic example for this situation occurs in the Bible itself, in Paul's discourse on the Areopagus. There he preached to the Athenians: "What you worship as unknown, this I proclaim to you" (Acts 17:23). He preached the message of the unknown

12 *KM*, II, p. 211.

God now revealed in Jesus Christ. The perpetual problem of the Christian mission is to find a point of contact between religion and Christ.

This means that myth is not only temporally prior to Christ, but that its content and multiple expression contain a pre-understanding and insight into every revelation. It reaches a climax in Christ. This prior insight is interpreted and made intelligible in mythological terms because Christian revelation addresses every man who comes from the world of myth. This "prior insight," prior to revelation, takes place as myth excites questions which touch human existence. The biblical images of Christ as light, life, savior, rock, vine, bread, water, shepherd, lamb, the talk about expiation and deliverance, would be neither possible nor intelligible were there not a prior understanding of them. This prior understanding is no trivial one; it is a religious insight expressed in myth, rooted in existence, and related to the divine.

By using these expressions the Bible indicates that Jesus Christ is the one about whom myth asks. He is the one of whom images and symbols speak, but who cannot be found in the multiplicity of myth. In Jesus Christ the mythical pattern becomes identical with the historical person.

Myths are not focal points of error, darkness, and paganism, but of light. They are scattered lights radiated by that Light which enlightens every man who comes into this world (see Jn. 1:9). In their role as prior understanding myths exercise a preliminary function and fulfill Clement of Alexandria's daring idea: All the lamps of Greece burn for Christ the Sun.[13] From this point of view it was possible to express the reality of Christ in the vocabulary of myth, not only in familiar mythical images but in the very names of gods. Jesus Christ was spoken of as the true Hermes, Orpheus, Heracles, Odysseus, Theseus, Helios. Hans Urs von Balthasar observes that ridiculing the gods was

[13] See H. Rahner, *Greek Myths and Christian Mystery* (New York, 1963), p. xvii.

42

not something for the Christian faith to be proud of.[14] According to Greek patristic thought, Christ realized and incarnated the meaning which myths and theophanies tried to present. In this way, in Christ, *mythos* is "elevated" (*aufgehoben*), realized in its manifold depth, freed from a rambling lack of definition, and vitalized in the here and now of Jesus Christ. These processes, however, are much more a mythologizing than a demythologizing. The dynamism of myth is elevated, freed, and illumined towards reality and theology. Christian theological truth has a universal reference: it manifests the fact that Jesus Christ is the word and salvation for all.

Myth's second positive relationship to theological truth is to give verbal expression to historical revelation. Historical revelation speaks a different word than myth, but myth investigates the locale where man asks his questions and where revelation encounters man. The revelation of God culminates in the Son of man's becoming man. In the incarnation and in the person of the God-man, in whom the divine and the human are present inseparably but unconfusedly, one of the aims of myth is achieved and far surpassed. Incarnation figures in a variety of ways in myth, the appearance of God in human form and the mythical, confused mixture of divine and human destiny.[15] This too is a positive relation of myth to Christianity.

Mythology speaks in graphic terms, in pictures and symbols, in drama and narrative. And, the reality expressed in human speech as Christian truth cannot dispense with images and similes, for every conception takes its start from images. There is no work without a corresponding representation. Man is dominated by his senses. Even if he wants to speak in a negative fashion of the supernatural, of the hidden things of God, he cannot dispense with images and pictures; he can speak of the reality and the mystery of God only in similes and paradoxes. He sees things in a mirror, dually (1 Cor. 13:2); the mystery of

[14] H. Urs von Balthasar, *Herrlichkeit,* I (Einsiedeln, 1961), p. 482.
[15] See C. Koch, *Religio: Studien zu Kult und Glauben der Römer* (Nuremberg, 1960).

the divine love which surpasses all understanding (Eph. 3:19) can be only represented in images. The images and similes should not be stripped down like concepts (not that the function of concepts in theology with respect to theological truth is something to be feared). The images should communicate the height and the depth (this, too, is an image, in fact, a mythological expression, yet we cannot speak without it) of the manifold wisdom of God (Eph. 3:10). In these images we see how the death of Christ is no ordinary death but the ransom, the sacrifice, the expiation, the atonement, the salvation for the world. Myth belongs to the "human voice in which the divine Word has humbly given itself to be understood."[16]

We cannot dispose of all mythological manner of speaking. No theology can be radically demythologized. The only thing we can do is to clarify and understand the pictures and images in their meaning-content. Mythological talk does not belong to a naïve and primitive stage of thought; it is part of the radical potentiality of man and of his capacity for expression. It cannot be suppressed even by modern cosmology. If the allegation is true that the old words and images mean nothing to us today, this does not mean that we should substitute some other mode of expression. Rather, we have become stunted in our human development. We must recover our origins and also go beyond image to meaning and reality.

The "concrete universal" found in Christ includes both the universality of general concepts and the concreteness of expressions in image, likeness, and symbol. The only suitable expression of the revelation culminating in Christ is one in which *mythos* and *logos* meet. Jesus Christ is at once the *Logos* (Jn. 1:1), the Word of God, and the *Eikon,* the image of God (2 Cor. 4:11; Col. 1:15). He is divinity present in image.[17]

Myth and mythology do stand in opposition to theological truth. That is why demythologizing is an approach to theologi-

---

[16] J. Bernhart, *Bibel und Mythos* (Munich, 1954), p. 63.
[17] S. Otto, "Bild," *Handbuch theologischer Grundbegriffe, ed. cit.,* I, pp. 160–68.

mythos + logos meet

cal truth. Myth levels the distinctions between the divine, the worldly, and the human, and it proclaims an undifferentiated unity of the three in being and becoming, in action and history. This mystical presentation is different from the revelation of the one and triune God beside whom no other gods exist. In the recognition of this truth the absolute sovereignty and transcendence of God over against the world of man find expression. The world and man are defined in an entirely unmythical way as the free unconstrained work of God's love. The teaching of the creation myth is an intrinsic contradiction. Likewise, the end and consummation of things is the free action of God. In this way Christian faith is a transition described by Paul as a conversion "from pagan images to the living and true God" (1 Thes. 1:9).

Christian theological truth stands in opposition to myth, because myth allows for many gods and narrates stories of gods. It presents a certain religious fullness, but it decides on no one definition; it reveals no single pattern as normative. In its pantheon and stories myth multiplies and confuses the truly godly. In contrast to myth, revelation recognizes the obligatory open but summoning character of God's self-communication in Jesus Christ. In Jesus Christ alone is salvation (Acts 4:12); in him God has concretely decided in favor of the world and mankind. Revelation demands a personal response and existential decision given in faith. Yet this exclusiveness is found in the broadest universality.

Myth stands over against theological truth since myth's interpretation of man is different from the one expressed in revelation. Revelation does not define man as someone helplessly exposed by faith to the choices and influences of the gods. Rather, revelation defines man as the crown and master of creation, as a person, living in the world, as the free partner of the God who comes to meet him in word and love. This man experiences the action of God in Christ as freedom from all slavery, as liberation for his own benefit; he recognizes the almighty but provident choices of the sovereign God not as

45

restricting but rather as endowing true freedom. In all these areas demythologizing makes theological truth possible.

The Bible, at least the New Testament, is not written within the perspective of myth. The Bible means liberation from myth understood as the story of gods, the end of the vague mixing of divine and human dimensions as religions. This rejection of myth does not prevent the Bible from borrowing mythological ways of speaking, representations, cosmological schemes, images and categories, from using apocalyptic and gnostic sources, without thereby yielding to myth. For the Bible must use human language and the language of its time. The expressions borrowed from myth are applied to a completely unmythical subject: *Forma mythica antimythica dicuntur.* Myth and mythological language are not the same, and mythical language does not always imply a mythical religion. It is possible to demythicize without demythologizing; there can be simultaneously mythology and demythologizing.

Acknowledging the role played by the mythical in the New Testament and yet remaining faithful to the New Testament as the fundamental witness of God's non-mythical revelation, we can conclude that in the New Testament no fully developed myth is ever narrated as part of the New Testament's life and message. At best, "fragments" of the mythical are employed as the language, milieu, and formation of the different books demanded. Heinrich Schlier has shown how this is exemplified in the "Son of man" myth and the "proto-Adam as savior" myth. These found their unique fulfillment in the concrete person and historical life of Jesus Christ, but at the same time they were transcended as myths. "In the New Testament, myth is so transformed into history that by reason of its connection with Christ it ceases to be myth. Its understanding of God, the world, and man is thought out and clarified in order to give the historical revelation of the crucified and risen Jesus Christ a language appropriate to its circle of meaning. In this kind of critical use made by history itself in the interest of interpretation, myth comes to its end, but that end is its fulfillment."[18] Myth is not the field within which revelation unfolds but rather within revelation is the field where myth finds its place and takes on its full meaning.

The relation of God to the world cannot be described exclusively in terms of transcendence, the beyond, or the a-cosmic. There is no greater distance of opposition than that between the produced, creaturely being of the world and of man, and the unproduced, creative being of God. But, there can be no greater closeness, community, and intimacy than that between God the Creator and the world and man as creatures. The world is not God, but it belongs to God in complete dependence. Thus the absolutely transcendent God is at the same time the imminent God; God is above and within the world. When this latter dimension is left out of consideration, something essential is omitted from the free dynamism of God and the reality of the world. The fundamental connection between God and the world is rooted in creation and finds its conceptual formulation in the analogy of being. It was not taken away by sin, though it was encumbered.

God is both a yes and a no to the world. And the world, which is completely God's, affirms him. The world is not isolated, locked up within itself. By its very nature the cosmos is open to God and to his action in it. The miraculous, which Bultmann refuses to admit in view of the constitution of the world, is really, fundamentally possible, as it is a miraculous sign that God and his activity are close to the world and are manifesting themselves there in a "new creation." The secular world may hotly contest this possibility and claim independence from God, but Bultmann's position against an end to the world and a consummation of all history brought about by God's action is theologically unjustifiable.

Through the incarnation even more than through creation, God has made clear to all eyes the fact and the extent of his

[18] H. Schlier, "The New Testament and Myth," in *The Relevance of the New Testament* (New York, 1968).

cosmic and human presence. He has entered time and space as one of us, brother to each one of us, in all things a man (Phil. 2:7). Worship and sacrament are possible and meaningful as "visible signs of invisible grace." They are the ever present representatives of the "Word (*Logos*) made flesh," which Bultmann holds fast to. The same is true of the Church as the primal sacrament.

Dialogical terms are rejected by Bultmann—a-cosmic and cosmic; divine and human; beyond and here; yet both sides ground every theological mention of God. Without them we cannot speak of God, certainly not of the God of biblical (especially New Testament) revelation. So this means that we cannot speak of God except "mythologically" as Bultmann understands the term.[19]

When the Bible speaks mythologically, it is not describing something imaginary, but bringing the transcendent and authentic to life. Mythology so understood is one of the categories found in the Bible for expressing the cosmic, this-worldly, human side of God in creation and revelation without denying his transcendence and unworldliness.

Karl Rahner has made the astute observation that the truth about God and our conceptualization of the world are two very different things. Basically, the activity of God and his Word do not belong to phenomenology and the sciences; they belong to the presuppositions of the natural sciences but are unattainable by them. Thus the Word of God is beyond human science while remaining within human life and experience. If the divine truth of God's Word is expressed in human languages partially conditioned by a primitive cosmology, it does not follow that they must be demythologized. They continue to be meaningful even when the cosmology under whose suppositions and aid they were first elaborated has long been dead. The meaning is the same as that first intended. This is the reason for recognizing that "fundamentally the original expressions of faith

[19] H. Fries, "Myth and Revelation," *Theology Today,* ed. J. Feiner, *et al.* (Milwaukee, 1967).

48

did not identify the content they represented with the representational elements borrowed from a cosmology to formulate them. Neither do they stand as a guarantee of the truth of such a cosmology."[20]

Demythologizing challenges us to search out the *logos* from the forms, categories, and images in the biblical testimony of revelation. This effort must make the *logos* in myth present to us; it must let the underlying reality beneath myth enkindle our concern and life. To observe and delineate the difference between manner of presentation and meaning, between form and content in an expression, is part of the massive and unending task of exegesis, hermeneutics, and theology. But this labor is not just for specialists, but for every Christian who wants to understand the faith in preaching and commitment. There is no end to Christian hermeneutic and theology.

Certainly a very important disclosure of meaning has been achieved through the inquiry into the understanding and interpretation of human existence found in the Scripture. This is the "truth for me" and demands faith as my decision and response. But we cannot identify this subjectivism with myth or reduce the whole of theology's truth to this common denominator, for we have introduced a principle too narrow to admit the whole of revelation. There is the danger that a purely personal, existential understanding of revelation and faith will prejudice the content and style of revelation and that God's historical communication of himself will be transformed into insights about the intrinsic potentialities of the human mode of existence.

The question of demythologizing biblical hermeneutics and theological truth calls attention to the task of *understanding*, but it also calls attention to a question contingent upon understanding, the question of translating the message of revelation and faith for men of every age, for contemporary men having their own idea of the world, their own language, their own

[20] K. Rahner, "Science as a Confession," *Theological Investigations,* III (Baltimore, 1967), pp. 385 ff.

thought-forms. The translation of the Christian message for today must be open-ended; open towards the profound message of revelation and faith, and open to the sphere of language of men in every historical epoch. In every age man defines himself anew, and yet in every historical development, even in the breath-taking whirl of our own day, man remains. He retains something lasting through each change. Every man has the possibility and capacity to understand and appreciate what, thousands of years before, was said by men in human images and ideas.

It is not a question of changing or eliminating the object of theological truth through an imprecise process of demythologizing. Instead, it is a matter of calling man back to himself and reawakening his own potentialities. For man is known in the world. Life grows by means of sensible things and pictures which we sublimate into knowledge, *logos,* meaning, concept, and word. Man the inquirer is open to everything that exists; he constantly reaches beyond himself to the ground of his being. Thus he becomes the "hearer of the Word," which is not his word but contains the real answer to problematic man. Every man carries with him a perpetual desire for the meaning and salvation of his life. He shows thereby that he cannot himself provide that salvation towards which he strives but must have it offered to him. He is not sufficient unto himself; he can find his sufficiency only in the Infinite. He recognizes his striving and his limits, becomes aware of his finitude. This is man, it is also today's man; in his life, concept and image, *logos* and *mythos* interplay. From the depths of his heart and spirit he brings forth old things and new. Surrounded by so many sounds and media, he wants and struggles to hear the Word of God spoken to him in revelation and faith. No less than the men of the past or the men of the future, secular man must discern the Christ-event and its meaning for him in the New Testament, for he is called to be a hearer and son of that Truth which is Way and Freedom, Light and Life.

50

II. DEMYTHOLOGIZING IN THE SCHOOL OF ALEXANDRIA

By Jean Daniélou

Any attempt to transpose a contemporary problem into the past involves an element of risk. Yet it is remarkable to see how the same problems arise at different stages of history. While it is valid to make comparisons, at the same time quick identifications are dangerous. The question of demythologizing is characteristic in this regard. A certain equivalent can be found in the thought of ancient Christianity, but it was discussed in terms different from those of today. By situating this earlier problem in its own context, we may perhaps find some principles useful for today's problematic.

Originally demythologizing was in no way a specifically Christian problem. On the contrary, it was first posed by the Greeks. It is an inevitable consequence of the progress of scientific thought, which from the outset is defined by its opposition to myths. We find this opposition as early as Heraclitus and Xenophanes, and it continues throughout the whole scientific tradition. The problem became particularly critical at the beginning of our Christian era. We need only read the *Dialogues* of Lucian or the *True Discourse* of Celsus to be made aware of this fact. The early Christians made ample use of this pagan polemic to denounce the immorality and puerility of Greek mythology. It was a necessary chapter in every apology

51

whether of Justin or Athenagoras, Theophilus or Tatian, Clement or Origen. Earlier, Philo the Jew used the same tactic. But this polemical device could just as easily be used against the Bible itself. There were already skeptics among the Alexandrian Jews. The Jews ridiculed pagan myths, but they put themselves in a similar position. "How can you still respect the traditions of the Ancients as if they contained the canons of truth? The Books which you call holy themselves contain the same myths as those which you are so accustomed to deride when you hear them recounted by others."[1] The discussion of Celsus and Origen is characteristic here. Celsus tried to defend the pagan myths, and treated the biblical accounts as absurd fables. Origen defended the biblical accounts, and mocked Greek mythology.

But there was a common element in this criticism. Both agreed that certain accounts could not be taken literally. It is important to show that Jews and Christians alike saw this as true of biblical texts, just as the Greeks did for the texts of Homer. Thus for Philo, the literal interpretation of God's planting of the Garden of Paradise would be $\mu\nu\theta o\pi o\iota\acute{\iota}a$;[2] the formation of Eve from the side of Adam is mythical ($\mu\nu\theta\hat{\omega}\delta\epsilon\varsigma$) in the literal sense,[3] as is the role of the serpent in the temptation.[4] Philo was disturbed by the scandal which an historical interpretation of these facts cause in the pagans. By doing this they discredit the Word of God.[5] We find similar reflections in Origen. Gregory of Nyssa mocks those who, like Theodore of Mopsuestia, ask whether the tree of knowledge was a fig tree. "If its fruit was poisoned, how has it become edible? . . . Taken literally, the biblical account appears truly unreal and mythical [$\mu\nu\theta\hat{\omega}\delta\epsilon\varsigma$] to the uninformed."[6]

---

[1] Philo, *The Confusion of Tongues,* 2–3; IV, pp. 11–14. All references to Philo's works are to the Loeb edition (Cambridge, 1960).

[2] Philo, *Allegorical Interpretation of Genesis,* bk. iii, 14, 43; I, pp. 329 ff.

[3] Philo, *Ibid.,* bk. ii, 7, 19; I, p. 239.

[4] Philo, *Agriculture,* 22, 97; III, pp. 157–158.

[5] Philo, *That God Is Immutable,* 21–22; III, pp. 113–119.

[6] Gregory of Nyssa, *In Canticorum, PG* 44, 761.

52

Greeks and Christians shared the common problem of safe-guarding the value of their religious traditions which scientific criticism had shown to be fictitious. The solution is to show that these values are presented in a mythical form, and that it is not necessary to take them literally. At the same time it is necessary to show that they nevertheless contain a truth which we must discover behind the letter. In a proper sense this is demythologizing, the concern of hermeneutics, the interpretation of sacred texts. We are aware of the importance of hermeneutics in the exegesis of Homer and in Greek tradition generally. The Stoics, Pythagoreans, and Platonists were rivals in their search to discover in the ancient myths teachings on the universe and its structure, the soul and its virtues, God and his powers. The ancient Greeks reacted to rational criticism of the myths by means of allegory.

So, Jews and Christians alike adapted Greek hermeneutics. They were confronted with the problem of discovering the truth behind the symbol of the myths, and pagans, Jews, and Christians used similar language in their demythologizing. Clement of Alexandria explained that "poets often philosophize by insinuation [ὑπόνοια]." It was necessary for research to penetrate to the thought (ἔννοια) contained in the symbols for the reality to be discovered.[7] He used similar expressions to describe St. John the Baptist untying the straps of Christ's sandals, in other words, unveiling (ἐχχάλυψας) the thought (ἔννοια) contained in the symbols of the Old Testament.[8] Speaking of the serpent, Philo wrote that the mythical (μυθῶδες) element is cleared away and the truth discovered in exegesis which proceeds by allegories (ὑπόνιαι).[9]

However, a problem arises concerning the rules of this allegorical exegesis of the myths. We must keep in mind that the Fathers of the Church, and Philo before them, were influenced not only by the very principle of the necessity of a demythologizing, but by the content which the Greek philosophers had

---

[7] Clement of Alexandria, *Stromata,* bk. v, 4, 1–2; *PG* 69, 38 ff., 9 ff.
[8] *Ibid.,* bk. v, 8, 55, 3; *PG* 69, 71 ff.
[9] Philo, *Agriculture, loc. cit.*

given to their own myths. They were tempted simply to transfer the same interpretations to the biblical texts. This is most characteristic of Philo. We have seen that he affirms the necessity of demythologizing the history of the creation of Eve. This demythologizing interpreted Adam as a symbol of intelligence and Eve as a symbol of sensation. The sleep of Adam is intelligence turning from intelligible things. The rib is one of the powers of intelligence, the faculty of sensation; the formation of woman is sensing.[10] Clement and especially Origen made similar analogies.

Christian tradition, however, presented another possibility. Even before its confrontation with scientific thought questioned the value of the myths, there was a type of original symbolism contained in the perspective of salvation history. Paul in the Epistle to the Romans described Adam as the prefiguration ($\tau\acute{\upsilon}\pi o\varsigma$) of him who was to come, that is, of Christ. The Epistle of Peter presents baptism as the antitype ($\dot{\alpha}\nu\tau\acute{\iota}\tau\upsilon\pi o\varsigma$) of the Deluge. Properly speaking, this is not exegesis. And no question was posed as to the mythical or historical character of the events cited. Quite the contrary, since it concerned pointing out a correspondence between two moments in history, the very method employed and the comparison presuppose the historical character of the two events compared.

The fact remains that confusion between typology and demythologizing arose in the school of Clement and Origen. We just mentioned in passing a passage where Clement explains that St. John the Baptist unveiled the content ($\check{\epsilon}\nu\nu o\iota\alpha$) contained in the symbols of the Old Testament. The word serves to designate the reality contained under the veil of the myths. A transposition is made here. The symbols, the myths, are the realities of the Old Testament; the $\check{\epsilon}\nu\nu o\iota\alpha$, the contained reality, is the person of Christ. The Old Testament expresses in a veiled way what the New Testament reveals clearly. It remains questionable to what degree Clement was inspired by the view-

---

[10] Philo, *Genesis,* bk. ii, 8–11, 25–38; I. pp. 241 ff., 287 ff.

point found in Maximus of Tyre, who says that myths correspond to the Ancients, that is, to a still imperfect understanding, whereas λόγος corresponds to perfect knowledge.[11]

A text of Origen raises an important point. In *Contra Celsus* he wrote concerning the Jews: "What a wonderful thing it was for them to know the truth from their childhood. . . . These truths were as yet proclaimed in the form of myths [μυθικώτερον] because they were children and had only a child's capacity for understanding. But now, for those who seek for the true content [λόγος] and wish to advance therein, what was once so to speak myth [μῦθος] is transformed into the truth which was hidden [ἐναποκεκρυμμένη]."[12] The passage from the Old to the New Testament is also a passage from myth (μῦθος) to word (λόγος), from truth hidden in symbol to truth manifested in its reality. The error of the Jews is to remain with myth when the Word is present. True demythologizing is the passage from the Old to the New Testament.

This perspective is very interesting from the viewpoint of the content of the myth. The ἔννοια ceases to be a philosophical truth as it had been among the Greeks. It is transformed into the *Logos* himself, the Christian truth. But at the same time it entails a grave consequence for the μῦθος, which is amazingly extended. It is not merely the first accounts which could be termed mythical. The entire Old Testament becomes an immense symbol. Certainly, the historical character of the facts is not denied, but the literal sense is considered as a cloak for a hidden meaning, which is the real sense, the ἔννοια. The New Testament unveils the hidden meaning, which was already the *Logos*. Consequently, demythologizing by allegory would have to be extended to the whole of the Old Testament.

The meaning of myth is entirely changed here. In its usual meaning, myth is opposed to history; but in this interpretation it is not, because history can become myth. There is another

---

[11] Maximus of Tyre, *Discourses,* bk. x, 5.
[12] Origen, *Contra Celsum,* bk. v, 42; *PG* 11, 1246–1247.

way in which myth is opposed to *logos* (we have already seen this in Maximus of Tyre). The *logos* is the ground of being, the first reality. For Origen this reality was the Word of God and his mysteries, difficult to grasp, and wrapped in the veils of myth. This is the Platonic conception of myth. At any rate, this is how Origen interprets it: "If we use philosophy to search out what Plato expressed in the form of myths [ἐν σχήματι μύθου] we will find his thought. He withheld from the masses the profound doctrines which were manifest to him, and expressed them in the form of myths. Yet he did this in such a way that the elite could understand the truth hidden in the myths."[13] In short, by giving Christ as the content of this myth, Origen applied to the entire Old Testament the Platonic concept of myth.

Consequently, there could be two interpretations of the Old Testament. We could interpret it literally, which would be equivalent to taking the Platonic myths literally, without demythologizing, and remaining at the mythical level. This is the situation of the Jews and those Christians who defend the literal interpretation of the Old Testament. But Christian truths demythologized the Old Testament by allegory. "They show the profound and mysterious doctrines contained in Scripture, whereas the Jews read them superficially and as myths [μυθικώτερον]."[14] Moreover, "All the teachings of the Jews today are myths, fairy tales [λῆροι] because they have not the light of knowledge."[15] The Christians have escaped from Jewish mythology.[16] Christ has delivered them "from the myths of the Jews."[17]

So, for Origen, the Old Testament is the myth of which the New Testament is the reality. But we must beware of taking this opposition in a purely historical sense. Actually, for Origen, there were men in the Old Testament who already contemplated

13 *Ibid.*, bk. iv, 39; *PG* 11, 1090–1091.
14 *Ibid.*, bk. ii, 4; *PG* 11, 802.
15 *Ibid.*, bk. ii, 5; *PG* 802–803.
16 *Ibid.*, bk. ii, 6; *PG* 11, 803.
17 *Ibid.*, bk. ii, 52; *PG* 11, 879.

the *Logos* behind the veils, and there can be men in the New Testament who are still on the plane of myth. The problem of myth in the New Testament itself must be raised. This does not deny the historical character of the coming of Christ in the New Testament any more than the mythical character of the Old Testament excludes historical events. But this means that there was a knowledge of present or future truth in the Old Testament and that there can be ignorance of the present or past truth in the New Testament. In other words, for Origen, although there was progress in historical reality, there was no progress in knowledge. Or rather, the progress of knowledge is the passage from myth to understanding, and that has always been possible.

This problem is most acute in the area of eschatology. Origen knew Christians who interpreted the promises of Christ about the coming kingdom as describing an assembly of the saved in a Palestine flowing with milk and honey. This is the millenarianist doctrine, a position which was current at the time of Origen and expounded by such men as Irenaeus, Tertullian, Hippolytus, and Methodius. Origen rejected it. "The promised land running with milk and honey is not, as some say, the Judea of this world."[18] But it is that land which St. Paul, "a stranger to Jewish mythology [μυθολογία],"[19] speaks of in the Epistle to the Hebrews. St. Basil uses similar terms when he refers to the millenarianism of Apollinaris: "We find in the writings of this man, considerations on the Resurrection which are mythical [μυθικῶς], I might even say Jewish."[20] We see that the attack on "Judaism" always criticized the Jews' literal interpretation of Scripture.

We find here on the plane of eschatology the same attitude as that of "archeology." Demythologizing moves on two levels. First of all, it touches on the mythical, that is, the fantastic character of the representations and denies them historical

[18] *Ibid.*, bk. vii, 28; *PG* 11, 1459.
[19] *Ibid.*, bk. vii, 20; *PG* 11, 1447.
[20] Basil the Great, *Letter 263; PG* 32, 980.

reality. Further, and this was the general attitude of Origen, it redeems the truth contained in the literal sense, whether this be historical or not. The two points of view are obviously different, but the difficulty is to chart where they differ. It is not always easy to determine in the writings of Origen how far his demythologizing—as a penetration to the ultimate truth contained under the letter—does not imply a devaluation of the historical reality and a lapsing into a gnosis.

In conclusion, we can see that the similarities between the problem posed by the Alexandrians and that which concerns contemporary demythologizing is striking. In both cases the difficulty arises from the shock of scientific criticism which seems to disturb faith in the Word of God and obliges us to reclaim faith from representations which compromise it. But actually, the total relationship between *history* and *knowledge* is involved. The effort to separate the reality believed from its contingent historical context always involves the risk of removing faith from history. Yet, even when history is affirmed in its concrete reality, it risks being severed from being known. But, if both aspects engage in a mutual dialogue, the differences of each should prevent us from transposing one into the sphere of the other.

III. FORM-CRITICISM AND THE GOSPELS

By Rudolf Schnackenburg

THE PRESENT SITUATION OF RESEARCH

In 1962 Rudolf Bultmann published a second revised edition of his work, *The History of the Synoptic Tradition* (1921). Its extensive bibliography shows the immense amount of work in the field of form-criticism which resulted after the first edition. Since the second printing (1931), the main text of the book has remained unaltered, as has also, as far as essentials are concerned, the standpoint of Bultmann himself. For him many of the pericopes and logia of Jesus are nothing more than later "contributions of the community." It is mainly this skepticism which has brought form-criticism into disrepute with conservative scholars. Such skepticism still exists today, and leads, for instance, to the denial of the whole of Jesus's characterization of himself as Messiah, and to its explanation in the light of the faith of the community.[1] Yet, even in the Bultmannian school, a certain change has taken place, above all through the attention being given to the problem of the "historical Jesus." In an essay of 1954 in which he disassociated himself from the

[1] See *TNT,* I, pp. 26–32; E. Käsemann, "Das Problem des historischen Jesus," *ZThK,* 51 (1954), p. 150; H. Conzelmann, "Gegenwart und Zukunft in der synoptischen Tradition," *ZThK,* 54 (1957), p. 281; G. Bornkamm, *Jesus of Nazareth* (London, 1960), pp. 226–231.

school, E. Käsemann sketched this task, recognizing the interest of the primitive Church in the pre-Easter Jesus, and maintaining "that there are sections of the synoptic tradition which the historian must simply recognize as authentic if he wants to remain an historian."[2] Admittedly, as far as the synoptic tradition itself is concerned, Käsemann thinks that after all the work of form-criticism the reliability of the synoptic tradition can in general no longer be taken for granted.[3] So, this research-method's new approach to the "historical Jesus"[4] remains critical of the synoptic tradition as such; the presumption is against its genuineness, and the burden of proof that in each case a genuine tradition of Jesus is involved lies with its defenders.[5]

On the other hand, there are scholars who are prepared to prove genuine utterances of Jesus and traditions about him, whether on the ground of Jesus's originality of thought and attitude, or because of the Palestinian coloring of the presentation, or the Aramaisms, or the linguistic peculiarities of the sayings of Jesus, and so on.[6] Of course, these attempts are often rejected by opposing scholars as inadequate, since, for example, the primitive community, still Aramaic-speaking, would also have been capable of such presentations. But this patient historical and philological research merits greater attention, since it brings together many parts of the mosaic, which, at the

[2] E. Käsemann, art. cit., p. 152.

[3] Ibid., p. 142.

[4] See J. M. Robinson, New Quest of the Historical Jesus (Naperville, 1959); idem, "The Recent Debate on the 'New Quest,' " Journal of Bible and Religion, 30 (1962), pp. 198–208.

[5] See Käsemann, art. cit., p. 142.

[6] See J. Jeremias, "Kennzeichen der ipsissima vox Jesu," Synoptische Studien (Munich, 1954), pp. 86–93; idem, The Parables of Jesus (New York, 1963); idem, The Problem of the Historical Jesus (Philadelphia, 1964); N. A. Dahl, "Der historische Jesus als geschichtswissenschaftliches und theologisches Problem," Kerygma und Dogma, 1 (1955), pp. 104–132; E. Stauffer, Jesus and His Story (London, 1960); W. Grundmann, Die Geschichte Jesu Christi (Berlin, 1957).

very least, raise the historical credibility of the tradition of Jesus. Who in the primitive Church has such a power over words as many of the polished logia of Jesus display, who has such mastery in telling of parables, who has such an original wealth of religious expression?

To the form must be added the special content of the message: the announcement that the kingdom of God was near (which in this form was not absorbed by early Christian preaching),[7] the sovereign attitude adopted by Jesus towards the law, especially towards the prescriptions for purification and the sabbath, and his claim to be savior, which exploded every scheme of Jewish expectation. Some Son of man logia withstand the most severe criticism.[8] This kind of argumentation need not be removed from the form-critical approach, but should make clear in what way statements and claims of Jesus were delivered to the post-Easter Church, and how it received them and passed them on. It would be wrong simply to oppose all methods of form-criticism; rather, we must use them when possible, studying carefully the multiple influence of the post-Easter Church.[9]

Alongside these particular questions, which can check many critical judgments and yet use the same methodology, there are promising developments here, helps towards investigating certain basic positions of the approach of form-criticism. Those who are skeptical towards the tradition of Jesus think of the "chasm" which separates the work of Jesus on earth and the faith of the post-Easter community; they are led to the conclusion that there is no recognizable way back. How could there be, if it has to be proved from form-criticism and tradition-

[7] See R. Schnackenburg, *God's Rule and Kingdom* (New York, 1963), pp. 160–215.

[8] See A. Vögtle, "Jesus Christus," *LThK,* V, pp. 928–932; and "Menschensohn," *LThK,* VII, pp. 297–300.

[9] See B. Rigaux, "Die Zwölf in Geschichte und Kerygma," *Der historische Jesus und der kerygmatische Christus,* ed. H. Ristow and K. Matthiae (Berlin, 1960), pp. 468–486.

criticism that important traditions, above all the logia of Jesus, have their *Sitz im Leben* not in the situation of the Church but in the preaching of Jesus? Such a proof is not easy to give, as the words of Jesus were received by the primitive Church to be made fruitful for her life, so that the critical scholar can always maintain that he has before him the proclamation of the primitive Church.

Yet certain progress has been made in this direction. The Swedish scholar H. Riesenfeld caused surprise at the New Testament Congress in Oxford in 1957 with the thesis that neither the missionary preaching nor the community preaching constitutes the *Sitz im Leben* of the tradition, but rather the activity of teachers who passed on the words and deeds of Jesus in much the same way as the rabbis treated the statements of their authorities, as a "holy," inviolable word. The disciples of Jesus took over this manner of tradition from their Jewish milieu, as the technical use of the expressions for "tradition" in the primitive Church shows. The result is a view of the "origin" of tradition different from form-criticism. The discourse goes back close to Jesus himself.[10] A pupil of Riesenfeld has produced in the meantime a detailed work on this Jewish-Christian method of tradition.[11] There is much that can be said against this analogy from Judaism. But observations on the basis of synoptic comparison strongly confirm the existence of a form for the logia, even when their use in particular contexts cannot be supported.[19] Even G. Bornkamm, a pupil of Bultmann, recognizes the fact "that before all else Jesus himself makes use of established forms in his own preaching, such as were used in the prophecy, wisdom, and the teaching of the Jewish scribes."[13] On the Catholic side H. Schürmann has tried

[10] See H. Riesenfeld, *The Gospel Tradition and Its Beginnings* (London, 1957), pp. 16 ff.

[11] See B. Gerhardssohn, *Memory and Manuscript* (Uppsala, 1961).

[12] See G. Lindeskog, "Logia-Studien," *Studia Theologica*, 4 (1950), pp. 129–189.

[13] G. Bornkamm, "Evangelien (Formgeschichtlich)," *RGG*, II, p. 752.

62

to strengthen the "pre-Easter beginnings of the tradition of the logia" through argument and example.[14] One sees that form-criticism as such does not necessarily lead only to negative judgments about the credibility of the synoptic tradition, if its basic questions force one behind the fixed text to the consideration of the form, the meaning, the genuineness of the words of Jesus.

It also becomes clear that form-criticism is capable and in need of further broadening development. Exegetes are no longer inclined, as for example M. Dibelius was earlier,[15] to draw almost all the material of tradition from the early Christian "preaching," but they have recourse more readily to catechesis and liturgy.[16] For instruction in the faith within the Church the words of the Lord, indeed, the genuine, transmitted words of Jesus, had to have a fundamental meaning. It is possible that their arrangement could be the result of viewpoints other than historical reporting of particular sermons by Jesus; but there should be no doubt that their tenor and origin is from Jesus. The deeds and events of the life of Jesus did not always need to be handed on in their historical circumstances; it was much more important to draw out their abiding significance. If we conceive of a synoptic gospel as something of a "catechism"— each gospel perhaps with its particular emphases and objectives —then its particular form becomes obvious, and there is no need to doubt on that account the reliability of the material of tradition. Basically, our modern catechesis proceeds in the

[14] See H. Schürmann, "Die vorösterlichen Anfänge der Logien-tradition," *Der historische Jesus und der kerygmatische Christus, ed. cit.,* pp. 342–370.

[15] *From Tradition to Gospel* (New York, 1935).

[16] See K. Stendahl, *The School of St. Matthew* (Uppsala-Lund-Copenhagen, 1954); H. Riesenfeld, *op. cit.;* G. Schille, "Bemerkungen zur Formgeschichte des Evangeliums," *New Testament Studies,* 4 (1957–1958), pp. 1–24, 101–114; 5 (1958–1959), pp. 174–187; C. H. Dodd, "The Primitive Catechism and the Sayings of Jesus," *New Testament Essays* (Manchester, 1959), pp. 106–118; D. M. Stanley, "Liturgical Influence on the Formation of the Four Gospels," *CBQ,* 21 (1959), pp. 24–38.

same way, and it is understandable that Church instruction, as distinct from purely historical reporting, must proceed in this way to make the "history of Jesus," his Word and instruction, alive for faith. A positive use of form-criticism is not a faddish capitulation but a valuable tool for both exegete and theologian.[17]

ADVANTAGES OF FORM-CRITICISM

The suitability and usefulness of form-criticism can be shown and illustrated by the following examples. If we turn to the Gospel of Mark, we are struck by certain "disciple" pericopes in its first part: the calling (1:16–20), the choice of the twelve (3:14–19), and their mission (6:7–13). Considered purely historically, it is remarkable that the two pairs of brothers in 1:16–20 immediately leave work, home, and family on Jesus' (first) call to discipleship and attach themselves to Jesus. Also, we discover from the gospel of John (1:40–42) that Simon Peter and Andrew had already become acquainted with Jesus at the scene of John the Baptist's labors and joined his group of disciples. But Mark's report pursues a different goal: he wants to offer a "typical" calling of disciples, from which the essen-

[17] For further details, see E. Schick, *Formgeschichte und Synoptikerexegese* (Münster, 1940); F. M. Braun, "Formgeschichte," *DBS,* III, pp. 312–318; J. Huby and X. Léon–Dufour, *L'évangile et les évangiles* (Paris, 1954); J. Heuschen, *et al., Recherches bibliques,* II (Louvain, 1957); X. Léon–Dufour, "Formgeschichte et Redaktionsgeschichte des Evangiles synoptiques," *RSR,* 46 (1958), pp. 237–269; A. Wikenhauser, *New Testament Introduction* (New York, 1963), pp. 253–277; R. Schnackenburg, "Formgeschictliche Methode," *LThK,* IV, pp. 211–213; L. Randellini, "La formazione degli Evangeli sinnotici secondo la critica recente," *Divus Thomas,* 73 (1960), pp. 3–30. See W. Marxen, *Der Evangelist Markus: Studien zur Redaktionsgeschichte des Evangeliums* (Göttingen, 1960); W. Trilling, *Das wahre Israel: Studien zur Theologie des Matthäusevangeliums* (Leipzig, 1959); J. Gnilka, *Die Verstockung Israels: Isaias 6, 9–10 in der Theologie der Synoptiker* (Munich, 1961). As an example of how the form-critical, literary, and historical approaches can be combined, see X. Léon–Dufour, "Passion," *DBS,* VI, pp. 1419–1492.

tials of "calling" and "following" can be gathered, without questioning the calling of the two pairs of brothers which actually took place. In this way, through the sovereign call, to which those called responded by obedience, Jesus has drawn and gathered disciples to himself. This gathering of disciples, as the choice of the twelve shows (3:13–19), also has a particular meaning in salvation history: Jesus lays claim to the eschatological people of God (the number twelve). From the standpoint of the primitive Church, there is a special ecclesiological meaning: in the circle of disciples there is a portrayal of the later, that is, definitively constituted after Easter, community (Church) of Jesus.

The sending of the disciples is to be understood as similarly historical and yet at the same time anticipatory and permanently valid (6:7–13). Mark does not give the historically revealing directive of Jesus that the disciples are not to go to the pagans and Samaritans but only to the "lost sheep of the house of Israel" (Mt. 10:5 f.); but neither does he deëmphasize the historical character of this first sending of the disciples at the climax of Jesus' Galilean ministry (see the return of the disciples, 6:30 f.). At the same time, however, he wants to give his readers a lesson about the mission of the Church and the activity of its missionaries. The mission is the continuation of the activity of Jesus, the assumption of his proclamation and saving power. Mark demands the same spirit of missionary zeal, eschatological urgency, and human modesty that filled Jesus and his disciples. Perhaps the construction of this part, up to the scene at Caesarea (8:27–30), is arranged so that two levels of understanding become possible: the historical activity of Jesus with its echo among the people, and at the same time also the "doctrine" which results from it for the later community in its beginnings, life, and activity. The exposition of the "history of Jesus" becomes "transparent," reveals important aspects for the early Church's understanding of itself, as it sees its existence founded in the activity of Jesus, its experience anticipated in his experience, its tasks determined by his will. The great miracle of the feeding in the desert, the trips through Jewish territory, the scene with the heathen Syrophoenician woman, the conversation about leaven—all take on alongside the "historical" aspect another "actual" meaning. In other words, not only an interest in historical reporting but a many-layered "theological" interest directs the presentation.

Of course, all this requires more precise investigation and further reflection. That this approach, concerned with the direct interests of the community addressed throughout by the gospel, is warranted and intended by the evangelist, cannot be doubted for the section 8:31–38. From a purely historical viewpoint it is improbable that Jesus called at the same time "the whole group of disciples" (v. 34), in order to impress on that circle of hearers those three or four pregnant logia which are brought together in vv. 34–38. But it is theologically and didactically meaningful that at the first announcement of the sufferings of Jesus (v. 31), against which Peter protests in vain (vv. 32 f.), those statements demanding of the disciples of Jesus an equal readiness for the laying down of life, should be immediately added. On the other hand, it is precisely these logia which are raised above the suspicion of being later "contributions of the community." It is the paradoxically formulated words which betray the spirit and style of Jesus, but they are brought in at this point because they reveal here their deeper meaning and assume a greater force. Are not these sayings intended for the hitherto faithful disciples rather than for all the people? Matthew (16:24) has them directed "to his disciples," Luke (9:23) "to all." That is not inconsistent, if one bears in mind the particular intention of the evangelists with regard to these "frame-observations." For actually these once-spoken words of Jesus to his "disciples" retain their binding power "for all," for the whole later Church, which Mark would designate by the expression "the whole group of disciples."

Mark 9:33–50 cannot be understood except as a "collection united in a tradition," which had already been gathered together in the early Church as an instruction for disciples, or as a "rule for the community."[18] Looked at historically, this rapid succession of small scenes and different logia remains incomprehensible, but as a "catchword composition" they become clear. This archaic character of a collection of traditions, even if it resulted from a mnemonic process, guarantees the reliability of the tradition. Even so, the primitive Church would have been guided by a superior, realistic point of view which could without difficulty recognize that there are directions of Jesus to the disciples which retain their validity for the life of the community and on this level acquired even a new significance. We possess another, quite similar "rule for the community" in Matthew 18:1–20, which deals in part with the same tradition-material.[19] To be specific, the parable of the lost sheep (Mt. 18:12–14), which in Luke 15:3–7 illustrates God's all-merciful love of sinners, is related to the shepherds of the community and their duty of zealous care for "the little ones." Is it permissible so to use a parable intended originally by Jesus in another sense? For a strict historian, scarcely; but the primitive Church clearly thought otherwise. There are many examples of this changing of sense. In the Lukan account of the argument about rank among the disciples in the Upper Room and the appended words of Jesus (22:24–30), the intention is to give a lesson to the future community reading this report,[20] especially since the parallel passages report a quarrel among the disciples in another place but in relation to almost the same logia (see Mt. 20:24–27; Mk. 10:41–44; also, Mt. 18:1–4; Mk. 9:33–37; Lk. 9:46–48).

[18] See L. Vaganay, "Le schématisme du discours communautaire à la lumière de la critique des sources," *RB*, 60 (1953), pp. 203–244; R. Schnackenburg, "Markus 9, 33–50," *Synoptische Studien, ed. cit.*, pp. 184–206.

[19] See W. Trilling, *Hausordnung Gottes: Eine Auslegung von Matthäus 18* (Düsseldorf, 1960).

[20] See H. Schürmann, *Der Abendmahlsbericht Lukas 22, 7–38 als Gosttesdienstordnung, Gemeindeordnung, Lebensordnung* (Leipzig, 1955), pp. 69–75.

Returning to the Gospel of Mark, we find that the large section 10:1–45 was likewise composed with an eye to the primitive Church, which guarded the word and command of Jesus as a binding heritage. In it are united five pericopes dealing with: divorce (vv. 1–12); Jesus and the children (vv. 13–16); the rich young man and statements about rich and poor (vv. 17–31); the third announcement of the passion (vv. 32–34); the request of the sons of Zebedee and words about commanding and serving (vv. 35–45). At this time Jesus restricted himself more to the group of disciples (see 9:30 ff.), so it is strange that the introductory passage is, "the crowds gathered to him again" and he "taught them again, as was his custom" (v. 1). Should not Jesus be emphasized here as the "teacher" (as so often in Mark), in order to bring out not only what he then taught among the Galilean people, but his abiding teaching office in the Church? In any case, the themes are large and important for the life of the community: the attitude towards marriage, children, ownership, and power. Other important sayings of Jesus, which could have been uttered at other times, are from time to time combined with particular scenes from Jesus' work. Before the request of the Zebedees, ambitious and deluded by worldly dreams, the last and longest announcement of the passion of their master is effectively introduced as a contrast. This forms a small, vivid catechism on important questions of the moral life, the life of the community in this world.

We can see how differently these pieces appear when considered only as historical reports from the life of Jesus. The basic decision of Jesus on the question of marriage was so important for the early Church that another special instruction for the disciples is appended (vv. 10–12), by means of which all doubt about the absolute prohibition by Jesus of divorce is excluded. We meet in verse 12 the formula, "when a woman divorces her husband." This does not correspond to Jewish marriage law, in which the man alone has the right by a letter of divorce to divorce his wife, but it refers rather to Roman divorce practice. The evangelist brings to his Gentile-Christian readers the sense and scope of the decision of Jesus with unmistakable clarity. What are the consequences of this procedure of the early Church? It not only transmits the historic, revolutionary answer of Jesus that marriage according to God's basic will is indissoluble, but adds its own "commentary," which excludes all misunderstanding. The process is therefore important, because in modern times doubts are expressed as to whether and to what extent the radical demands of Jesus in the sermon on the mount are to be literally or metaphorically understood. In the light of Mark 10:2 ff., we cannot agree with Bultmann when he says, "Whoever appealing to a word of Jesus refuses to dissolve an unendurable marriage, or whoever offers the other cheek to one who strikes him, *because* Jesus said so, would not understand Jesus."[21] Bultmann's second example is certainly an instance of the renunciation of revenge; but the first, according to the understanding of the early Church (see 1 Cor. 7:10 ff.), is a strict prohibition in the literal sense. But now we have the problem of how to draw from the gospels as far as possible the *bruta verba et facta Jesu*. We should be grateful to the early Church that it did not have another conception of how to pass on the words of the Lord. Following the intention of Jesus, it did not wish to fix them mechanically, but at the same time it did want to establish their meaning.

Jesus' blessing of the children is no mere idyllic scene but a serious piece of doctrine for the community, an answer to the question, "What is the position of children; have they any share in the kingdom of God? What place belongs to them in the community?" Many modern exegetes go so far as to say that in verse 14 ("Hinder them not") there is a formulation which became liturgically significant: the reply of Jesus was grasped by the community as approval for infant baptism.[22] Similarly

---

[21] *JW*, p. 92.
[22] See O. Cullmann, *Die Tauflehre des Neuen Testaments* (Zürich, 1948), pp. 65–73; J. Jeremias, *Infant Baptism in the First Four Centuries* (London, 1960), pp. 51 ff.

important, in view of the words and actions of Jesus, was the question of attitude towards worldly possessions. He had spoken harshly against riches, and with hyperbole said it was extremely difficult for a rich person to enter the kingdom of God (v. 25). But, the disciples asked (and later believers asked with them), who then can be saved? The answer of Jesus was encouraging and consoling: with God all things are possible (v. 27). Along the same lines, Jesus' answer to Peter's question about the reward for voluntary poverty is, in the formulation of Mark, instructive. As distinct from Matthew 19:29, there is here the question of a hundred-fold reward "now at this time," even though it comes "with persecution." The primitive Church thought of the many spiritual "brothers" who receive the disciple into the community after he has left his worldly family (see Mk. 3:34 f.). But here also there is a warning about exaggerated expectations in the present time, during which the disciples must still reckon with persecution. Finally, the early Church comes to realize in the basic attitude of Jesus to worldly power (Mk. 10:42 ff.) the law of service, which is put to the community as a new commandment ("but it shall not be so among you"). The Church looks to its Lord, who as the expiatory servant of God has given it the greatest model of service and self-denial (v. 45).

Let us, finally, take a look at the section Mark 12:13–37. The long discussions between Jesus and the ruling circles in Jerusalem during the few days after his entry into the holy city have always been thought unusual. Even exegetes who are particularly interested in the historical sequence of the life of Jesus consider it possible that discussions are reported there which took place during an earlier visit to Jerusalem; otherwise, the synoptic presentation provided no opportunity for such discussions. In the form-criticism school the "Jerusalem collection of controversy dialogues" (Mk. 2:27–12, 40) was readily seen as a foil to the "Galilean collection" (Mk. 2:1–3, 6), whose five parts were assembled according to subject matter rather than historical sequence.[23] Of course, many different kinds of material were included in Mark 12, and particular conversations, such as that of the greatest commandment, would have to be characterized as "scholastic dialogues." Recently, the Jewish law historian D. Daube has advanced an interesting thesis. According to him, the "four questions" handled successively in Mark 12:13–17 (the Pharisees on tax, the Sadducees on the resurrection, the Scribes on the greatest commandment, and the Messiah as Son of David), are different in their own way and correspond to a Jewish schema, which was observed, for example, in the Pasch-Haggadah. It is possible that this arrangement in the synoptic gospels also has a liturgical *Sitz im Leben,* perhaps an early Christian passover celebration for which Jewish Christian circles took over Jewish usage.[24] This thesis will appear to many as strange or daring; but H. Schürmann, in his investigations of Luke 22, has shown it to be likely that there did exist an "adapted" Christian passover and an old "account of the passover meal"[25] (from the Last Supper of Jesus). But even if one prescinds from a direct liturgical influence, the Jewish "question schema" (demonstrated by Daube) may have had a bearing on the form of this section. The early Church's collecting of important pericopes under a theological aspect does not endanger historical genuineness. The question of the Son of David is particularly suspect as being a contribution of the community, for it seems to reflect debates in the community concerning the messiahship or divine sonship of Jesus.[26] In this regard, Daube's observation is useful

[23] See M. Albertz, *Die synoptischen Streitgespräche* (Berlin, 1921), pp. 16–36; V. Taylor, *The Gospel According to St. Mark* (London, 1952), pp. 101, 468.

[24] See D. Daube, *The New Testament and Rabbinic Judaism* (London, 1955), pp. 158–169.

[25] See H. Schürmann, *Der Paschamahlbericht Lk. 22, 7–14, 15–18* (Münster, 1953); *Idem,* "Die Anfänge christlicher Osterfeier," *Theologische Quartalschrift,* 131 (1951), pp. 414–425; J. Jeremias, "πασχα," *TWNT,* V, pp. 900 ff.

[26] *HST,* pp. 136 ff.

71

—there were Haggadah questions for which the deeper agreement of two apparently contradictory passages was discussed; why should not Jesus himself have argued in this way? Precisely the indirect testimony of his messianic claim corresponds to his behavior in other ways.

These examples illustrate the value of form-criticism. It need not destroy the historical reliability of the synoptic tradition, but can illuminate it, render it more understandable, and frequently explain the divergences among the synoptics. Above all, it gives us along with the tradition of the words of the Lord the understanding of the primitive Church. It allows us to hear the living voice of this Church in its proclamation. Form-criticism has many consequences for today's theological situation, to some of which we now turn our attention.

THEOLOGICAL CONSEQUENCES

Form-criticism has made the formulation of fundamental theology more difficult, but not impossible. It is no longer enough to show textual integrity, relative origin from the evangelists named in the tradition of the Church, an early time of composition, and so forth, in order to work with the gospels as reliable historical documents. Unique though these sources may be, the history of their own traditions must be taken into account. We must study the origin, the *Sitz im Leben,* the formation of the individual pieces of tradition, the original form and meaning of tradition, the possibility and probability of words attributed to Jesus, their integration into the entire Christian proclamation, and in the case of explanatory material, its credibility in the framework of the life and activity of Jesus, and, finally, any other influential tendencies. But does not all this involve theology in a hopelessly difficult task?

We should recall that the role of fundamental theology is to work with the means available to reason, and so to explore the empirical and philosophical grounds of our faith. It must enter into the postulates and methods of secular science, particularly of history without giving up the message of faith. It would lose credibility if it rejected in advance, or with bad apologetics declared as unreliable, the methods developed by other disciplines.

In view of the uniqueness of the gospels we cannot characterize form-criticism as hostile and illegitimate. According to the facts ascertainable in the gospels themselves, this method concerns itself with collected and juxtaposed tradition-material which is subject to the same rules and laws as other "developed" traditions, even though its special character as a "holy" tradition, one to be preserved faithfully according to the supernatural faith of the primitive Church, is to be respected.

The Catholic theologian cannot and need not associate himself with some scholars' non-exegetical prerequisites when they prescind from revelation, inspiration, and canon. He avails himself of the methods of historico-critical research when they are suitable. As with all scientific questions (for which there can never be a complete absence of prerequisites), the answers and results will come out differently. But these must be supplied in the frame of the possibilities offered by critical research.

The historian must use his sources according to their particular nature. Even with the "tendencies" he discovers in the text's presentation he can still critically investigate events and facts. It would contradict the principles of sound historical research to reject in advance as completely unusable any source containing such "tendencies." The gospels were written by believing authors for communities that believed in Christ. The problem lies in the question of the extent their "tendencies towards faith" can and do allow a really correct, historically reliable exposition. To show this is a task for theology today.

This changed situation consists in the fact that a theologian's efforts to ascertain historical events, to reach and grasp the once spoken words of the revealer, Jesus Christ, have hitherto been too readily and simply equated with the object of the gospels.

73

Now, however, he must realize that these words reflect the kergymatic, catechetical, and other living interests of the community. Of course, Jesus' aims, history, and word are embedded and preserved there because the primitive Church wanted to render reliable information and witness. But the theologian does not stand immediately before the Jesus spoken of and dealt with in the sources, but rather immediately before the proclamation of the primitive Church. With the Church he looks back to the words and deeds of Jesus.

However, we should not look at the question exclusively from the point of view of theology. The consideration of the gospels from the point of view of the history of their traditions can broaden our vision theologically, and this new approach to the gospels, perhaps at first disturbing, can, as far as theology is concerned, reveal its fruitfulness, as the examples given above illustrate. We should approach these inspired writings in the manner best suited to them. As witnesses of the primitive Christian proclamation and instruction they offer us the fruit of the theological meditation of the primitive Church, or of the evangelists, something all the more valuable in that it is given us by the apostolic witnesses and interpreters of the revelation of Jesus Christ, by the inspired authors of the New Testament. In this way it is possible to draw out the oldest, really basic theology connected closely with revelation. This is the rich task of New Testament theology.

There can be misunderstanding when the doctrine and message of Jesus are designated as prerequisites of New Testament theology and are not considered as pertaining to its essential content.[27] We should recall that the theological contemplation

[27] See H. Schlier, "Sinn und Aufgabe einer Theologie des Neuen Testaments," *BZ* (NF), 1 (1957), pp. 12 f.; there Schlier says: "Of course, the final conclusion of the person, deeds, and word of Jesus preceded the theology of the New Testament authors, so that there can be no theology of the New Testament without this conclusion. But how did it precede the theology of the New Testament? Briefly, the history of Jesus awakens faith and makes possible the theological statements of the New Testament because it is firmly grounded in something beyond both of these."

74

of the primitive Church builds on the word of Jesus and his saving act bound to his person, and so the revelation of Jesus has a basic meaning. The Catholic viewpoint differs from that of theologians who consider the words and deeds of the "historical Jesus" as irrelevant, and occupy themselves only with the question of the "kerygma."[28] Naturally, one must distinguish between the immediate revelation of Jesus and the proclamation of the early Church which receives it, interprets it, and penetrates it theologically. But this is legitimate only as long as we are aware that under another aspect the proclamation of the early Church, formulated in the inspired writings of the New Testament, must be recognized as "revelation," since Scripture with its assertions is, specifically, a source of revelation. How the direct message of Jesus in the framework of a "New Testament theology" is to be brought to expression is another question. Perhaps this would be best done in connection with the oldest proclamation of the primitive Church which received it and passed it on.

Form-criticism of the gospels enables a broader development of the ideas implicit in the word of Jesus, for example his community, the Church. If we were to stop short at the spoken words of Jesus handed down in the Church, we would not find a great number of statements. Jesus first of all and directly addressed his contemporaries. He wanted to win all Israel for his message. Only after a rejection by the people of the old covenant could the foundation of the new salvation-community (see

[28] Bultmann writes: "By tradition Jesus is named as bearer of the message; according to overwhelming probability he really was. Should it prove otherwise, that does not change, in any way, what is said in the records" (*JW*, p. 14). In a more recent work, he clarifies his position without changing its basis: "For the Christ of the kerygma is not a historical figure which stands in continuity with the historical Jesus. Certainly, the kerygma which proclaims him is a historical phenomenon, but there can be a question of continuity only between this kerygma and the historical Jesus" (*Das Verhältnis der urchristlichen Christusbotschaft zum historischen Jesus* [Heidelberg, 1962], p. 8). For a criticism of the existential kerygma-theology by a Protestant, see P. Althaus, *Das sogenannte Kerygma und der historische Jesus* (Gütersloh, 1958).

Mt. 16:18), be visibly and expressly addressed by Jesus. Only his atoning death realized the "new covenant" concluded "in his blood" (Lk. 22:20; see Mk. 14:24), and only with the mission of the Holy Spirit did the "Church" enter effectively into life. But the primitive Church, cognizant of itself as the community of Jesus, now saw in retrospect how Jesus' word and act were directed to this foundation, and understood in a much deeper sense that its existence was depicted and anticipated in the circle of disciples.

The mind and activity of Jesus are rendered much more accessible here than in a purely historical exposition. We can recognize in the gospels the basic features of the "Church," as the primitive Church itself saw them. The same applies to the self-revelation of Jesus as Messiah and Son of God. It can scarcely be disputed historically (for the historical understanding of the behavior of Jesus it is essential) that it was only with great caution that he revealed the secret of his person. Here the primitive Church was able and obliged to bring to the fore unmistakably the witness of Jesus to himself in the light of his resurrection (and as illumined by the Holy Spirit). This unfolded for its believers the deeper meaning of the words of Jesus and, above all, of his deeds, his behavior, and his fate. The risen Lord himself did this for the disciples on the road to Emmaus (Lk. 24:25 ff.). Christological statements attain a greater fullness and clarity without losing their authenticity based in the self-witness of Jesus. All of Christology is implied in the self-witness of Jesus, but it is more strongly and explicitly expounded by the primitive Church. (This is clearly the case with the Gospel of John.)

We could offer many other illustrations—for example, the doctrine of the Holy Spirit, of baptism and Eucharist, of the parousia of Christ—of what was more strongly and deeply grasped by the primitive Church than by the disciples at the time of Jesus. The Gospel of John gives us the theological principle that it could not have been otherwise. Jesus says to his disciples in the Upper Room: "I have yet many things to say to you, but you cannot bear them now. When the Spirit of truth comes, he will guide you into all the truth" (16:12). That was the authorization of the apostolic witnesses to the activity of Jesus (see Jn. 15:27) for their presentation of the activity of Jesus (not misrepresenting the historical events but throwing light on them) and for their witness of the word of Jesus, which was a tradition and an interpretation. This allows us to understand better form-criticism's consideration of the gospels, the backward glance to their *Sitz im Leben* in the primitive Church.

In conclusion we must say something about the value of the information gathered in this way. The primitive Church shows us by its procedure that the words of the Revealer served as an abiding and direct voice to all hearers. His deeds and divinely decreed destiny are to be presented in their existential meaning for us and for our salvation. This is clear not only through the preaching of the apostles handed down in the Acts of the Apostles and the epistles, but also in the way the Church presents the report of Jesus' life, doctrine, and activity in the gospels. Such a report could not and should not be a purely historical account, but a "gospel," God's message of salvation, the message of salvation of and by Jesus Christ (see Mk. 1:1). Along with the primitive Church, the Church of all time should give knowledge and witness to the word and activity of Jesus. For this the gospels offer us not only the material but a vital lesson as to how this can be done. No one will deny that this makes our present task of proclaiming the truth easier than if we had only historical reports, a "documentary account" something always imperfect and open to misunderstanding. With gratitude we receive the gospels in their present form from the hand of the Church. They bring us that "Word of life" (Phil. 2:16), which once rang out, was immediately effective, and remains ever true. The gospels let us encounter the "Word of Life" in person (1 Jn. 1:1).

77

IV. BULTMANN AND THE GOSPEL ACCORDING TO JOHN

By Josef Blank

Whoever undertakes to analyze Bultmann's interpretation of the Gospel of John—an interpretation which has had considerable influence in the study of this Gospel—must be concerned with this Gospel's complex development. He must try to see Bultmann's interpretation in its various components, tendencies, and intentions. He must be conscious that in this area he is deeply involved with the problem of interpretation, the "hermeneutical question." Finally, the importance of the historical-critical method in the interpretation of the New Testament, its entire scientific problematic as well as the intellectual, philosophical, and theological situation during the first half of the twentieth century in Germany (for example, Dilthey, Barth, Heidegger, phenomenology, dialectical theology, existentialism), must be kept in mind.

Many studies on Bultmann suffer from the fact that they look only at one side (usually the less difficult side) of his theology, his "existential interpretation" of the New Testament. They do not pursue his theology or interpretation to its foundation, his exegesis. These works remain provisional since they do not touch the foundation of Bultmann's theology, the New Testament text itself. Karl Barth remarks rightly: "Bultmann is an exegete, but I do not think that a person can discuss with him

78

only on terms of exegesis, because he is, at the same time, a systematic theologian to such an extent that at almost every step in his exegesis, regardless of the text, axioms of his theological thought are evident."[1] But this emphasis on Bultmann's theology should not lead to a neglect of his exegesis. The confrontation of his exegetical interpretation with the New Testament text offers the possibility to see more clearly the contours of his own theological understanding, "the axioms of his thought."

As we compare Bultmann's exegesis with the text, we will be able to judge more easily whether his exegesis is verified and substantiated by the New Testament text. Moreover, the principles of his interpretation of the New Testament are active in the individual sections of his exegesis. So, proceeding from another direction, an individual examination of basic aspects of his exegesis should cast light on the question of its principles. As exegesis, his work should be tested by the text of the New Testament; in the following critical dialogue, the role of judge falls, then, to the text of the New Testament.

THE QUESTION OF HERMENEUTIC

The basic criterion for the critical analysis of a text remains the confrontation with that text itself, in our case the Gospel according to John. It would, of course, be naïve to think that we could simply develop our exegesis from "what is there." Rather, the critic who refers himself to this text immediately has a definite relationship to the text. He does not exist without a "preliminary understanding" (*Vorverständnis*). How, then, can we say that the text itself is the criterion? First of all, as a reality before its interpreters, the text has its own reflective aspect, for it is a definite understanding of revelation, an articulated exegesis of God, Jesus Christ, world, man, and history in a complex and manifold linguistic and conceptual form. The text brings its own horizon of understanding with itself. The "reality" expressed here is already, to some extent, set forth by the text. It is not a

---

[1] Karl Barth, *Church Dogmatics* (Edinburgh, 1960), III/2, p. 445.

completely dark chaos illuminated only through exegesis or interpretation, but a totality basically thought through and structured by its author. If a text were not itself structured in a meaningful way, no interpretative attempts could make any sense out of it. But because of the text's linguistic and reflective structure, the text itself presents a certain reality which interpretation tries to penetrate, a demand which the exegete must accept in order to be led into the process of understanding this text.

A discussion of Bultmann's hermeneutical view is unavoidable for our question. His essay "The Problem of Hermeneutics"[2] illumines his interpretation of John. Here he explains his important idea of "preliminary understanding" (which is totally different from prejudice). Every interpretation is "constantly orientated to a particular formulation of a question, a particular objective."[3] It is "never without its own presuppositions," but is "governed always by a preliminary understanding of the subject." The preliminary understanding as including an interest in the subject makes interpretation possible; it is its condition. Preliminary understanding is grounded in "the interpreter's relationship in his life to the subject"[4]; it is an understanding grounded through my interest in the subject, my existential relationship to it. "And in the same way it is understandable for this reason, that every interpretation incorporates a particular preliminary understanding—namely, that which arises out of the context of living experience to which the subject belongs."[5] This relationship to our life means "that a condition for exposition is the fact that the expositor and author live as men in the same historical world, in which 'human being' occurs as a 'being' in an environment, in understanding intercourse with objects and our fellowmen."[6] Bultmann develops here along with the idea of living experience the historical dimension of existence. Historicity is an "existential-ontological" aspect of man. All of this leads to and attains depth in self-understanding.

[2] *EPT*, II, pp. 234–261.   [3] *Ibid.*, p. 239.
[4] *Ibid.*, p. 241.   [5] *Ibid.*, p. 242.
[6] *Ibid.*, p. 243.

"Interpretation is intended to bring comprehension of the possibilities of man's being . . . [as revealed in the text]."[7] The direction of interpretation (*Woraufhin*) is "the possibilities that belong specifically to the one who understands."[8] This understanding is concerned with the understanding of man's being, his existence in history.

Bultmann says that without this understanding the text is mute. The hermeneutical problem is deeply related to the epistemological problem with the added factor of historicity. The self-understanding present and objectified in the text and the understanding of the text ending in a new self-understanding correspond to each other. "The 'most subjective' interpretation is in this case the most 'objective,' that is, only those who are stirred by the question of their own existence can hear the claim which the text makes."[9]

In contrast to Barth, Bultmann says that the Scriptures' subject is not God's action (of which we would have no preliminary understanding), but man's existence. "In the same way the comprehension of records about events as the action of God presupposes a prior understanding of what may in my case be termed the action of God—let us say, as distinct from man's action or natural events. . . . We have to reply that *man may very well be aware who God is, namely, in the inquiry about him.*"[10] Man's existence is troubled, moved by this question, otherwise he would not be able to know God in God's revelation. In human existence there is a vital existential knowledge about God, formed in a concern with happiness, salvation, meaning, existence, and so forth. This knowledge can attain concrete form. It is the New Testament which responds to the question, unfolds this knowledge. But it is the mission of philosophical (in the terms of existential) analysis to develop and unfold human existence. It precises the preliminary understanding brought to the text. "It is a mistake to think we can understand a word of the New Testament without such a prior understanding and the concepts which emanate from it, if it is

---

[7] *Ibid.*, p. 246.   [8] *Loc. cit.*
[9] *Ibid.*, p. 256.   [10] *Ibid.*, p. 255.

to be understood as the Word of God."[11] Bultmann concludes: "The exegete is to 'interpret' Scripture, after he has responsibly 'heard' what Scripture has to say! And how is he to 'hear' without *understanding?* The problem of interpretation is precisely that of understanding!"[12]

Bultmann's understanding of the problem of hermeneutic is important for understanding his hermeneutical position with regards to the Gospel of John. His leading principle of interpretation is an existential understanding of man, a new self-understanding to be gained in terms of an existential dimension. This opens the horizon for interpretation and this is interpretation's principle. This preliminary understanding is for Bultmann "a condition for the possibility of understanding." We cannot here go further into the implications of Kantianism which might lie in this view of understanding, but we should note that the principle-concept experiences here a remarkable modification. "From the interest of the subject arises the nature of the formulation of inquiry, the *direction of the investigation and, therefore, the hermeneutical principle.*"[13] The principle is, simply, the type of questioning, developed here as an understanding of existence. Clearly, Bultmann means something different with the word "principle," and not principle in the Aristotelian or medieval sense of *principium.*

THE HERMENEUTICAL PRINCIPLE IN THOMAS AQUINAS'S COMMENTARY ON JOHN

In order to develop Bultmann's particular hermeneutical point of departure more clearly, let us compare it with a view of medieval theology, that of Thomas Aquinas.[14] Here the "prin-

11 *Ibid.*, p. 258.
12 *Ibid.*, p. 261.
13 *Ibid.*, p. 252.
14 Thomas Aquinas, *Super Evangelium S. Ioanis Lectura*, ed. R. Cai, O.P. (Rome, 1952).

ciple" is the ultimate sustaining ground of being and reality, "truth itself," *veritas ipsa,* the ground of meaning, the light (*lux-illuminans*) of all understanding. Truth itself must be God who in his Word and through his Word is the principle of revelation to men.[15] As the light of men revelation comes to realization. *Non solum manifestatur hoc vel illud, sed ipsa veritas, quae manifestabilis est et manifestiva omnium.* This theology is often developed with the example of John 8:25 where the Vulgate identifies Jesus with the "beginning" who speaks to us.[16] In and through Jesus the divine origin speaks to us.[17] While God reveals himself in Jesus, at the same time he remains the principle of revelation and its understanding, for through the Spirit he opens its truth and raises men to its understanding.[18] In this theology the principle of understanding the biblical text as the word of God is ultimately God revealing himself in Jesus Christ, who through his Spirit makes our understanding of his word possible, working in man through faith. Doubtless, we encounter in the biblical text the Word of God, but as a written word this is not simply identical with Christ, but is a relational analogue to Christ. The word is itself a sign and not the immediate reality. The reality is much more Christ himself and, at the same time, Christ as God revealing himself, so that while faith certainly orientates itself towards the written and preached word, it does not stop directly at the formula or expression, but goes rather "*ad rem,*" to the reality itself.[19] The understanding of a text can but need not neces-

---

[15] *Ibid.,* p. 20.

[16] *Ibid.,* p. 221.

[17] "*Ad hoc ergo quod immediate ipsum divinum Verbum audiremus, carnem assumpsit, cuius organo locutus est nobis*" (*loc. cit.*).

[18] Concerning the Holy Spirit, Aquinas writes: "*Cum enim sit a veritate, ejus est docere veritatem, et facere similes suo principio*" (*ibid.,* p. 397). This means that the Spirit "teaches" the truth of God inasmuch as he suits this truth to men, harmonizes man's understanding with the reality to be grasped. Man does not bring this propensity to understanding with him because as sinner and man he is a stranger to revelation which is not similar to him.

[19] Thomas Aquinas, *Summa theologiae,* II–II, q. 1, a. 2, ad 2.

sarily be identical with the understanding of the reality which this understanding of the text unfolds for faith.

The basic difference between Aquinas's view and Bultmann's is that Bultmann begins with the dimension of the historical, placing the question of understanding in the horizons of the historicity and the self-understanding of man whose existence is encompassed by history. An example might be God revealing himself. How should man come to an understanding or, better, to a knowledge of God in his revelation, to faith which always includes a moment of understanding? (Revelation comes to this; it does not necessarily begin here.) This indicates (the question was not, of course, asked in this way in the Middle Ages) the historical dimension of the question of revelation and faith. What is the historical facet of understanding, of man's understanding, of the historicity of all understanding even in faith and theology? The central problem can be phrased in this way: If scriptural exegesis today must follow in the path of the historicity of understanding, will it still give us access to the reality in a text which is the Word of God, to a revelation of God in Jesus Christ? And, how will it do this? A non-historical view which would set aside the historical nature of the mediation and interpretation of faith, Scripture and dogma, is no longer possible now that the historical conditions of holy Scripture are recognized. It is the difficult question of the historical in theology, and this is the context of Bultmann's work.

FURTHER ASPECTS

How does Bultmann's hermeneutical principle, existential understanding, apply to this or that text? We have seen that the text itself has a particular meaning and structure. A preliminary understanding before a text cannot be simply *my* preliminary understanding. Then every interpretation would be superfluous; it would be an unrelated self-interpretation. Bultmann rightly introduces here the concept of the reality itself. Preliminary understanding is an *understanding in the reality* and must let itself be questioned by the text. We cannot simply cut the reality out of the text. The reality appears in the horizon of the text given and mediated by it, for example through the kind of eschatological conceptuality, or in a language and thought-pattern formed by the Old Testament with Hellenistic and gnostic elements added to it. Bultmann certainly thinks that this conceptuality can lead us to a basic, underlying understanding of human existence where reality is joined to text and interpretation. But does this do justice to the problematic? Since reality and language cannot be separated in the text, the problem of interpretation becomes more complex. Reflection through a historical distance, a distance of 2000 years, reminds us that both of these horizons, the horizon in the text and the one brought by me, are distinguished in understanding. An attempt simply to meet "what is there" is open to the danger of misunderstanding. H. G. Gadamer has pointed out this fact at length in his work *Wahrheit und Methode*.[20] He has developed the concept of active history and active-historical consciousness.[21] "The distance in time is not something to be overcome." Rather, "the distance in time must be recognized for its positive and productive potential."[22] The text comes to me and determines with myself my own horizon. The horizon of today is not formed without the past. There is neither today's horizon nor various historical horizons. *"Much more, understanding is always the process of fusing various horizons which previously seemed, incorrectly, to be self-sufficient. . . . The process of tradition is constantly taking place."*[23]

To return to our question, the text of the Bible has produced a history of exegesis, a history of Christian theology, even the history of the Church.[24] The Church's tradition of teaching is a

[20] Tübingen, 1960.   [21] *Ibid.*, pp. 284 ff.
[22] *Ibid.*, p. 281.   [23] *Ibid.*, p. 289.
[24] See G. Ebeling, *Die Geschichtlichkeit der Kirche und ihrer Verkündigung als theologisches Problem* (Tübingen, 1954), p. 81; there he defines church history as "the history of the exegesis and interpretation of the Holy Scriptures."

landmark in the process of exegesis and preaching. Catholic, Reformed, or Lutheran traditions are elements which determine our preliminary understanding and they can never be totally excluded from interpretation. These traditions, however, are not just negative moments but can be seen as positive possibilities. The argument about the interpretation of definite texts (for instance, the reports of the Last Supper) shows that a theological preliminary understanding as well as one coming from liturgy and piety has been drawn into interpretation. We see that the text reveals a series of possibilities of understanding, that there are different interpretations: the more diverse the content of the passage is, the more rich it is. We designate the content as the reality, as *the truth of the text;* still, this truth is not one-sided but complex. It is not a mathematical formula which has only one sense. Its truth is the Word of God, and the text seen *analogously* (and not immediately in a literalistic sense) explains the text as inspired. On the other hand, if interpretation never exhausts the truth of the text, it can bring many facets to expression. It always remains respectful before the truth of the text. At the same time it explains the text, points something out, says something new. In some way it goes beyond a pure statement of the text. (Bonaventure says: *Theologia fit per additionem.*) Unavoidably it adds something new to the text and contributes to the active history of this text. The interpretor places in his interpretation his own personal answer to the address of the text: he does this in a historical-personal way, and not simply as the automatic voice of a tradition. De Lubac has summarized this dialectic of interpretation well:

In one sense the commentary, if it is to be at all penetrating, is always going to go further than the text since it explains what it finds there. . . . But in another sense, more important, the text in its concrete richness goes deeper than the commentary; the latter can never cease returning to it. It has an ever present virtual infinitude.[25]

[25] H. de Lubac, S.J., *Nouveaux Paradoxes* (Paris, 1955), p. 22.

There is a moment of free choice, various alternatives, in every interpretation of a text, and there is responsibility, yet the spirit of truth does not let itself be exhausted in letters. The text has a fullness, an abundance, presenting a horizon of meaning which is broader and deeper than the hermeneutical principle through which I question the text. This does not mean that this principle, the understanding of our own existence, is necessarily false or unsuitable to explain the text. It cannot explain the entire text with all of its potentiality. From one aspect it can be correct, but it can also be false, unemployable, or insufficient from another.[26] The dangers for Bultmann seem to be clear. Above all, the hermeneutical principle is here absolutized, made into an exclusive critical standard. We have seen that for him this principle would explain everything, and this would be the only horizon for explaining the text, for interpretation. Bultmann's hermeneutical principle itself can limit to an extreme degree the important realities contained in the text.

One last reflection. Bultmann wants to explain the biblical text according to the principle of an understanding by and for human existence. The text speaks only inasmuch as it is interpreted existentially. The text is something *pro nobis, pro me,* faith speaking to man's existence. How often Bultmann cites the sentence of Melanchthon: "This is to know Christ, to know his benefits for me."[27] Obviously, this "for me," as a soteriological pinnacle, must enter into any statement of faith. The statement of revelation is only understood when it goes beyond its objective content. It must be understood in its meaning for me, for my salvation. The question is how should this "for me" be understood? Does it refer primarily to the individual believer or does it mean the believer within a community of believers, the Church? If the latter is the case, then existential understanding must also include an ecclesiological understanding of the hermeneutical principle. When we look at the New Testament, this is not exactly an unreasonable demand. Fur-

[26] See T. W. Adorno, *Noten zur Literatur* (Frankfurt, 1963), I, p. 12.
[27] *GV,* I, p. 267.

ther, since the Bible speaks of God's action in Israel and in Jesus Christ, is not a salvation-historical understanding or a Christological understanding conceivable and justified?

With regard to the historical, the Bible is not embarrassed by history because here history, man in his history, is seen as the place and the goal of revelation, God's saving event. Man is not conceived in a non-historical or essential way, as a human nature always the same. The God whom the Bible witnesses is not *ipsum esse* or *ens a se,* but the Lord of the world, of history, of man in history. Does not history, as it appears in the Bible, show itself theologically in a different, more profound, and truer light? We recognized this because of our contemporary consciousness of history and through the philosophy of historicity. Is it not possible to experience what history really is from the Bible?

Now we can look critically at Bultmann's interpretation of one book of the New Testament. We must examine what his interpretation is as compared to other possible exegeses and interpretations. The recognition of certain limits, even significant ones in Bultmann's interpretation, does not mean it is completely false, but indicates that in the area of exegesis there will never be one absolute manner of interpretation but rather many ways of critically approaching a text.

BULTMANN'S INTERPRETATION OF THE GOSPEL ACCORDING TO JOHN

What is Bultmann's method of interpreting John?[28] The problem of the Gospel text's order can offer us a point of departure, because this implies first of all that the text of the Gospel of John we have before us is not the original. Bultmann recognizes that it is necessary in several areas to change the order of the text. For example, he sees the "eucharistic section" of the

[28] For an orientation on the method-history of interpreting John, see S. Schultz, *Untersuchungen zur Menschensohnchristologie im Johannesevangelium* (Göttingen, 1957), pp. 39–95.

discourse on the bread of life (Jn. 6:27–58) as added through an ecclesiastical redaction, as is the end of this section where we have a reference to the resurrection on the last day. Any theology of sacraments or statements about future eschatology belong, according to Bultmann, to the final "ecclesiastical redaction," not to the original Gospel. This and other examples show that text order and the reasons for it are seldom derived from motives of real literary criticism, as, for instance, is the reversal of chapters 5 and 6.[29] Theological motives also play an important role in Bultmann's understanding of the discourses in John, discourses following the form of "gnostic discourses on revelation." The changes in text order are therefore a part of his literary, critical, but also of his theological view of John.[30]

The changes in textual order point to the question of the literary composition of the Gospel of John. Bultmann sees five sources in John: (1) revelation-discourses, which go back to a gnostic original document; (2) the sign-sources, narrative sections, especially reports of miracles; (3) the evangelist as redacter to whom we owe the first, basic summarizing document of the Gospel; (4) the "ecclesiastical redaction" to whom we owe, especially, those sections which edit the Gospel in such a way that it can be used by the world-wide church—these are mainly didactic sections about sacraments and eschatology; (5) tertiary glosses.[31]

This critical appraisal of the literary form raises other background relationships. The discourse source is closely bound to the question of comparative religion, for it is seen mainly as a document of intense gnostic influence, and therefore it should

[29] For the change in order, see *J*, p. 163.

[30] An example of the role which theological perspective and judgment play in Bultmann's reordering of the text is verse 6:23 where the phrase is eliminated because it is missing in some manuscripts (e.g., D), although it is in the major codices. The reason is clear; it could point to the Eucharist. Similarly, 3:5 (the phrase "from water") is eliminated because "the evangelist consciously wishes to eliminate sacramentalism from the church's piety." But textual tradition and criticism are not taken into account (*J*, p. 98).

[31] *J*, pp. 559 f.

be interpreted according to the scheme of gnostic revelation-discourses. The problems of form-criticism also enter here. The miracle as sign-source is related to the question of the origin of John's report of miracles, primitive Christian tradition. In this area as well as in the report of the passion the question arises concerning the relationship of John to the synoptic tradition. How does John interpret this tradition? The evangelist worked the discourse—and the sign-source—into his own written product, and we find their stamp throughout his theology. He consciously and always understands miracle as sign.

Bultmann conceives this evangelist as a man who interpreted the Christian faith with the help of a conceptuality impregnated with gnosticism. He sees theology as a theology of the Word dominated by the situation of preaching, preaching which presents a radical eschatology already present right now. To move from one area of Bultmann's work to another, we see that the work of the evangelist himself in John gives us the point of departure for demythologizing. The Gospel of John offers an excellent example of it. The gnostic myth which lies at the basis of the revelation-discourses serves *the evangelist* as a form by which he can express the event of salvation. The highlighting of gnostic concepts and thought-patterns through the study of comparative religion offers *us* the possibility of understanding the mythical pattern of language and thought and of lifting from these mythical forms the understanding of human existence radically intended by the *evangelist*. This substratum freed from mythical additions is the point of departure for existential interpretation. There an eschatological self-understanding according to a radical historized eschatology develops with the help of existential conceptuality a theology meaningful and valid for men today.

The ecclesiastical redaction in John attains a twofold character. By adding things it has preserved the fourth Gospel for wider use in the church. The evangelist originally presented a pure word and faith piety, but this was not sufficient for the ecclesiastical redaction. This redaction joined the sacramental practice of the church with the evangelist's theology and added the resurrection to the historized eschatological viewpoint. Naturally, this has obscured the radical standpoint of the evangelist which must now be critically exposed. We should recall that the historized eschatology in the Gospel of John is for Bultmann the ultimate and purest level of eschatological thinking in primitive Christianity. His interpretation would like to set aside the ecclesiastical redaction and other foreign elements and bring the pure character of John's eschatology to life.

Bultmann has certain predecessors. For instance, his interpretation of John's eschatology can be found in the work of Wilhelm Bousset.[32] For Bousset, John is the representative of a mystical-gnostic religion, which moves "the good of salvation from the future totally into the present. The few nuances which still retain the eschatological dimension have no organic connection with the basic conviction of the Gospel; perhaps they were added by a redactor."[33] Mysticism and sacramental devotion for Bousset determine Johannine Christianity. Its significance is that it hinders "any resolution in the consciousness of Christians of the discrepancy between the synoptics' picture of Jesus of Nazareth and the early Church's preaching of the *Kyrios Christos.*"[34] Bultmann, however, has given up Bousset's concepts of spiritualization and mysticism, and he has expanded the role of the ecclesiastical redaction with regards to the theology of the sacraments. There were various reasons for this, among which is a new understanding of God's Word and faith developed for us by the school of dialectical theology. Bultmann has employed in his commentary the idea of the kerygma as a word to man coming from outside and has made this the center of his interpretation.[35]

[32] *Kyrios Christos* (Göttingen, 1913); the fifth edition of 1965 has an introduction by Bultmann.

[33] *Ibid.*, p. 177.

[34] *Ibid.*, p. 162.

[35] See *TNT,* II, pp. 60 ff.; here we have the decisive difference which separates Bultmann from "liberal exegesis." As word, revelation places human self-understanding in question and leads the hearer to decision in faith, a decision on death and life.

What significance does the early Jesus have for Bultmann? "The Revealer appears *not as man-in-general,* i.e., not simply as a bearer of human *nature,* but as *a definite human being in history,* as Jesus of Nazareth. His humanity is genuine humanity; 'the word became flesh.' "[36] The eschatological and gnostic conceptualities serve to express "that Jesus is the eschatological salvation-bringer, that *his coming is the eschatological event.*"[37] Here is the paradox of revelation: "God Himself encounters men in Jesus, a Jesus moreover who is a man in whom nothing unusual is perceptible except his bold assertion that in him God encounters men. In that fact lies the *paradoxical nature* of John's *concept of revelation,* paradox which John was the first to see clearly."[38] This paradox reaches its peak with Bultmann in that revelation does not say anything other than a pure "that." "If the revelation is to be presented neither as the communication of a definite teaching nor as the kindling of a mystical experience of the soul, then all that can be presented is the bare fact of it."[39] "The Revealer is nothing but a definite historical man, Jesus of Nazareth. Why this specific man? This is a question that must not, may not, be answered—for to do so would destroy the offense which belongs ineradicably to the Revelation."[40] The paradox says that this "that" of revelation is simply an assertion; there is no further content, no special relationship of Father to Son, Jesus to God. The categories of preëxistence, the sending of the Son into the world, the unity of Father and Son, are for Bultmann ways of saying through objectifying but mythological language the significance of the "that" of the existence of Jesus on earth. These categories are primarily significant as a hermeneutic for our faith. Basically they interpret the Jesus of history only as the eschatological event in which they retain the paradox of revelation as scandal.

With regard to the concept of the "paradox of revelation" in Bultmann's thought and its influence on contemporary

36 *Ibid.,* p. 41.   37 *Ibid.,* p. 37.
38 *Ibid.,* p. 50.   39 *Ibid.,* p. 67.
40 *Ibid.,* p. 69.

eschatology, the scandal-character and the retrogressive nature of the Gospel's teaching on the sacraments, Bultmann is highly influenced by Kierkegaard. In every discussion of Bultmann's existential interpretation, Heidegger's influence is noted, but that of Kierkegaard is often overlooked. We should recall that Kierkegaard is the primary source both for Heidegger and for Bultmann. Heidegger lifted Kierkegaard's thought out of its theological presuppositions and secularized it in a formal and general analysis of human existence. In Bultmann, the theological motives remain more deeply active, especially in his exegesis of John, an exegesis which cannot be understood apart from Kierkegaard.[41]

The Kierkegaardian paradox consists in the unity of the absolute difference between God and man in a historical man who is at the same time God. Relationship to the absolute paradox is possible only in faith. To come to this relationship, man must go through the possibility of scandal. The concept of the "present moment" belongs to paradox. The "moment" is the unity of time and eternity, the presence of the eternal in time. For Kierkegaard, faith develops along with paradox, not in the sense of an immediate historical simultaneity of time but in the simultaneity of time corresponding to paradox. This kind of temporal simultaneity with paradox is not historical but something pertaining to faith. Faith makes every believer exist at the same time with the paradox; it can diminish the importance of the historical distance. The question, then, of historical mediation and authenticity is relativized. Also, the concept of the Church in this connection has a diminished significance. What is decisive here is an idea of faith where the individual

---

[41] In *J* the following works by Kierkegaard are cited (page numbers refer to citations in *J*): *Christian Discourses* (p. 449), *Works of Love* (p. 405), *The Concept of Dread* (p. 339), *Training in Christianity* (pp. 161, 275, 331, 469), *Philosophical Fragments* (p. 104). The last two mentioned works are theologically the most important for Bultmann. Both works, orientated towards John, contain an exegesis stemming from the pietistic movement. This strain in Kierkegaard is a heritage from his father.

achieves an existential relationship to the paradox and then exists contemporaneously with it. For Kiekegaard, through a paradox which is a unity of time and eternity, of God and man in the God-man, the paradox becomes contemporary. With regard to the present, the contemporary past and future lose, in a certain degree, their difference. With this view of the paradox Kierkegaard wanted to solve the problem of the historical in Christianity. But actually Kierkegaard's thought here remains totally in the horizon of metaphysics; in the last analysis it cannot solve the problem of history because this solution is unhistorical.

Bultmann takes over not only the paradox but also the understanding of today as a point present right now, the point of simultaneity. This is the "that" of revelation and the existential idea of faith. We must concede that this development of Kierkegaard's categories is significant for many important New Testament facts. However, we should notice that Kierkegaard treats the absolute paradox in the light of the traditional Christology of two natures and one person. Influenced by historical-critical studies in the history of religions, Bultmann, naturally, does not retain this background but transfers it into the "that" of *the statement of the address of the kerygma to man.* Faith as existential self-understanding becomes the hermeneutical principle, a formalization of the paradox which is not totally alien to Kierkegaard. Bultmann's interpretation takes place in the horizon of a theological anthropology, and Kierkegaard's thought on the eternal in history is, at the least, weakened by Bultmann's view of the existential-historical (*Geschichte*).

Bultmann gives eschatology a new tone by joining aspects of the Old Testament expectation to existential analysis. "Eschatological existence" retains the moment of the historically meaningful for faith; this tends to remove faith from a concrete existence in the world, from expression in secular categories to a decision for the "that." The following sentence from Kierkegaard is important for understanding Bultmann: "When there is a subjective questioning of the truth, there is also a subjective reflection on the relationship of the individual; if only the 'how' of this relationship is in truth, then the individual is in truth, even if here it is actually a question of non-truth."[42] In other words a subject, a subjectivity in a rightly understood truth, has the right relationship to truth. At the same time it extrapolates truth as objective. Under these conditions subjectivity can and must become the criterion of truth. There is perhaps no sentence which so clearly expresses the approach to existential interpretation as this formulation of Kierkegaard.

In Bultmann's thought there are, also, certain presuppositions taken from the field of comparative religion. In his commentary on John, Judaism (the Old Testament, eschatology, apocalyptic and rabbinic literature), Hellenism (Philo, Hellenistic mystery religions, hermetic literature), and gnosticism play important explicative roles.[43] Bultmann owes a debt to Hans Jonas, who with the help of Heidegger understood gnostic mythological statements as the objectification of an underlying gnostic understanding of human existence.[44] The mythological is not an ultimate reality for gnosticism but only a sign on the way. The believer accepts the deeper existential message beneath the objectification. The assertion that the mythological is a form of objectification within gnosis itself permits us to see the gnostic myth as presenting an understanding of self and existence. As we noted we find here the basic scheme of demythologizing already formulated.[45]

The gnostic understanding of existence offered within a

[42] Kierkegaard, "Afterword," *Philosophical Fragments* (New York, 1936), p. 284. See J. Heywood Thomas, "The Relevance of Kierkegaard for the Demythologising Controversy," *Scottish Journal of Theology*, 10 (1957), pp. 239–252.

[43] *TNT*, I, pp. 160 ff. Especially important are the Mandaean texts published by M. Lidzbarski; see also, Bultmann's "Die Bedeutung der neuerschlossenen mandäischen und manichäischen Quellen für das Verständnis des Johannesevangeliums," *Zeitschrift für neutestamentliche Wissenschaft*, 24 (1925), pp. 100–146.

[44] H. Jonas, *The Gnostic Religion* (Boston, 1963).

[45] See *NTM*, pp. 3–9.

parenthetical statement the possibility of mediating an eschatological existence, and therewith the possibility of making these
gnostic texts fruitful for the interpretation of John (for example,
the gnostic discourses on revelation could be a model for the
Johannine discourses). Gnostic conceptuality in the Gospel of
John serves to retain eschatology for today. In this eschatological conceptuality, the future moment (as Paul shows) was
dominant. What the gnostic ideas achieve is mainly presenting
the eschaton as present right now. So it is clear that statements
in John about the future are later ecclesiastical additions to the
Gospel. The grand schema which encompasses everything and
makes this interpretation possible is existential understanding.
Bultmann says that John has an eschatological existence or an
eschatological self-understanding, not simply a self-understanding or a gnostic self-understanding. The eschatological existence
remains; not everything is given up, for faith does not want to
become this gnosis. The key retention is the moment of historicity. John's eschatology is referred to history, while gnostic
thought is radically anti-historical. This is how Bultmann joins
John's eschatology and gnosis, bringing them both together in
the aspects of historicity and today. Both refer to faith as an
understanding of existence, for faith is authentically being-in-
history. It makes possible the relationship of today as simultaneous to the revelation once preached in the kerygma, and
now preached in a sermon today. The past and present form
the paradox of faith, the paradox "that a historical, individual
man is the revelation, the eschatological event."

CRITIQUE

A critique is difficult because the varied lines of Bultmann's
interpretation flow together and form an impressive continuous
system. As we said, what we are comparing is this interpretation
with the text of John. This comparison seems to show that

Bultmann's interpretation has limited the text, and that there has been an oversimplification of the problem of interpretation along with a narrowing of the theological view.[46]

The best way to look at Bultmann's position from a critical standpoint is to consider John's Christology, to begin with a simple fact which strikes the unprejudiced reader of the fourth gospel: the decisive content, the message of this text, is Jesus Christ himself. If we study the horizon of meaning opened in the gospel, then the text leads us to Jesus Christ as its center. Faith understands itself in light of Jesus Christ, and so our first question is whether the principle of interpretation of the text as an understanding of our own existence does justice to this. Further, does not this limit what the text could say, limit it to only one aspect? And this aspect through its elevation to the hermeneutical principle excludes other possibilities of explaining the text. The text can no longer say everything it wants to say. Under these circumstances a critique of Bultmann must try to bring his work on John out of the narrowness he has placed it in. An example of this process might be the discourse contained in the sixth chapter of John.

Bultmann's Interpretation of the Discourse in the Sixth Chapter of John

Bultmann begins with the observation that the handed-down succession of chapters 5 and 6 cannot be original.[47] He opts for the original order as 4, 6, 5, 7. He offers among others a

---

[46] In this area see E. Ruckstuhl, *Die literarische Einheit des Johannesevangeliums* (Fribourg, 1951); F. Mussner, *ZSLH, Die Anschauung vom Leben im vierten Evangelium* (Munich, 1952); A. Corell, *Consummatum est, Eschatology and Church in the Gospel of St. John* (London, 1958); C. H. Dodd, *The Interpretation of the Fourth Gospel* (Cambridge, 1958); L. van Haringsveld, *Die Eschatologie des Johannesevangeliums* (Assen, 1962); J. Blank, *Krisis* (Freiburg, 1964).

[47] *J*, pp. 340–346, 155–161, 215. Bultmann separates verses 60–71 from the rest of chapter 6 and places them between chapters 12 and 13.

theological argument: chapter 6 shows revelation as the crisis of man's longing for life, while chapter 5 shows it as the crisis with man's religion. Chapter 6 follows the dispute with the people, while chapter 5 follows that with the people's leaders.

To the first section Bultmann gives the title "Feeding and Traveling by Sea." A comparison with Mark 6:31–51 shows a previous tradition which certainly was not at hand for Mark. Bultmann notes the uniqueness of John's view, a multiplication of loaves where Jesus seizes the initiative. Jesus knows what he will do; he sets this whole event in motion by a question; the embarrassment of the disciples is emphasized more strongly; the preparation of the miracle becomes more complicated. The story of Jesus' walking on the water is for Bultmann an earlier stage in the tradition active within John. Absent are the motif of the storm and its quieting along with the disciples' lack of understanding; instead, we have a motif of their miraculous landing and a particular form of faith in miracles at the end. Bultmann concludes that the evangelist has taken this section from the sign-source, adding to it (verse 4 is an indication of the approaching paschal feast; verses 14 ff. refer to the future knowledge of Jesus; verses 23 ff. to the misunderstanding of the crowd). Bultmann does not accept that the evangelist has before him oral or written traditions which he has worked over. However, a comparison with Mark 6:32–52 (parallel in Matthew 14:13–33) gives the impression that tendencies cited by Bultmann—the tendency to a Christological concentration and the tendency to increase the demonstrative power of the miracles— found their origin in the *composer* of the fourth gospel. The same tendencies can be seen in the other reports of miracles in John. The understanding of the miracles as signs of revelation does not appear as an added interpretation, but goes back to the very formulation of the reports of these miracles.

The second part, "The Bread of Life" (6:27–59), includes the discourse itself.[48] Bultmann sees the incorrect order of the

[48] *Ibid.,* pp. 161–177.

text to be explicable only by a redactor who by external destruction has changed the order of the text into another order. First, the section on the Eucharist (6:51b–58c) is removed, "for here we are talking about the sacramental meal of the Eucharist, where the Lord's supper is understood as the φάρμαχον ἀθανασίας, 'the medicine of immortality' " (Ignatius of Antioch[49]). For Bultmann this is contradictory to the entire view of the evangelist. The revealer himself is the Bread of Life. The demand for faith does not need any more sacramental act through which the believer touches life. Bultmann interprets the verses which speak of the future (39, 40, 41). Verse 54 is the organizing center of the section, but it does not fit in with the rest of the discourse. "Its insertion is an attempt by the redaction to subject the entire discourse to the viewpoint of the verses 51–58."[50] This redaction is an ecclesiastical redaction; the viewpoint is sacramental. If we look at the change in the text order, then we see that its result gives a totally defined systematization of the text.

The discourse on the bread of life begins with verse 27. The warning (whose background is John's dualism) directs itself to the struggle of man for life, and states that life is not assured through early nourishment. If man wants to have an eternal life he must find a nourishment which is not transient, a miraculous nourishment in an understanding of his own existence. Man is always his own life. This preliminary understanding objectifies itself in mythical pictures of the bread of life, the food of life. The request that Jesus would give this miraculous bread expresses the misunderstanding of the hearers. Jesus' answer is formulated in the revelation-formula, and it says that his person is what they are asking for. Bultmann understands this formula as a "recognition-formula."[51] The "I am" is the predicate and stands in contrast to false revelation. In this

[49] *Ibid.*, p. 162; the phrase is from his *Letter to the Ephesians*, 20; *PG*, 5, 661.
[50] *Ibid.*, p. 162.
[51] *Ibid.*, p. 167.

answer "the entire paradox of revelation is contained . . . Jesus gives the bread of life in as much as he is it; in his own person he is nothing, but he is in the service of the Father for men."[52] Whoever wishes to receive the bread of life must "come to him," believe in him.

The world, however, in the face of this demand for faith wants a sign. The Jews ask for a miracle like the miracle of manna because they are still thinking of material nourishment. Their thoughts might be expressed in that they wish "to have at their disposal a criterion on which revelation depends, while the revelation of God destroys all the pictures man's mind wants to make of it, and it is exactly the test of an authentic desire for salvation to believe even when God speaks differently than man expects."[53] In verse 47, the tone of a promise frames the demand for faith: "Jesus is the bread of life." The promise of faith includes a demand for faith. The true bread of heaven is contrasted to manna. Manna could not give life, nor can any of the mythical pictures of man's desire for life. This presents and concludes the first part of the discourse, where Jesus presents himself as the real bread of life and the demand for faith is raised.

In the second part of the discourse *"the possibility of faith* becomes the express theme."[54] The contradiction of the world corresponds to the claim of revelation. "It is scandalized because revelation is in history, because the world in the sphere in which it is at home encounters the revealer, and the world knows his origin." From the point of view of the world the claim of the revealer is absurd, but the knowledge of the world "is turned around into unknowing insofar as the divine act of revelation is conceived as a constant supernatural phenomenon rather than an event which reduces man to nothingness."[55] Revelation confesses the absurdity of a normal man asserting that he is the revealer. To understand revelation, man must let go of

[52] *Ibid.*, p. 168.
[54] *Ibid.*, p. 170.

[53] *Ibid.*, p. 169.
[55] *Ibid.*, p. 171.

security ("Security means to be able to judge the divine and the human as objective phenomena").[56] Revelation is interpreted existentially as non-objectifiable. Therefore, the evangelist says, security must be given up; "as long as man clings to security, he is blind to true revelation."

The Father draws man and this is the paradox which makes faith clear. Faith can have no support except itself. For Bultmann faith has its object; something is believed. But what? Bultmann speaks of "promise," but he is certainly thinking mainly of the word of revelation. Bultmann speaks of relationship, but what is this relationship to Jesus? Is this relationship the existential moment? A special and direct relationship to God does not seem to stand within the possibility of man. So we ask: Is Jesus only the mediator of this relationship to God, its occasion, its condition, or is he himself constitutive in a basic and unrepeatable way for this relationship to God?

Jesus' discourse ends. The world has seen but not believed. It did not understand the sign of the feeding. In the sign, the possibility to see was given but it did not take place. Faith did not follow what seeing there was. "Even if the world sees, it does not believe."[57] Finally, the evangelist concludes with various thoughts on seeing and believing, on the relationship of faith to the revealer in history. He makes clear that God's work with men is nothing else than his activity within the act of faith.

The movement of thought in the discourse on the bread of life can be summarized in this way. At the beginning there is the discourse on revelation in which Jesus says: The bread of life in which man may take part is I myself. A demand for faith follows immediately, in the mythical picture of the bread of life the salvation of man is objectified—the question of the authenticity of his existence. But the world demands a legitimation, a proof, which must be rejected because the demand for faith has

[56] *Loc. cit.*
[57] *Ibid.,* p. 172.

come forth without any conditions. Revelation now can only be spoken out again in the challenge of faith which is at the same time the promise of faith. The question of the possibility of faith for man becomes important. The contradiction of the world is hidden behind the appearance of "knowledge." It does not and cannot conceive that revelation is not a fact, no objective reality. All worldly security must be given up and only then is faith possible. In other words, we come to faith only through our faith as we are believing. Faith is "decision" as the Father draws us not behind but in the decision of faith. Still, faith has its own kind of security: In what is believed is the word of revelation itself. The paradox of faith corresponds to the paradox of the assertion of the revealer that he is the bread of life. The sign can give rise to faith, but it can also give rise to a rejection of faith. Here there is no real point of departure for a future eschatology. Faith does not need it, and any support from a theology of the sacraments is opposed to this idea of faith, for revelation is not objectifiable in this world.

In the sacrament, a "thingification" takes place. Bultmann sees the redactor as moving the meaning to a secondary relationship to the Lord's Supper. The redactor has copied the style and the conceptuality of the discourse on the living bread. "The technique of the evangelist serves the redactor as a pattern but the imitation is clear."[58] The Lord's Supper as a "medicine of immortality" is quite different. "The one who is taking part in the sacramental meal has the potentiality which guarantees him resurrection."[59] The redactor uses a formula, "he in me and I in him"—a formula which John otherwise uses to describe the relationship of faith to the revealer.[60] There are other examples of the introduction of sacramental elements here which Bultmann sees as additions, because he understands sacrament as a kind of magical guarantee of salvation in the style of the Hellenistic mystery cults.

[58] *Ibid.*, p. 175.
[59] *Loc. cit.*
[60] *Ibid.*, p. 176

The problem could be stated differently. Exactly because the formulations in the discourse on life's bread are accepted (or, better, retained), we should ask whether there is here only an external relationship to the discourse on bread. It is possible, even likely, that these formulations give a definite Johannine understanding of the Lord's Supper, an understanding which cannot be summarized either by a single phrase (the "medicine of immortality") or by Bultmann's understanding of sacrament. The irreconcilability of the discourse on the living bread and the Eucharist could have its source in Bultmann's own *theology*. Bultmann's exegetical interpretation must be examined to see whether it comes from an exegesis of the text or from a theology of what sacrament cannot mean.

The Sixth Chapter of John from Another Perspective

Let us return to the text of John itself in order to reflect on Bultmann's interpretation. The text must be our judge with its own factual structure of meaning. A change in textual order is only justified if the present pattern of the text has no meaning. This meaning can lie deeper than what appears at first sight. Our point of departure is that the text at hand does not need a change in order and that the concluding verses 68–71 belong to the original text.

It has been shown that the style of this chapter is unified, and that this chapter can offer very few criteria for deciding on specific sources.[61] If John 6 has a unity stylistically and critically, that means that the chapter also has an author who conceived

[61] See E. Ruckstuhl, *op. cit.*, pp. 220–271. With regard to the relationship between the first (bread of life) and second (Eucharist) parts of the discourse, he says: "We must read the first section in light of the second, and the second in light of the first" (*ibid.*, p. 268). For a lengthy discussion of the unity of this section, see R. Brown, *The Gospel According to John* (New York, 1966), pp. 261–304.

this unity. (It does not mean that the author did not work over the material which he received and *interpret* it.) This section has some relationship to the synoptic tradition; a background related to primitive Christian tradition is more prominent there than appears in Bultmann's interpretation.[62] The role and the place of Peter's confession at the end is important because it is in a different place in the synoptics. There is no reason to remove it from the sixth chapter of John and place it between the twelfth and thirteenth. Naturally, John has worked over theologically the tradition which he received. The story of the feeding is evidently interpreted in the sense of a Christological climax. An interest in the Eucharist seems to play a role here just as the synoptic tradition also shows an interpretative revision with regards to a eucharistic understanding of the bread.[63] Similarly, the signs also go back to the evangelist. In John miracles have the character of a "Christological revelation-sign." The union of sign and discourse is typical.

To understand the background in its relationship to the tradition present, we must understand the tradition of the Lord's Supper in the primitive church. The language here is highly determined by it.[64] John 6:51 joins together the discourse on bread and the discourse on the Eucharist; it is the cornerstone of the entire discourse. This verse cannot be removed without removing the unity of the whole, and so this shows that the Evangelist interpreted the tradition of the Lord's Supper in the sense of his own theology. We must speak of a specifically Johannine theology of the sacraments. It expresses itself linguistically in the turns of speech it has in common with the first part of the discourse. Now, from the beginning, an "eschatological view" belongs to the Lord's Supper in the New

[62] See R. Schnackenburg, *Das Johannesevangelium* (Freiburg, 1965), I, p. 18.
[63] See Mk. 6:41; Mt. 14:19; Lk. 6:11; Mk. 8:6; Mt. 15:36.
[64] See H. Schürmann, "John 6:51c – Ein Schlüssel zur grossen johanneischen Brotrede," *BZ* (NF), pp. 244–263; Ruckstuhl, *op. cit.*, pp. 220 ff.

Testament. In Paul, this eschatological view has already been precised by a looking towards the coming Lord (1 Cor. 11:26). With John, there is a similar change. Whoever eats the flesh of Christ and drinks his blood has eternal life, has a gift today of salvation. In this form, the fourth gospel presents the eschatological view. It is possible it received it from the future-eschatological view of the tradition of the Lord's Supper and worked it into this first part of our discourse. The text gives us no justification for cutting the future eschatological perspective out as a redaction.[65] It is here that Bultmann's theological hermeneutical presuppositions are at work. It is his preliminary understanding of revelation which gives rise to this cutting up of the text.

What stimulates too little discussion in Bultmann is that this discourse on bread is basically *Christology.* Behind the whole discourse there is a unified Christological thought determined by John's Son-of-man Christology and his kerygma. Dodd has rightly noted: "It is as Son of Man that Jesus says, ἐγώ εἰμαι ὁ ἄρτος τῆν βίος."[66] Nowhere does Jesus as Son of man, the eschatological bringer of salvation and giver of life, enter so clearly as in this chapter with the tone of chapter 3 of the Son of man descending and ascending in the background.[67] The Son of man and the bread from heaven are joined. These concepts— coming down and going up—encompass in John's language the saving event, its point of departure and goal. Naturally, for Bultmann, this is "mythological" with a gnostic myth of redemption behind it.[68] However, this descending as John uses the word does not appear in gnostic writings, and John's formulation stands in sharp contrast to gnosis. What is important is that according to John the Christ-event is history, a history which has its goal and origin in God himself. John does not know a historical Jesus in the sense of today's discussion, and the

[65] Blank, *op. cit.,* pp. 172–182.
[66] Dodd, *op. cit.,* p. 248.
[67] See 6:33, 38, 41, 42, 50, 51, 58; 6:62.
[68] *J,* p. 107.

105

paradox of revelation is that Jesus of Nazareth is the Son of man come from heaven and returning to the Father through cross, resurrection, and exultation. Bultmann neglects the cross; he sets it aside as a later addition. This removes the most difficult objection to his view, for the cross (indicated in 6:51) would make it fully impossible to understand the discourse on bread as following the scheme of a gnostic discourse on revelation. Gnostic thought is quite different from an event on the cross. The cross was the test whether the incarnation was to be taken seriously. Gnosis helped to raise these problems about the union of the human and the divine in Jesus.

Also the conclusion (6:62 ff.) cannot be separated from the whole. Verse 62 contains the indication of the ascending return of the Son of man, "to where he previously was." There is no doubt that we are to think here of Jesus' resurrection and ascension. Certainly verse 63, when it says "What will you make of it, if you see the Son of man ascending to the place where he was before?", poses the question of how this entire discourse on bread should be understood. The Christ of John who speaks in this discourse is not the "historical Jesus" but the glorified Christ alive today who, however, is identical with the Jesus who lived on earth. The discourse in its totality is conceived in a situation taking place after Easter and it presents a unique union of kerygma and tradition about Jesus, something which is typical for the entire Gospel of John.

In this connection the "I am" discourse is clear.[69] It is concerned with the discourse on revelation in a special sense, and I personally think that in the background there is the divine self-enunciation of the Old Testament.[70] The bread of life (one of many images complementing the revealer[71]) presents a development of the absolute "I am." This imagery is for the purpose of giving self-witness to the self-revelation of Jesus. In

[69] See H. Zimmermann, "Das absolute ἐγώ εἰμαι als die neutestamentliche Offenbarungsformel," *BZ* (NF), 4 (1960), pp. 54–69, 266–276.
[70] See Ex. 3:14; Is. 41:4–10; 42:13; 45:5, 6, 18.
[71] See John 8:12; 10:7, 9; 10:11–14; 11:25; 14:6; 15:1.

106

the imagery of bread we understand the meaning of Jesus for man's salvation. This significance, however, is grounded in his person and divine origin which cannot be removed. The religious background of the discourses using such imagery is controversial. Bultmann finds it in the various images of the bread of life and the miraculous mythical food of life, but an exegete might turn first from the text of John to Jewish tradition.[72] Bultmann has distracted our attention from this tradition, but the text itself shows a connection in the mention of manna. Jewish and Christian eschatology are joined together. The evangelist uses the phrase "bread from heaven" in order to make clear to the Jewish expectation of the Christ that Jesus himself is the true bread from heaven. This salvation-historical dimension is eliminated by Bultmann at the benefit of his general, anthropological, existential understanding.[73] But exactly in reading the sixth chapter of John we cannot doubt that something of Exodus 16 stands in the background in an antithetic typology.

We can divide the discourse on the living bread in this way: (a) I am the bread of life (vv. 25–35); (b) the controversy about Jesus as the revealer and the mediator of God's salvation and faith (vv. 36–50); (c) the eucharistic discourse (vv. 51–59). Only if a theologian understands word and sacrament as two mutually excluding realities can he eliminate the eucharistic section. But this alternative is always the result of the theologian's own motives; the text does not necessitate it. A unified Christological background makes it clear how Christ through his Word and the Lord's Supper is present in the community, present as the eschatological giver of life.

If the Christological background (including its soteriology) is kept in mind as the discourse on the bread of life or the entire Gospel of John is examined, we shall be able to recognize that a position of existential interpretation has its own relative rights. It is obvious, for Bultmann, that the point of departure

[72] See Ps. 78:24; Ps. 105:40; Wis. 16:20 ff.
[73] Bultmann writes: "The history of salvation perspective as a whole is lacking in John" (*TNT*, II, p. 8).

for existential understanding begins with anthropology, with faith seen theologically as a subjective decision. Christology and theology are understood in light of anthropology and they derive their criteria from it inasmuch as they are accessible to an existential interpretation. The conclusion of this is a striking abbreviation of Christological and theological thought in John.

The assertation of the "that" of revelation enters with a theological foundation, but this theology is seriously close to the irrationalism of a subjectively qualified theology of pure assertion. The universal, cosmic relationship and breadth of faith seems to be gone, while the over-all impression of John's theology (and the same is analogously true for Paul) seems to be clearly that faith and believing existence are understood as grounded in Jesus Christ. Anthropology must be theologically understood in Christology. Otherwise, as with Bultmann, we fall into the acutely dangerous situation that the believer is being addressed in a way which strictly speaking is valid only of Christ. This is true of eschatology. When future eschatology is eliminated, then the situation of faith in time is incorrectly understood. The believer is not the glorified Christ. Christ is the completion; he is the eschatological giver of life as the crucified and glorified Son of man. The believer still lives in time, and his own fulfillment as well as his completion of faith is still ahead of him. The pattern for faith's completion is the risen Christ who himself is "the resurrection and the life" (Jn. 11:25). He will bring the believer's present life through faith in salvation to fulfillment as he, sent from God as the bringer of life, wakes all of the faithful on the last day (Jn. 5:19–30).

The role of time for the believer is retained through the eschatological statements about the future. John's formulations make it clear that the pattern for the future of the believer is the risen Christ (Phil. 3:21). The existence of man on earth is closely joined to the role of time. The elimination of a theology of sacrament, especially the Lord's Supper, signifies a dangerous lack of recognition of the significance of the earthly and

108

corporeal for the concrete act of faith. It seems that (despite many assertions to the contrary) the Incarnation, in the last analysis, is not really being taken seriously, because it may not be announced in a tangible visible sign but is reduced simply to a "that." We have to ask whether Bultmann's anthropology corresponds to that of the Bible, to the Gospel of John, or whether it is penetrated to a great extent with spiritualistic characteristics which only a great deal of effort can harmonize with the Johannine variety and depth.

V. BULTMANN AND THE
OLD TESTAMENT

By René Marlé

For Bultmann, the problem posed by the existence of the Old Testament and its meaning for anyone who reads it helped to bring primitive Christianity to a definition of its own faith.[1] As an exegete and theologian of the New Testament, Bultmann tried to account for this Christian faith. He has never studied the Old Testament for itself alone, but rather to determine what a Christian could seek and find in it. This is a question to which he returns several times in his work,[2] and which offers a characteristic orientation in his theology.

To determine what the Christian faith can and must seek in the Old Testament, Bultmann eliminates at the outset several ways of considering it which he deems either unacceptable or without theological significance. The Old Testament can obviously be looked at from other points of view than faith. The historian can see in it the testimony of one or more stages

[1] See *TNT*, I, pp. 92 ff., 108 ff.
[2] See "Die Bedeutung des Alten Testaments für den christlichen Glauben," *GV*, I, pp. 313–336; "Christ the End of the Law" *EPT*, pp. 36–66; "Prophecy and Fulfillment" *EPT*, pp. 182–208; "Ursprung und Sinn der Typologie als hermeneutische Methode," *Theologische Literaturzeitung*, 4 (1950), pp. 205–212; *TNT*, I, pp. 108–121; "History and Eschatology in the New Testament," *New Testament Studies*, 1 (1954), pp. 5–16.

in the development of religious ideas and experiences. This type of consideration is legitimate only on condition of recognizing it for what it is: a positive study, leaving in doubt the final theological significance of its results. These limits abstract from the fundamental affirmation of the Christian faith, that everything is connected with God and is linked to the person of Jesus and that there is no real religion apart from him. If the historian's point of view is the final and definitive point of view, it necessarily implies a relativist concept of the bases of history, which amounts to a rejection of faith.[3]

Along with the consideration of the Old Testament from the point of view of historical development, there are other unacceptable views of the Old Testament made impossible by the historical-critical method.[4] This is true of the attempt to study it as a book of prophecies. "The so-called prophecies of the Old Testament are not genuine prophecies; they pertain neither to Jesus nor to the Christian community; they express uniquely the Israelite and Jewish hope for the future."[5] The prophets of the Old Testament were not thinking of the events subsequently interpreted as their fulfillment. Moreover, in order to furnish a suitable prophecy most of the texts have to be taken in a sense contrary to their original meaning. Recourse was had to a version of the Septuagint which differs from the Hebrew text where the sought-for transpositions would not even have been possible.[6]

Along with this kind of manipulation of the original texts, the interpretation of the Old Testament as a book of prophecies stimulated a method borrowed from Hellenist culture: allegorical interpretation. It permits both the extraction from the whole Bible of a number of selected sayings and also an interpretation of the entire content of the Old Testament as prophetic of what is realized in the New Testament. Bultmann knows that there is a distinction between true allegory and typology, the moral

[3] See *GV*, I, pp. 313–317.
[5] *GV*, I, p. 335.
[4] See *EPT*, p. 185; *GV*, I, p. 335.
[6] See *EPT*, p. 185.

111

sense, and so on. He has had occasion to delineate the technique proper to these different methods, noting how often they are mingled.[7] But the point which is of interest to us here is that all these procedures, whose use is not specifically Christian, have not withstood criticism. These methods leave the text to the interpretation of the exegete and tend to fantasy or puerility.[8] At most, they can express differently what one knows already. We cannot expect much to come of it.[9]

More modern attempts at interpreting the Old Testament in its relation to Jesus Christ are much more persuasive, viz., the one developed in the nineteenth century by J. C. Hofmann in his work *Weissagung und Erfüllung*. For Hofmann it was not so much the words of the Old Testament nor each detail of its content which have prophetic value but rather the dynamism of the history given us by the Old Testament. The history of Israel appears to Hofmann as prophetic in the measure in which it is a movement leading to a goal and continually containing this goal in itself. It is only from its completion onward that history can be understood as prophetic, as it manifests precisely the purpose of its movement. For Hofmann, Christ is effectively the meaning and purpose of the history of Israel and therefore of the history of the world, which can be seen as stretching prophetically towards him.[10]

It is important, remarks Bultmann, to ask what theological significance such a consideration can have. Obviously, it cannot establish the importance of Christ since it has its beginning in him. And if we object that this importance springs from the simple fact that history would be centered in him, we grant that a religious truth can be backed up by a consideration drawn from the philosophy of history. This betrays a radical misunder-

[7] See "Ursprung und Sinn der Typologie als hermeneutische Methode," *art. cit.*; see *TNT*, I, pp. 113–114.
[8] "All allegory is either a game or nonsense" (*GV*, I, p. 335).
[9] See *loc. cit.*; *EPT*, p. 188.
[10] See *EPT*, pp. 188–190.

112

standing of the transcendence of faith and of the realities on which it has bearing. "According to the New Testament, Christ is the end of salvation history not in the sense that he signifies the goal of historical development but because he is its eschatological end."[11]

A final way of viewing the Old Testament is more legitimate. It opens an understanding of the Old Testament which in certain respects cannot be surpassed, as it manifests a *fundamental possibility of human existence,* and a particular understanding of that existence. Like every historical document the Old Testament is an invitation, a challenge addressed to us.[12] Our past has been conditioned above all by biblical tradition and by Greek humanism; they condition the situation through which we have to realize our freedom.[13] More precisely, Biblical tradition awakens us to this understanding of historic existence, without which it would be vain to dream of reaching a true understanding of faith. And in this regard, the content of the Old Testament harmonizes perfectly with what we find in the gospels and epistles. Both testaments show us that time or "history" constitutes the very being of man, that man's ideal is not a contemplation, a theory of the divine nature, but attention to the Word of God and to the demands which it manifests to me at this very moment. The Old Testament as well as the New reveals no other rapport with God than that of faith, a rapport created by a living fidelity, obedience, and confidence.[14]

Does this last way of approaching and understanding the Old Testament permit us to give an account of what the Old Testament really means for Christian faith? Has it only one meaning, different in its content but of the same order as Platonic philosophy or Greek humanism? On the other hand, although it testifies to an understanding of existence which is basically the same as that of the New Testament, does not the latter represent for Christians in its relation with the Old something

---

[11] *Ibid.,* pp. 190–191.   [12] See *GV,* I, p. 318.
[13] *Ibid.,* pp. 322, 332.   [14] See *ibid.,* pp. 323–324.

essentially new? Until these questions are answered, we cannot pretend to have determined what the Old Testament means for Christian faith.

Bultmann thinks that during the times which kept up a genuinely historic relationship with the Old Testament, the understanding of existence expressed therein was opposed to the Christian understanding in the antithesis: Law and Gospel. A personal and existential tradition starting with St. Paul but strongly marked since then by the genius of Luther[15] determines the precise sense in which the Old Testament can and ought to be received by the Christian faith.

To understand the opposition of Law and Gospel which must be the principle of the Christian interpretation of the Old Testament, it is important to formulate precisely what can be the meaning of the Law with which the Old Testament is identified. The Law is not only a composite of ordinances which expressed for the believing Jew the will of God. If the Gospel is substituted (by the Christian faith) for the Law, if Christ is its "end," this does not mean that the period of its divine commands is for us a thing of the past. Faith itself is "obedience" and he who lives by it ought not to "yield [his] members to sin as instruments of wickedness . . . but to God as instruments of righteousness" (Rom. 6:13). Faith does not free one from the Law as from an intolerable burden. And Bultmann notes in this regard that it is a mistake to read Paul with the eyes of Luther. For Paul, as for the majority of Jews, the Law was never really a burden and it is not as such that he shakes it off.[16]

Does not Paul (and do not we) distinguish between the Law's accidentals (cultic or ritual ordinances), and the parts which would remain valid and living (purely moral prescriptions, corresponding to the interior voice of conscience)?[17] It is

[15] On the complex problem of Luther and the Old Testament, confer H. Bornkamm, *Luther und das Alte Testament* (Tübingen, 1948).

[16] See *EPT*, pp. 36–37.

[17] It is true that this distinction is possible. With regard to positive ordinances bound to the historical and sociological context in which they

not to the fundamental content of the Law that the Gospel is opposed, it is not this which Paul attacks, but rather its fundamental attitude giving man the opportunity to lean on it in order to glorify himself before God. What is in question in the New Testament, what the Christian faith opposes, is the idea that the fulfillment of the Law is a way of salvation. The Christian message, the Gospel of which Paul makes himself the herald, is that of a salvation, a justification attained by faith alone, given gratuitously by God.

Law and Gospel express two fundamental ways of life, two forms of existence. When they are opposed, there are two facets, or a twofold principle of life: life guided by the desire to glorify oneself, depending on one's own strength, or, on the contrary, a life conscious of its essential powerlessness and nothingness, expecting everything from the pardon and grace of God.[18]

These two types of existence condition each other, and it is impossible to understand one without understanding the other. Only the man who has experienced his own powerlessness and sinfulness can experience grace. He must repeat that experience unceasingly, because grace is never a thing possessed. It is pardon continually renewed, from an action unceasingly renewed by which we make ourselves sinners.[19]

Can the message of the Gospel be understood by one who

---

were formulated, Bultmann himself says that the expression of essential moral needs corresponds to the nature of the human condition as it is and particularly to its fundamental characteristic of existence-in-common. These latter needs evidently remain valid for all times and places. But they do not have any intrinsic link with the Old Testament, even if the Old Testament has helped them to be seen more clearly. See *GV,* I, p. 320. At any rate, what we should especially note in all of this, Bultmann tells us, is that Paul's reflections on the Law have no bearing on this distinction and that in this regard "his fundamental attack against the Jewish Law is of a different kind than Jesus" (*EPT,* pp. 40–42).

[18] See *EPT,* pp. 41–49.
[19] See *GV,* I, pp. 319–320.

does not understand what the Law is? Does this amount to saying that it is also absolutely necessary to pass through the Old Testament in order to understand the Gospel and make it one's own? Does not the Law manifest itself elsewhere? The answer seems obvious to Bultmann. When Paul, explaining the message of the Gospel to pagans, seeks to convince them of their powerlessness and their sin, he does not need to invoke the Old Testament. He knows that pagans, who do not have the Law, know by nature what the Law ordains; their conscience is the witness that the word of the Law is inscribed in their hearts. To put it in other terms, the preliminary understanding of the Law, which is necessary for the Gospel and which is offered by the Old Testament, can also be obtained from other realities through which the divine law is manifest. "Everywhere opportunity is given to man to become aware of his nothingness and thus to become humble or give up all hope of himself; everywhere also is the temptation to make of a moral obligation the means of obtaining personal virtue and to think that by struggle, actions, self-education, one may fashion for oneself a moral personality and thus attain one's authentic being, or at least have the potentiality and the urge to attain it. Everywhere there can develop a zeal for God which Paul calls an unenlightened zeal (Rom. 10:2) which the message of the cross definitely encounters."[20]

If the Church still uses the Old Testament in her preaching, it can only be for pedagogical reasons. No other place shows so forcefully the meaning of the moral exigencies of man's responsibility before others and God, the importance of immediate decision.[21] This essential moment of the past in the Old Testament has formed us and we should return unceasingly to see the possibilities of existence which we must embrace and to realize fully this existence in history where the Christian faith

[20] *Ibid.*, p. 321.
[21] See *loc. cit.*

116

must exist. But all of this does not make the Old Testament a holy book, the living expression of the very Word of God.

The foregoing observations are all dependent upon the identification of the Old Testament and the Law. Is this conclusion legitimate? Is the relation of the Old Testament to the New adequately expressed by the opposition of Law and Gospel? Existence under Law and existence under grace are certainly mutually dependent. The Law must be known in one way or another or the Gospel is not possible. Only he can truly know what the Law is who is enlightened by the true light and liberated by it. Does not the experience of the Law postulate in the Old Testament itself a certain experience of what is in the Gospel?

Bultmann recognizes that the Old Testament is far from ignoring grace. The gift of the Law itself appears as a grace. Israel knows that it is not primarily obedience to the Law to which it owes existence but to gratuitous divine election. Israel has been able to survive in spite of innumerable infidelities only because of pardon unceasingly renewed by a God as merciful as he is just. Even if we note the considerable differences among various books or authors of the Old Testament, there remain incontestable testimonies of a true ontological appreciation of sin and of the divine pardon which alone can absolve it.[22] In their "tragic" history and in their conviction that the action of God was to be interwoven with the destiny of his people, the Jewish people saw themselves spontaneously projected in a sort of mad hope, even to the end of time. The Jew was able to anticipate what the Christian faith considers as now realized.[23] Therefore may it be said that "from its own point of view the Old Testament is at once Law and Gospel."[24]

[22] See *ibid.*, pp. 326–330.
[23] See *ibid.*, pp. 330–331; see also *EPT,* pp. 191–205, where Bultmann develops this point more precisely with the ideas of alliance, kingdom, and people of God.
[24] *GV,* I, p. 333.

117

But this can no longer be true for us. The history of Israel is no longer our history; we can no longer lean on it as the foundation of our faith in the eschatological intervention of God our savior.[25] The essential quality of Christian faith is to recognize in Jesus Christ that eschatological intervention which puts an end to any idea of a religious history confused with the history of a people. This eschatological intervention is not like those by which Yahweh chose Abraham, freed his people from slavery in Egypt, guided their journey in the wilderness. It does not proceed from the events of the history of Israel, to which it marks the end. Our faith is not nourished by memory, as Jewish faith could be, by recalling the gift of the Law on Sinai, the passage of the Red Sea, the entrance into the Promised Land. The essence of our faith is not expressed in the continuity of the history of a people nor in the tradition which continues and guarantees that continuity. "The message of pardon granted through Jesus Christ by the grace of God is not the historic account of a past event but the Word of the preaching Church being addressed at this very moment to each of us as the Word of God in which Jesus Christ is present precisely as the *Word*."[26]

We cannot find the revelation of God directly in the Old Testament, in the history which it recounts for us, or in the experiences which it describes for us.[27] The Old Testament cannot make us understand the living Word of the grace of God. As with the concept of our nothingness it can only help us to plumb the depths of the mercy and forgiveness of God, of our radical helplessness, poverty, and sinfulness.[28] In any case, it

25 See *ibid.*, pp. 322–333.
26 *Ibid.*, pp. 331–332.
27 See *ibid.*, pp. 333–335.
28 Bultmann remarks that we also meet outside of the biblical sphere the idea of the non-being man. Man is seen as a fool for trying to compare himself with the divine power, thanks to which through grace he has been freed. It is true that the attitude which conveys this basic ideal is different in Hellenism (e.g., temperance, the mean, modesty) than in the Bible (e.g., confidence). Bultmann sees this difference (see *EPT*, p. 59) but does not note all of the conclusions which suggest themselves.

should not in any way be confused with the Gospel of grace which indicates its end.

Can we recognize in the Old Testament the expression of the Word of God and, in a traditional way, the prophetic announcement of what the Gospel proclaims? The Old Testament is, in fact, prophetic, effectively prophetic for one who recognizes the inner contradiction which runs all through it, or, the radical failure necessarily implied in its essential contradiction: the wish to enclose a God who is not of the world (a divine, truly eschatological action) in the personal history in the world of a particular people. For man only the checkmating of his own ways can have a prophetic value, only his realization of the impossibility of entering during his history on earth into direct possession of God, or of identifying this history with the action of God. The Old Testament becomes revelation, the work of God, for the Christian who finds in it the tragic disavowal of the human plan to appropriate God to oneself.[29] The Old Testament is always indirect.[30] Faith in Christ subsists independently of the Hebrew Scriptures, and this is why they are not indispensable for Christians and why the reading of them brings the Christian believer nothing for his faith which he does not already possess substantially.[31] The writings of the New Testament itself do not allude with equal frequency to the Old. There are several writers who almost ignore it.[32] This fact only confirms the true nature of eschatological faith.

It is not simply the results of critical research that compel us to recognize that the Old Testament is not a book of extraordinary oracles written by the finger of God. Faith itself must reject this concept, for faith is apart from external props, which are inimical to the very nature of faith.[33]

Exegetical subtleties aiming to evoke faith through marvels can

[29] See *EPT*, pp. 205–208; *GV*, I, pp. 335–336.
[30] *GV*, I, p. 335.
[31] See *ibid.*, p. 334.
[32] *Ibid.*, p. 336.
[33] See *ibid.*, p. 335; *EPT*, pp. 187–188; *TNT*, I, p. 114.

only obscure and destroy faith. Awakened in the heart of man, faith is able to use the Old Testament as it can use any reality, but faith cannot be grounded on it.

Critics have said that there is a certain Marcionism in Bultmann.[34] This must be qualified but the fact remains that in his theology there is a strong tendency to undervalue the Old Testament. Bultmann himself underlined the importance for the primitive Christian community of preserving the Old Testament as a holy book. If it is true, he says, that the Judeo-Christian communities tried to regard themselves only as a new sect within Judaism, the temptation for the Hellenists was entirely different. They saw themselves as a new religion, distinct from Judaism and from paganism, distinguished by progress in the knowledge of God and in the pursuit of moral ideals. To this too natural tendency, the possession of the Old Testament was to bring a valuable counterpoise. "For to the Old Testament, God is not cosmic law available to thought and investigation, but *the God who reveals himself in the course of history.*" The Old Testament offered opposition to the attempt to elaborate a "natural theology." "Thanks to the Old Testament the idea that God reveals himself in what he does was retained; that is the beginning of the understanding of the person of Jesus and his cross. This position enables us to understand what an eschatological event is, if it is true that it is not merely a myth." The Old Testament furnished an answer to the elaboration of any natural theology, an answer also centered in the idea of virtue and personal perfection. It defined the sense of a genuine religious ethic in which the Good is nothing other than the expression of the concrete demands of the will of God.[35]

[34] See J. B. Soucek, "Die Entmythologisierung in der tschechischen Theologie," *KuM,* IV, p. 26.

[35] See *TNT,* I, pp. 114–116; see also "History and Eschatology in the New Testament," *art. cit.,* 10.

120

Does Bultmann escape these dangers of a Christianity which, if not cut off from history, meets it only tenuously?[36] The Old Testament ought to be and always has been distinguished from the New. Our faith sees in it, however, more than a human treasure, valuable but unnecessary. It is more than an illustration of the antithesis of Gospel to Law. It furnishes the material for the Gospel.[37] The New Testament may unfold the meaning of what is announced and prefigured in the Old Testament, but the New Testament never reveals itself to us other than as the fulfillment and transfiguration of the Old. If then we can hear Jesus speaking while we reread the Old Testament, as Bultmann grants,[38] it is not simply because any reality can agree with the faith of those who already believe; it is first and essentially because Jesus himself is assimilated to it after, having taken his body of flesh, he revealed all its mysterious sense when he delivered his body on the cross and poured out his spirit on our world. Bultmann seems to reduce if not destroy the mystery of Jesus' Cross, Easter, and Pentecost. It is impossible to contemplate the mystery of salvation without accepting the divine wonders which it reveals ("the eschatological realities"), the human, historic realities in which Christ is revealed, which he transfigures.[39]

The authors of the Old Testament were able to announce (in a manner veiled to the understanding of their contemporaries and even to their own understanding) the coming of Jesus and his destiny. Jesus put an "end" to this history of salvation interwoven with the people's history. He completed that "teaching" by which God progressively prepared Israel to recognize the

[36] On Bultmann's "occasionalism," see R. Marlé, S.J., *Bultmann et l'interprétation du nouveau testament* (Paris, 1956), pp. 182 ff.

[37] See H. de Lubac, S.J., *Histoire et Esprit* (Paris, 1950), pp. 381 ff. See also J. Levie, "Les limites de la preuve d'Ecriture sainte," *Nouvelle revue théologique*, 71 (1949), pp. 1012–1013.

[38] See *GV*, I, p. 336.

[39] For Bultmann, wherever the message of the New Testament is expressed in all its purity, history is completely swallowed up in eschatology: "History and Eschatology in the New Testament," *art. cit.*, 11.

121

gift which he gives them, himself in the person of his Son. Was this teaching opposed to what the Messiah represented (to faith as well as to history), the purpose of this long historical approach? It is important not to confound the point of view of the believer with that of the philosopher or the historian. We cannot establish the reality of Jesus as Messiah and the fulfillment in him of the prophecies in the same way we prove a truth of science. But can the simple objective study of the Scriptures prepare for the decision of faith and bring to it a reasonable justification? The traditional "argument from prophecy" in a new existential form retains something of its theological value.

It is mysterious fulfillment effectively accomplished in Jesus Christ which gives historical basis to this "allegorical" exegesis, whose authentic reality Bultmann does not recognize.[40] It is true that the method may be abused, especially by departing too quickly from the literal sense. Once the minimum effort has been made to overcome the undeniable differences of culture, can we relegate to the rank of puerilities or unacceptable fantasies the exegesis of Origen, Gregory of Nyssa, or St. Augustine?[41] Must we eliminate or deprecate the innumerable examples of (allegorical) exegesis which much of the New Testament itself offers us and which explains the exegesis of the Fathers?

It is not just for reasons of scientific criticism that Bultmann rejects everything which can make us attribute too great a value and significance to the Old Testament. His position is grounded on a truly eschatological faith which defines the proper importance of the Gospel. To affirm the transcendence and the absolute newness of the revelation fulfilled in Jesus Christ, Bultmann stresses the definitely outmoded character of the Old Testament and the purely "indirect" and negative significance which it can assume for faith. However, by a curious reversal, it is that very transcendence and newness which are threatened

[40] There are different kinds of "allegorical exegesis" and various meanings of the word "allegory." See de Lubac, *op. cit.*, pp. 384 ff.

[41] It was necessary to emphasize this point several times in my study of Bultmann, *op. cit.*, pp. 69, 131, 180.

here. The newness emphasized by the New Testament has nothing in common with any development of man's religious consciousness. For him, such a consideration has no bearing on faith, no properly theological significance. The more open Israelites of the Old Testament were able to hope for that future realized in the coming of Jesus.[42] The transcendence and the newness of the Christian faith hold to the recognition of this *now*[43]; they imply no new knowledge of God. But can it be said in this case that our situation has, compared to that of the Jews, really changed? Perhaps salvation is signified for us in another way than it is for them: through the scandal of the cross of Jesus instead of through the defeats and contradictions of an impossible history. The relationship to God established by the Christian faith remains (as it was for the Jews) superior to all the realities of our worldly existence. The reality of salvation is yet to come.[44]

Can the entire New Testament lead us back to the recognition of this eschatological *now* linked with the Resurrection of Jesus? At the same time that it is the message of salvation is not the New Testament the living manifestation of a person? Has not Jesus by fulfilling the messianic hope of Israel also revealed himself?[45] This wholly new light cast on his mission, which had its source in his messianic consciousness (whose existence Bultmann denies),[46] is what the authors of the New Testament have tried to transmit to us. It is this revelation which disconcerted the contemporaries of Jesus. It is this revelation which continues to make men responsible for their choice before the Gospel. This permits us to penetrate beyond what was opened by the Old Testament towards the mystery of the Messiah, a mystery which is love as God himself.[47]

[42] See *GV*, I, p. 331.

[43] See *GV*, I, pp. 204, 265.

[44] Bultmann makes use of the teaching of a purely "forensic" justification, so essential to Lutheran theology; see Marlé, *op. cit.,* pp. 136 ff.

[45] See de Lubac, *op. cit.,* pp. 441 f.

[46] See *TNT,* I, pp. 26–32.

[47] After having noted the orientation of Luther's Christology, less intent on the internal mystery of Christ then on hearing his call and promise, Yves Congar underlines the "Semitic, biblical, and prophetic"

123

In the mystery of Jesus we have not just the announcement of pardon for our whole sinful existence. Pardon is accomplished because he has lived it in his body. The body of Christ and not only his message, his Word, becomes the true principle of the new creation. Like many Protestant theologians, Bultmann hesitates to pass from a revelation announced, to an incarnation realized and a Pasch consummated. The sacrament of the gift which God makes himself, and of the Easter to which he invites us now—this is the body of Jesus Christ nailed on a cross. He nourishes our faith, but simultaneous with him the entirety of the Scripture feeds us, those writings which alone can reveal the indescribable riches of God.

---

character of this view. He adds that it is still necessary to reflect on the Old Testament because "it seems evident to me that with Jesus Christ the interior mystery of God (glimpsed beforehand) has been revealed to us. Faith has now assumed a new dimension of knowledge" "Dogme Christologique et ecclesiologie," *Das Konzil von Chalkedon,* ed. L. A. Grillmeier and H. Bacht (Würzburg, 1954), III, p. 483.

VI. NEW INSIGHTS INTO FAITH

By Gotthold Hasenhüttl

WHAT ABOUT BULTMANN?

Few other Protestant theologians have been so diversely judged as Bultmann.[1] In the Lutheran Church, especially among theologians of the older school, he has sometimes been called heretical or even apostate. The judgment of Catholic theologians has been no less harsh. Because of his theory of "demythologizing" his thought has been termed a theology of disbelief. On the other hand, there has been repeated recognition of his worth on both sides; his intellectual achievement has even been compared with that of St. Thomas. Some maintain that his theology is derived from Luther, others from Calvin, or Heidegger, or Jaspers. These opinions arise out of the very

[1] In 1963 the author published *Der Glaubensvollzug* (Essen), in which he examined Bultmann's thought to discover whether it might be fruitful for Catholic theology. Rudolf Bultmann himself wrote the "Foreword" to this book where he said: "I have been asked whether I recognized this interpretation [by Dr. Hasenhüttl] as pertinent and adequate. I am extremely pleased to be able to answer in the affirmative without reservation. . . . It is a joy for the Protestant theologian when his assertions are approved in discussion with a Catholic theologian. In the present case our mutual understanding has helped us to clarify the meaning of 'the act of faith.' How far this common ground extends is a difficult question to decide, but it could be very far. The author obviously interprets my work from the Catholic understanding of faith, and there is throughout a critical element in his exposition, which becomes explicit at the end. All the same, there is also an understanding

125

nature of Bultmann's theology, which is so easy to misunderstand.[2] Why is this so?

Bultmann's theology has something in common with modern art. Anyone contemplating Michelangelo's "Last Judgment" will be deeply impressed by Christ as Judge of the World, but this impression is not the result of any effort on the part of the viewer—the painter himself guides the viewer's understanding of the work to such an extent that he just has to let himself be captivated. But the cooperation of the onlooker is very essential to the appreciation of modern art. Without it no understanding of the picture is possible; one is merely aware of detached forms that give the impression of chaos. But if we stop objectivizing and are willing to transcend subject and object, we are suddenly drawn by the artist into shaping with him a small portion of being.

Bultmann's theology should be approached in a similar way. Deeply moved by absolute truth, yet involved in the history of the becoming of all created being. Bultmann certainly had no wish to deny this truth—he sought life everywhere. His theology is sometimes "without fixed results" and when it is so judged it is open to misunderstanding. The key to his theology is the word "historicity." "Encounter" is an ever recurrent concept in his writing and he never tires of talking about "understanding." It is not out of place to see reminiscences of Aquinas here, because understanding, in the sense of the "to-be-with-it"

which can only come from a common understanding of the matter itself. . . . Future discussion will be all the more fraternal and fruitful the more the atmosphere in which it takes place is determined by a fundamental agreement on the essence of the fulfillment of faith. That the present book has contributed in a special way to the creation of this atmosphere is to my mind its greatest service" (pp. 9, 10). On *Der Glaubensvollzug*, see G. Bornkamm, "Die Theologie Rudolf Bultmanns in der neueren Diskussion," *Theologische Rundschau* (NF), 29 (1963), pp. 33–141; also J. Korner, "Katholisches Votum zur existentialen Interpretation," *Theologische Rundschau* (NF), 31 (1965), pp. 316–335. In the present essay the author summarizes *Der Glaubensvollzug* and attempts to engage Bultmann in further dialogue.

[2] G. Hasenhüttl, *Der Glaubensvollzug, ed. cit.,* pp. 18–22.

(*Bei-sich-sein*) of the human intellect, is always and everywhere active realization and never purely passive registration.[3] We have to bring a fresh perception to the study of Bultmann and not be frightened by his terminology which for many Catholic readers seems to indicate unbelief.

Nevertheless, precisely because it is a question of truth, there may be a danger here: is it permissible even to consider such an understanding and presentation of the truth? Bultmann gives the answer himself: "I think it is irresponsible to discuss the theme—I should say: the catchword—'demythologizing' in the presence of the laity. This is a theme which the laity either cannot understand or necessarily misunderstands because a previous theological education is essential to grasp its meaning."[4] I would add that even a theologian is under a great handicap if he has only recently come to know (or better, come to accept) genuine existential philosophy. In my book *Der Glaubensvollzug* I have tried to open new perspectives to this new sort of theological reflection in order to make it accessible to the Catholic theologian. It does not attempt a final solution; it is meant to be a contribution to the problem in the form of a discussion which may have something important to say for mutual understanding. Obviously, this understanding does not imply an unreserved acceptance of each single proposition. Though it is possible to discern a great amount of common ground in Catholic and Protestant thought, the questions of the Church's proclamation, of its office and rights, await future discussion.

THE OUTLINES OF BULTMANN'S ENDEAVOR

In the following statement of Bultmann's theology, "demythologizing" will be referred to only insofar as it is identical with "existential interpretation." Bultmann himself is always careful

---

[3] "*Intellectus nec per se nec per accidens passibilis est*" (St. Thomas Aquinas, *Quaestiones disputatae de anima*. q. 3, a. 1, ad 7).
[4] *KuM*, I, p. 8.

to confront his reader with the actual, decisive question, which is not one of terminology, but of how to respond to preaching, that is, the question of the full act of faith.

A Pre-Understanding for God's Revelation

Through the Church's proclamation the message of God's saving act in Christ reaches modern man in his own clearly defined historical situation. Can he understand this message? Can he hear the Word of God? He can, because the search for light, for life, and for truth is alive in him. In all forms of human desire and activity, balanced or perverted, this search is alive, urging man on towards his limit. If this questioning and drive in man is allowed full play, it will lead him to the question about God and thereby to a preliminary understanding of God's revelation. This revelation is not yet a reality in his life; he is still blind, but he is aware that the light exists, and because human existence implies *the ability to be* he can already stretch out his hands to it.

The answer which Greek philosophy gives to this search can be very confusing to modern man's ability to hear, because it takes for granted that man is master of himself and can dispose of himself at will. His concrete existence is glossed over, lowered to one case of the universal and lost in the cosmos. God is seen merely as the explanation of the world, and the world gives the key to the meaning of life and death. Man's concrete, ever renewed crisis-situation is thus dissolved into world membership and his preliminary understanding is deceived with an apparent answer.

But how easily existential philosophy also can give a false answer! Man is always tempted to provide an answer himself, substituting a self-made certainty for the searching quest of his preliminary understanding, and so he misses the real answer. Nevertheless, the existential approach, because of its ambiguity and openness, allows man to catch sight of the decisive point, which cannot be answered by anthropology.

Theology, on the other hand, recognizes the question confronting man. It looks for the answer in the direction of man's concrete existence but at the same time it rejects the idea that man as such can give the answer to his own existence—the essence of life is beyond his grasp. However, the human quest within him drives him towards his final meeting with the answer. In practice though, he will not wait for this meeting, but gives the answer himself and so becomes a sinner. In this way he misses his real being. "All have sinned" (Rom. 3:23), and "the Scripture consigned all things to sin" (Gal. 3:22). So man is darkness instead of light, alone, abandoned to his own devices and unable to free himself from this state of affairs. The option which surpasses all the other decisions in life is for darkness. This option is the basic cause of sin, in it man misuses his preliminary understanding of God's revelation. From this abuse arise worry, fear, and doubt. Man cannot save himself from this situation, but this very sickness unto death can become the occasion for God's grace. Also, even in the depth of his abandonment, man is still moved by his quest for real existence, for the meeting with God.

The Encounter with God's Saving Act in Christ

Man is powerless to bring about this meeting—God does it for him: the Word of God becomes flesh. The bearer of God's salvation and revelation is a real man. No grandiose natural display takes place, which could overwhelm the individual; a man appears, he lives in history and kerygma (*Historisch* and *Geschichtlich*); Jesus is the Redeemer. It is not primarily a teaching which was brought to us through him—a new knowledge about God, man, and the world; rather, it is that through him a Person becomes decisive for our life and salvation. (It is therefore not essential that we should remember each single

129

event in his life.) On the other hand, this Person who reveals God to us has not come to lead us to a purely human encounter with him within our individual personal history; ultimate, final salvation happens to us and is spoken to us in this encounter. Man is made into a new creature through God's Word, through Jesus Christ. Time and history are led to their eschatological end through this salvation event and both receive a new meaning from it. If I accept this new dimension, which enlightens us about everything within the world, then salvation has been granted me and Christ becomes *constitutive* of my new mode of being.

How is this possible? It is possible in that, with faith, I receive and confess Christ as the Truth and as the innermost reality of my being. Something takes place which was hitherto beyond man in his radical sense: a man, Jesus of Nazareth, who is the Word of God, becomes for me the basis of a new choice of being, becomes absolutely necessary to my new existence. If the human lover finds something of his own existence in the being of the loved one and from it advances to discover new reality, this can be only an analogy for what happens between the believer and the Word of God. This theme is extremely important in Bultmann's theology and could also initiate a fruitful research in Catholic thought. It is not memory, not learning, which primarily bring Christ to us; if this were so, the teacher would become superfluous once the teaching had been grasped. God shares his own Person, speaks him forth: he will be remembered above all things that have ever been expressed and will remain forever present in genuine contact.

It could be objected that this throws the content, the "what" of God's word into the background. Certainly Bultmann's presentation does seem to lend weight to this objection, but at bottom, in the full sense of this "what," this is the correct place for it. Jesus of Nazareth, in history and kerygma, is one with the Word of God—there is "paradoxical identity," in the words of Bultmann. The mysterious Union of human and divine reality sees the essential in the revealing Word which God speaks, but at the same time he is aware of his human-kerygmatic condition. In this encounter with Jesus Christ, God no longer shows himself only as the outermost limit of my existence, but I am met as a person in my very being, I am spoken to and God's Word becomes effective in my life.

The Proclamation of the Church
as the Meeting Place with Christ

But how do I encounter his Word today? Does it just live on in my memory? Where can men living in the twentieth century encounter Christ? Bultmann answers: in the kerygma, in the proclamation of the Church. We have access to Christ only in the kerygma, without it Christ's death would have been lost in the past and could never have been made present in its fullness. It is only from the Revealer whom I encounter in the Church's proclamation that I receive my new existence. So Christ's Word—that it is to our advantage that he has returned to the Father—holds good today, for the community was grounded in his death and exists through its proclamation, and I have entered into Christ's life and death.

No other Protestant has insisted so strongly on the unity between Christ and the Church as Bultmann has, and it is precisely because of the whole relationship which he defends that his theology has been—and still is—so violently attacked. Is this attack justified? Bornkamm writes: "This thesis is so constantly emphasized and is theologically so important for him that it is hard to see how Christ and the salvation-event make the kerygma and the Church possible and are the *critical instance* for both; after all, the proclamation and the Church must in all times be judged and measured by the Christ event. However clearly the concept of the paradoxical identity avoids Platonism, however distinctly he may show that the event proclaimed belongs essentially to the salvation event (see 2 Cor.

131

6:2!), and that the Church is thus the place where Christ is present now, it remains misleading and problematical so long as he has not brought out the critical *difference* between Christ and the Gospel *as distinct from* the proclamation and the Church."[5]

There is no doubt that there is a real problem here which still needs a good deal of study. Nevertheless, the "for" and "against" seem to tear open a rift between Christ and the proclamation which no longer throws any useful light on the whole question of the relationship between them. As a "critical instance," the saving event in Christ cannot be set over against the saving event in the Church. The presence of salvation in preaching is the presence of Christ, whose death and Resurrection is present in the kerygma. Bultmann's "critical instance" does not seem to me to hold up. The bride of Christ, the community of the faithful, is not judged, but loved by Christ, who according to John's Gospel saves those who believe in Christ from coming into judgment. It is precisely when the unity of the Christ event with the Church's proclamation is stressed that the essential coördination of the members to Christ, their Head, becomes apparent.

There is no weakening of the Christ event when it is proclaimed in the Church. On the contrary, it brings out the unique place Christ holds in our vocation from God. Jesus Christ is there as the Word of God become word. Bultmann does avoid going into the differentiating question of whether Christ is God "in himself" or only "for me," for this distinction has been introduced into his thought and was not original to it. If we reflect that God is not a particular instance of being but is in his essence Event, living personal relationship, then it becomes clear that Jesus Christ as the Word of God is always this Word as being-uttered-to-us by the Father, and therefore as Word he is truly God. Thomas, overpowered by his meeting with Jesus Christ, exclaimed: "My Lord and my God" (Jn. 20:28). This is the completely fitting confession before the Risen Christ; much stronger than "Master," it recognizes God

5 G. Bornkamm, *art. cit.,* 135.

himself in Jesus. "He who has seen me has seen the Father," Jesus said (Jn. 14:9; see 12:45). Thomas beheld Jesus as he wanted to be seen and should be seen. The final confession of faith in the Gospel brings out in its ὁ θεός μοῦ that Jesus is the *Logos,* who has returned to where he was before the Incarnation, who has been glorified with the glory which he had with the Father before the world was made (17:5); he is now recognized as the God he was before the beginning (1:1).[6] And this confession is ever renewed in the acceptance in faith of the proclamation.

Justification through Faith in Jesus Christ

The fulfillment of faith is the answer to the encounter with Jesus Christ in preaching. But this answer must come from the whole of man's existence; his decision of faith fulfills itself in this existential answer. The encounter with the saving act of God takes place neither "before" nor "after" this decision but *in* it. Thus faith is bound up with its object, so that reference to Christ is constitutive for the fulfillment of faith. "Faith is not an act which can be consummated by man on his own initiative as if Jesus were only the 'impulse' towards it. Rather it is exactly Jesus towards whom faith is directed: he who is the way, the truth, and the life and without whom no one comes to the Father."[7] The object of faith is included in the fulfillment of faith, it is always referred to its object, to God's saving act in Christ. It can never be degraded to a mere "attitude of the soul" or to a "holding for true what the Church teaches." So that *fides qua creditur* is what it is only in relation to its object, *fides quae creditur.*[8] It is not a matter of indifference "what" a man believes; faith is always *in* Jesus Christ, who died for us and rose again. It cannot be reduced to a general faith in God.

6 *J,* pp. 538 f.
7 *TNT,* II, p. 76.
8 *GV,* I, p. 88.

Only in Christ is existence in faith taken seriously, is it genuine. This faith alone creates a new way of life which renews the believer in the core of his being.

This faith in God's Word in Jesus Christ, because in it God gives us the power to live a new life, is the condition for receiving the grace of justification. "Faith is the condition for the reception of grace: but yet not in such a way that the believer might think he has fulfilled this condition and can lay claim to God's grace."[9] Grace is always a pure gift which comes to man in his encounter with Christ. Apart from this encounter man has no access to grace because he has forfeited it through sin, but in his meeting with God's saving act the condition for salvation is fulfilled in his case. God's free gift of faith is also the condition for man's justification, which is a forensic occurrence. Justification is not from within man, as though he could in any way justify himself; it comes to him from God, before the forum, and he is answerable to God for it. Man is justified through the judgment of the loving God and this shows us the source of our salvation; it comes to us from God. But the place where the saving event takes place is Jesus Christ; it is the eschatological event, and so justification is qualified as an eschatological occurrence. This last event takes place here and now in the encounter with God's Word. Justification from this viewpoint is a present occurrence.

This forensic, eschatological, present justification happens through the act of God working effectively in man, not in the "as though" fashion once incorrectly introduced in some Protestant theological circles. Bultmann insists strongly on its being understood as really actually happening. Man *is* just, because God's acquittal makes him really free. When man considers himself, he sees himself to be caught up and bound by sin, but if he considers God's act of love in his Son, man is saved, justified, and set free. He is free to make a genuine decision, in which he no longer chooses according to his human measure from among the attractive possibilities in life; these will

[9] *EPT,* p. 176.

134

be placed in the balance, and he can no longer choose from selfish motives but must opt for his real chance, which is offered to him from the cross of Christ. "If the decision of faith takes place before the cross of Christ which offers us life, then it is obvious that it will not be a choice between worldly possibilities springing from worldly motives."[10] Man will choose the eschatological event of the cross; in other words, he will choose the end and ground of his existence. And man can make this decision on the ground of his being loved by God.

Then he will not only experience newness but will become radically new; he will be born again. Man can exchange his origin, his derivation, in the course of his justification; he can become a new creature and reach his true being. In this eschatological event not only can he acquire new "qualities," he can enter into a new mode of being. He has to live in a new way, because he has become a new being, he has been born again. We may be tempted to ask Nicodemus's question: "How can a man be born when he is old? Can he enter a second time into his mother's womb and be born?" (Jn. 3:4). From the human point of view it is absurd to speak of this new birth, but seen from "God's point of view," as he encounters us in Christ, it not only has meaning but is our salvation. God in his saving act, in Jesus Christ, lovingly calls man to a new mode of being: he is no longer to live of the world, but he lives in Christ. God puts an end to "this world" in that he makes man new, gives him a new existence, and this places man before a decision. Through faith human existence experiences its eschatological aspect as graced, and if he accepts God's justifying grace, man moves into the eschaton, into his final mode of existence. This is the moment in which man responds to the encounter with God's salvation in Christ and so passes from death to life. "Truly, truly, I say to you, the hour is coming, and now is, when the dead will hear the voice of the Son of God, and those who hear will live" (Jn. 5:25).

In spite of all this, man remains in the world. He is im-

[10] *TNT*, II, p. 23.

prisoned in time and history, and has to keep struggling for his eschatological, unworldly existence in a repeated option for God's justifying grace. "The work of the revealer becomes effective, not in being in the world, but only in the eschatological existence apprehended by faith. But this means: only in a constant overcoming of existence in the world."[11] And precisely because of his paradoxical mode of existence, it is impossible for the believer to withdraw from his concrete situation and forget the world. "Faith, πίστις, does not shun contact with existence in history, it realizes an eschatological existence in temporality. Christian existence in πίστις is thus *the paradoxical eschatological existence within man's historical Dasein.*"[12] "*It is the paradox of Christian being* that the believer is taken out of the world and exists, so to speak, as unworldly, and that at the same time he remains within the world, within his historicity."[13] "The paradox that Christian existence is at the same time an eschatological unworldly being and an historical being is analogous with the Lutheran statement: *Simul justus, simul peccator.*"[14]

The Inner Structure of the Complete Act of Faith

The acceptance of God's justifying grace in man's new eschatological existence includes, as its innermost structure, the moment of *self-giving.* In the fulfillment of faith the believer gives himself up to God's Word. He does not give God some thing but *himself,* and he includes his whole existence in this gift. He also gives himself as a sinner; all vanity and boasting must be renounced in faith. The believer knows that recognition can come to him only from God, because no one can glorify himself before God (see 1 Cor. 1:26 ff). Man can

[11] *J.* p. 454.
[12] Bultmann, "πιστεύω," *TWNT,* 6, pp. 222–223.
[13] *HE,* p. 152.
[14] *Ibid.,* p. 154.

attain his real existence only by forfeiting it to God. The Christian faith knows that man can receive himself only from God and that this can take place only when his renunciation of the world (and this in the last resort means his self-renunciation) is radical.[15]

Man is always fighting against this renunciation, and we know even from our human experience how difficult total surrender is. "Many human beings long for friendship and love, and in this they basically long for surrender of themselves, in which their being is to be fulfilled. Yet they are incapable of taking the decision of unreserved surrender in the encounters of life, or of trusting simply, without being able to hold on to a support, without a guarantee. Many a friendship and many a marriage is wrecked by a man's inability to win this victory over himself. And the relationship of so many human beings with God is wrecked just here too. For it is only for such surrender that God's grace becomes effective."[16] This total self-surrender cannot be achieved by man once and for all, so that from then on he can live in security. It must be constantly renewed and the believer always remains the unprofitable servant. In this renunciation of his sinful existence, and in his perpetual living in dependence on God's saving act, man must also include the surrender of all security in the world. *All* glory, not just self-glorification, is excluded before God. Man knows that he has nothing which he has not received, and since he has received it he cannot glory in it, he must refer it all to God. But this always includes the painful moment of giving away, when man comes to God out of his sinful condition. So Paul declared that all that he had held dear until this moment was as nothing: "But whatever gain I had, I counted as loss for the sake of Christ. Indeed I count everything as loss because of the surpassing worth of knowing Christ Jesus my Lord. For his sake I have suffered the loss of all things, and count them as refuse, in order that I may gain Christ and be found in him, not

[15] *EPT,* p. 175.
[16] *Ibid.,* pp. 174–175.

137

having a righteousness of my own, based on law, but that which is through faith in Christ, the righteousness from God that depends on faith" (Phil. 3:7–9). Every human bond must give way before this surrender, which also includes the readiness "to enter into a solitariness in which the world fades away, in which all links, relationships, even the most binding and the dearest, are loosed and where we stand confronted by God alone. We must come into the presence of God bared and naked, divested of all to which we would fain cling, stripped of the rags with which we would cover ourselves . . . and only he who is ready to enter with Jesus into the dread hour of Godforsakenness on the cross, will be allowed to share in the joy of the Risen Savior."[17] The risen life, which frees man from an existence doomed to death, remains enveloped in darkness, however; dark because of the renunciation of all false, erroneous light, and dark also because man cannot look into the blinding light of God's grace. The attitude of the believer in God's loving hands can only be one of *obedience* to him. Faith in its innermost structure is not only total self-surrender but also complete obedience. Even this is the gift of God's grace, given in the fullness of faith, of which it is a part. Man can never forego this obedience, for just as he possesses his life through faith, so he also has it only if he listens to God, hears and obeys him. "The acceptance of God's grace is ὑπακοή, because this grace encounters man in the paradoxical form of the cross of Christ—in others words, because the divine act of grace implies at the same time the judgment carried out on man on the cross, with his sins as well as with his striving for righteousness—or for wisdom. Faith is then the obedient acceptance of the divine judgment on man's previous independence."[18] This obedience is the opposite of Adam's act. No man can hide from God's inexorable scrutiny, but in Christ there is at the same time the call of his grace, by which man is transferred from his lost state into

[17] *TWB,* pp. 194 f.
[18] Bultmann, *art. cit., TWNT,* 6, p. 218.

God's love. Obedience thus contains two elements: the renunciation of sin and conversion to God in a radical placing of one's self at his disposal. In faith man fulfills his being by turning from the disobedience of sin and surrendering entirely to God's demands. He thereby abandons all human security. This new understanding of faith goes beyond the Jewish concept that I must obey all that God has commanded but am free to do as I like where nothing has been commanded. To act in this way is a mechanical righteousness which is not radical enough for the obedience of faith—man is at God's disposal at all times. As long as I obey only because it is commanded and would act otherwise if it were not commanded, I am not in harmony with the exigencies of the law. I am entirely obedient only when I understand all the exigencies of the law and agree with them from within.[19] Radical obedience is present "only when a man inwardly assents to what is required of him . . . where the whole man stands behind what he does; or better, when the whole man is *in* what he does, when he is not *doing something obediently,* but *is* essentially obedient."[20] When a man is obedient in this way in his being, his obedience coincides with the fulfillment of faith and is its innermost structure. There follows, then, as the third characteristic essential to the life of faith: self-knowledge. The obedience of faith is not a blind obedience. No sacrifice of the intellect is exacted from man, he fulfills his faith in an understanding decision. Man's response to God's saving act must be given with his whole being, but at the same time he must understand what he is doing, so that his entire way of life, renewed and reoriented, can be brought into it. A genuine call to faith must be understood if it is to involve the whole man and not just elicit an acquiescence in incomprehensible statements. "The genuine call is simply a word which shows man to himself, teaches him to understand himself . . . opens up to him a situation of existential self-knowledge, which in fact he has

[19] *PC,* pp. 59, 79.
[20] *JW,* p. 77.

to have. This call does not put me before a free choice of just anything, but before the necessity to decide; my real self is as it were the only available choice."[21] "Therefore the believer does not understand revelation as *something* new, but understands it only insofar as he has a new understanding of *himself* in it. Existence in faith fulfills itself through a new understanding of what it is to exist."[22] Acceptance of the Good News gives me a new being and so gives me myself. The self-understanding which comes to me in faith lights up my whole existence. In the light of faith man really understands himself, and all unreal, false understanding comes to an end. Man understands himself in a new way, has a fresh relationship to himself, but not only this: he also forms a new relationship with his fellow men and the world around him, so that he can realize his existence in time.

The Freedom of Faith

The main characteristic of the believer's new relationship to the world is freedom. Before he has been graced in Jesus Christ, man is not free. "Truly, truly, I say to you, every one who commits sin is a slave to sin. The slave does not continue in the house forever; the son continues forever. So if the Son makes you free, you will be free indeed" (ὄντως—in your essence) (Jn. 8:31–36). Certainly, mankind had freedom of choice before Christ, but it is only through man's acceptance of the proclamation in faith that he is able to choose himself anew. The relative freedom which every spiritual being has in the moment of decision is not lost through sin; what is lost is the absolute freedom which gives the possibility of genuine self-choice. This can become a new reality only through the encounter with the Word of God. For the self has this freedom, not in an inner independence, but only in an encounter with the

---

[21] *GV*, I, p. 283.
[22] *Ibid.*, p. 297.

Thou. And the freedom which comes to me in this way constitutes my existence in Jesus Christ. Man is responsible for his being, and every encounter brings with it the decision as to whether man will respond to God's call to him in the actual moment or whether he will shut his ears to it and so lose his ultimate freedom.

But if man is forfeit to sin without grace (Rom. 7:14), then is his fate decided beforehand, is he predestined? Certainly, his own decisions bind him, for the bad tree bears evil fruit (Mt. 7:17). But in the encounter with Christ this selfish isolation is broken down and he can receive himself anew from the divine Thou. There is no decision without man's acquiescence and no man without God's Word: God speaks his saving Word and man responds in an encounter. All attempts to explain what happens through predestination are speculations originating in a false Cartesianism and do not understand a freedom which arises only in encounter and is immediately obedient. Thus grace and freedom, choice and acceptance of salvation, form a unity which is previous to all separation.

Human relationships provide a good example of this kind of freedom. Even in human friendship and love, the trusting gift of self to the other is genuine only when it is a free decision, yet the giver knows that actually he is receiving himself wholly from the other. He knows that his friendship or his love is not something for which he will *deserve* a return of friendship or love. The other is as free as he is and his friendship and love can only come as a free gift. "In friendship and love all I do for the other in the way of love has the purpose of revealing me to him, and not that of earning his love. If my love is returned and it comes to the free act of surrender, then I know that even this surrender of mine is a gift of the other: I am 'chosen,' so that I actually exist from my friend . . . what happens in this way between men is a pattern of what happens between God and man. But what happens between man and man never covers the whole of our existence . . . the relationship with God embraces the whole of human existence and innocence and newness are pure gift from his forgiving grace."[23] The freedom which God gives is not only absolute, but it is at the same time ultimate possibility, eschatological reality. Because of God's enduring coming, man can be sure of the future, and because of God's forgiving grace, he can be sure of the past, so that the moment of man's free, God-given decision will involve both the past and the future. This ultimate freedom does not come from any worldly impulse, it comes only through union with Christ: Christian freedom is the fruit of the *break with the world*. But this does not imply any asceticism which flees the world or turns away from it. It does not imply an escape from the bonds of law and order, but a binding to the Lord, who loosens man from the chains of the world. In the encounter with Christ "man is de-secularized by God's direct pronouncement to him, which tears him out of all security of any kind and places him at the brink of the End. And God is 'de-secularized' by understanding his dealing eschatologically: he lifts man out of his worldly ties and places him directly before his own eyes. Hence, the 'de-historization' or 'de-secularization' both of God and of man is to be understood as a paradox: precisely that God, who stands aloof from the history of nations, meets each man in his own little history, his everyday life. . . . De-historicized man (that is, naked of his security within his historical group) is guided into his concrete encounter with his neighbor, in which he finds his true history."[24] Christian freedom becomes a dialectical relationship in which man remains at a certain "distance" with regard to everything mundane. He meets the world in the attitude of the Pauline "as if it were not." He is the master of all things in the world, for he remains in the world, but he is no longer of the world.

But his fidelity is constantly tested in the matter of today's existence. In Scripture the word "today" is always the time of decision, decision in freedom about the whole of existence.

[23] *EPT,* pp. 178–179.
[24] *TNT,* I, p. 27.

142

The encounter with Christ in the Church's preaching lends the fleeting moment of life this absolute meaning. "The encounter with him [Christ] turns the 'now' into eschatological time. If the passing moment were to become permanent, it would no longer be eschatological, but worldly time. It is precisely this fact which gives the 'now' which man meets the burden of responsibility; it turns it into the moment of decision over life and death."[25] This moment is not always at man's command; God's offer is not a perennial sun in a Platonic heaven of ideas; salvation breaks in on us now; a decision must be made precisely now, neither earlier nor later. We do not find Christ when it so pleases us. Our encounter with him is always and only when we meet him as he is proclaimed in our neighbor. And the time of the encounter with Christ is always fulfilled time, fullness of time, which itself is no longer a moment of linear time, but transcends it. This concentration on the present moment, for which Bultmann also provides a good philosophical grounding, we also find in great saints, who were fully conscious of its importance, for instance Thérèse of Lisieux.

Faith as Hope and Charity

It would seem that hope no longer has any meaning if everything hangs on the moment of decision. Can the future hold any promise for us when salvation or perdition takes place in the present? The future promised us in Christian hope is not a human possibility, a dream conjured up by man's desires and longing in which he can forget his present needs. Hope, which springs from faith, is a deep-rooted expectation which has renounced all wishful thinking but still moves joyously into the future because it is turned towards God. Although the future is not a mundane future and is fundamentally inaccessible to human knowledge, it nevertheless awakens a deep trust in the

[25] *J.* pp. 270 f.

believer, a trust which can wait on the promises of God as
Abraham did. Hope is the watchfulness of the five wise virgins,
who waited until the bridegroom came. "The one who waits!
Thus may we characterize in general terms the life of the
Christian; the description fits him just as does that which
qualifies him as the *viator,* the pilgrim. . . . The Christian is
a pilgrim who is engaged in a journey, who has turned his back
on the old world and is directing his steps to the future and so
we could describe him as the one who waits."[26] This expectant
hope of the Christian springs from his situation. An example
will make this clear: We say that a woman is expecting a
child; that is, she hopes once she has conceived the child. The
man of faith is expecting the true life in the same way, because he is already rooted in Christ. Expectation, trusting
hope, grown out of the fact that he is already in possession of
the future, that he *abides in Christ,* that he is faithful to what
God has done for him. This abiding gives our existence an
openness towards the future and from this comes a joyful
expectation. This abiding, this stillness before God, is a fore-
taste of the future, which in faith we can already possess
through revelation and we must keep it ever before us.[27] So
all things belong to the man of faith, present and future, and he
is Christ's and Christ is God's (1 Cor. 3:22–23). This dimension of the life in faith, constantly renewing the promise of the
future and speaking of God to the believer, sets him free to
love the Thou whom he encounters. His love shows whether
his faith and hope are real. In carrying out the commandment
to love, the believer becomes aware of his eschatological existence. "If there is anything at all which distinguishes the man of
faith in the world and proves the renewal of his life, it is
love . . . love is the only criterion by which the believer can
know that he has ceased to belong to the old world: 'We know
that we have passed from death to life, because we love the

26 *TWB,* p. 209.
27 *GV,* I, pp. 150–152.

144

brethren' (1 Jn. 3:14)."[28] The basis of this love is God's love for man: "For God so loved the world that he gave his only Son, that whoever believes in him should not perish but have eternal life" (Jn. 3:16). He loved us first and not we him; he received us as sinners into his love. And "the essential message of Christianity is that the love of God has been manifested in Jesus Christ. There it emerges from its hiddenness and in word and deed is proclaimed to all who in the torment of their distress and sorrow long for freedom. The love of God which takes us not as those who we are now and into whom we have made ourselves, but as those who we are not, who we ought and wish to be, who we shall be. And by this means the divine love makes what we are, apparent only, and bestows in its stead our genuine and true life.

"This love of God is not a goal towards which we strive—who could ever obtain it by striving?—but it is the power which already enclasps and enfolds us, and to which our eyes have only to be opened, and we are to turn our gaze and our mediation on Him in whom it has appeared incarnate, Jesus Christ."[29] "Our love is rooted in his love."[30] "We love because he first loved us" (1 Jn. 4:19). The reason why we are free to love is Jesus Christ in whom God's love has appeared. Our acceptance of Christ's love is the basis and norm of our own love. Christ's love for us and our love for him are deeply reciprocal, as is shown in the parable of the Good Shepherd: he knows his own and they know him. The object of love, however, is not immediately and directly Jesus Christ, but our present, tangible neighbor. "There is no such thing as a direct love for Jesus. Otherwise, love would not have understood him as the Revealer, that is, as the one in whom we encounter God. Love directly for God does not exist (see 1 Jn. 4:20 f.). Jesus' love is not a personal affective love, but a liberating service. Our return of this love is not a pietistic awareness

28 *PC,* p. 205.
29 *TWB,* pp. 80–81.
30 *GV,* III, p. 29.

of Christ,"[31] but the "love one another!" The commandment to love God forms an inseparable unity with the commandment to love our neighbor as ourselves. The measure of our love of God is always our love of our neighbor, and man experiences his encounter with Jesus Christ in his neighbor. How are we to love our neighbor? "As thyself" shows that it must be with the same love with which we ourselves are loved. Kierkegaard explains this clearly: "If one must love his neighbor *as himself*, then the commandment opens the lock of self-love as with a picklock and the man with it. Were this commandment expressed in some other way than by the use of this little phrase, 'as thyself,' which is at once so easy to use and yet has the tension of eternity, then it could not master self-love. This 'as thyself' does not vacillate in its aim, and so it enters with the condemning inflexibility of eternity, into the secret hiding place where a man loves himself. It does not leave self-love the least excuse, the least loop-hole open. How strange! Long and shrewd speeches might be made about how a man ought to love his neighbor, and self-love would always know how to bring forth excuses and ways of escape, because the subject had not been entirely exhausted. All alternatives had not been canvassed; a point was not exactly expressed because something had been forgotten or not accurately and bindingly enough expressed and described. This 'as thyself'—no wrestler can get so tight a hold on his opponent, as that with which this commandment binds selfishness."[32] We find the way to our neighbor in that we encounter him without reserve and accept the "as thyself" with all that it implies.

But who is my neighbor? We do not distinguish him on the basis of good qualities we meet, nor is he included under any philanthropic notion we may have. He is the entire, concrete, living man with whom I come in contact. The parable of the Good Samaritan in Luke, interpreting the double command to love, shows us how to love. Love is found on the way from

[31] *J*, p. 404.
[32] Kierkegaard, *Works of Love* (Princeton, 1946), pp. 15 ff.

Jerusalem to Jericho, where the man lies stricken to the ground. Love is the simple readiness to accept the existence of the other. It does not choose which man is to be my neighbor. The only valid principle for choice is the situation in which I find myself and in which I must prove myself, if I am to be true to my own being.

But it would be a wrong attitude if one were to love one's neighbor only "for God's sake," if God were the only direct object of our love and our fellow man were misused as the means to this end. On the contrary, we encounter God only in our neighbor; God is present when we encounter our neighbor as a Thou. A text from Simone Weil will make this clearer: "Love for our neighbor descends from God to man; it precedes the love which rises from man to God. God urges us to go out to the unfortunate. He is everywhere present where the unhappy are loved for themselves. God is not present, even when we call upon him, where the unfortunate are only an occasion for doing good and are loved for this reason. . . . Such expressions as 'to love our neighbor for God's sake' are misleading and ambiguous. The deepest kindness of which one is capable is just enough for us to reach the loveless and ragged bit of humanity begging on the street corner; this is not the moment to direct one's thoughts to God. Just as there are moments when we must think only about God and forget all creatures, without exception, so there are others when we must necessarily be preoccupied with the creature and not think directly on the Creator. In these moments God's presence in us is so hidden that it remains a mystery even for ourselves. There are moments when the thought of God would separate us from him . . . real love is not just that we love the unfortunate in God, but that God loves them through us."[33] When we turn our eyes from our neighbor to see *what* is to be done, then the usual commandments come into force. Love itself, however, is not aware of any over-all "what" to be carried out; it dis-

[33] Simone Weil, *Das Unglück und die Gottesliebe* (Munich, 1953), pp. 151 f.

covers what is to be done at the moment. "With a keen and sure eye, love discovers what there is to be done. Love is not so blind that it would have to weigh up conscientiously all the possibilities and consequences of an action in a given situation. But that which in view of these possibilities and consequences is demanded to be done at any given time cannot be imparted by any theory. On the contrary, it is love that reveals it."[34] St. Augustine also has deep, audacious words about love: "Love and then do what you will . . . let the root of love remain in you, nothing that is not good can spring from such a root."[35]

The Eternal Life of the Believer

At the end of these reflections on some of the themes in Bultmann's theology it remains to be asked whether this life in faith, hope, and charity will eventually come to an end. Man is accustomed to picture the future to himself and so he also has an image of what life after death will be like. This image is according to his present capacity for understanding it. Jesus speaks of it only in symbols, most often as a banquet prepared for us. The believer knows for sure only that life *itself* is promised him, that it will have no end, and that it stands in analogy to life in time and place. He does not claim to be able to discover "what the ζωή promised him is like. If the gift promised him bears the name of what man holds as his highest good, the name ζωή, then what he calls 'life' must be an indication of that other 'life.' But this is true only in the sense that this other life is the realization of all that his present ζωή *should be,* and *would like to be,* even if it is constantly hidden from him. This promised ζωή cannot be clearly described either as a 'spiritual' life in the ideal sense or as a phenomenon of the consciousness, of the soul's life. . . . Any representation of the content and manner of the promised ζωή could only speak in

[34] *EPT,* pp. 79–80.
[35] St. Augustine, *In Epist. Joannis ad Parthos,* vii, 8; *PL,* 35, 2033.

human language, and this even at its highest level would not be any more adequate than at its poorest level. For it is about promises which as eschatological, as ἀνάστασις καὶ ζωή, and these are beyond human description. Preparation for this life is the present acceptance of earthly death, that is, man's abandonment of himself as he knows himself and wills to be. This appears in the world under the mask of death."[36] But the believer knows that the risen life is his and that it will surely come. For he knows that his life is not fulfilled in time; real life, without any veil, is yet to come. He also knows, however, that eternal life has already begun here and now in faith and that it will have no end. True eschatological life does not appear in time. It is qualitatively more than the temporal and the visible. For this reason it cannot be so closely bound up with this life that it would end with man's visible existence; eternal life has no end because in it there is no death. The man of faith and love has really passed from death to life. When his earthly life ends, he is certain that in its last moment God's love will meet him and be with him forever.

It is the last moment which is filled with eternity, God's love is always active in it. When we have said that love is granted the believer in the hour of his death, no concept can surpass this statement: it has said everything that it is possible to express, for God is love and he who abides in love abides in God. And Jesus' words are verified in all their depth: "I am the resurrection and the life; he who believes in me, though he die, yet shall he live; and whoever lives and believes in me shall never die" (Jn. 11:25 f.).

CONCLUSION

This short indication of the most important themes in Bultmann's theology can perhaps serve as a guide to the direction his thought takes. Bultmann is careful in his theology to prove

[36] *J*, p. 308.

his points exegetically from Scripture texts, and they are well drawn from a philosophico-theological basis. At the same time, his thinking is filled with the joy of the Christian who, in hope and charity, is freed from the weight of sin and distance from God. Just as certainly as man knows that God encounters him in Christ, he also knows in the fullness of faith that his real life will have no end. He knows that he can hope that God's love will encounter him in the last hour of his temporal existence.

Man sets out in darkness, bearing in his heart the tormenting question about light and life. In his search a wonderful thing happens to him: God himself encounters him, speaks to him, heals him, and gives him, through his Son and through the proclamation of the Church, the light and brightness of his life. God's loving Word takes hold of the sinner and gives him the grace to hold his head up, to understand the world afresh in his light, and through his obediential capacity to attain to the obedience of faith and radical freedom.

There is a final unity and dynamism in Bultmann's theology. Can it be a starting point for a deepening of Catholic theology? I do not doubt it. But there is a danger here. For the deepest insights come from the most difficult work. My study of Bultmann's theology is an introduction to this work. Dialogue with theologians such as Bultmann always presupposes a certain sympathy towards really understanding what they are trying to say. Bultmann has said: "An understanding interpretation, even when it is critical, demands an inner sympathy between interpreter and subject; they are interested by the same problems, working in the same area. The greater the sympathy, the nearer both will come not only to an understanding of each other, but to a solution of the problem at hand."[37]

[37] Bultmann, "Foreword," in Hasenhüttl, *op. cit.,* p. 10.

VII. THE SACRAMENTS
IN BULTMANN'S THEOLOGY

By John L. McKenzie

The sacraments are not prominent in Bultmann's theology, and this itself may be important. He finds only two sacraments in the New Testament, baptism and the Lord's Supper, and his sacramental theology must be grasped from what he says of these. This will not be a vital point of difference although the septenary sacramental system is vital in Roman Catholic teaching. But the septenary system is the product of a vast and complex development of tradition and of ritual practice which has its beginnings in the New Testament and its progress in the post-apostolic Church. Standard theological arguments from New Testament texts which were intended to show that confirmation, penance, extreme unction, orders, and matrimony appear in the New Testament failed of their purpose for the simple reason that these sacraments do not appear in the New Testament with anything near the clarity in which baptism and the Eucharist appear. An effort to show that these five sacraments have equal standing with baptism and the Eucharist in the New Testament is doomed to failure before it is begun. If we do not meet Bultmann on this particular ground here, this implies no concession to his position; it implies only that his position on the number of the sacraments cannot be met from the New Testament alone.

Bultmann's treatment of baptism and the Eucharist in the New Testament is in many respects an excellent synthesis of New Testament teaching. He does not take the New Testament presentation of the sacraments as a static doctrine which reached fullness all at once, but as exhibiting development. Hardly any interpreter can disagree with the principle; but the question of the course which the development took cannot be traced so easily. Bultmann divides his treatment of the New Testament in *Theology of the New Testament* into the message of Jesus, the kerygma of the earliest Church, the kerygma of the Hellenistic Church apart from the Paul, the theology of Paul, the theology of the Johannine writings, and the development towards the ancient Church. The earliest Church was "an eschatological sect within Judaism."[1] Within this division the sacraments are not treated at all in the message of Jesus, and briefly in all other sections except the kerygma of the Hellenistic Church. Bultmann does not imply that there were no sacraments in the Churches represented by other New Testament writings, although it is clear that Bultmann does not think that they arise from Jesus himself precisely as sacraments. There are particular reasons why he places so much emphasis on the sacraments in the Hellenistic Church, and we shall have to question these reasons.

In the earliest Church Bultmann finds only one sacrament, baptism; the Eucharist had not yet become a cultic celebration, but was merely a common meal.[2] Baptism was at first a rite of initiation into the eschatological community, and its meaning did not differ greatly from the meaning of the baptism of John; it was a bath of purification in preparation for the coming reign. In both the Johannine baptism and Christian baptism purity from sin and not merely from ritual defilement was promised, and this distinguished both baptisms from Jewish rites of purification by water. Bultmann asserts that baptism was not

---

[1] *TNT*, I, p. 42.
[2] *Ibid.*, pp. 36–37, 57–58.

at first believed to establish a sacramental relation with Jesus as the Son of man; but it cannot be determined how early this conception arose. We shall meet this thesis again in the sacramental ideas of the Hellenistic Church.

How is it determined that this is the primitive idea of baptism? Bultmann's historical and critical arguments for the thesis are not impressive, and in fact are indirect rather than direct. He is convinced that other aspects of baptism are certainly original in the Hellenistic Church; therefore, they cannot be found in the earliest Church. The thesis does not rest even on critical arguments of the usual type. Yet, as we have noticed, the principle of development is legitimate. If baptism was a rite of initiation from the beginning, then it had a significance which is sacramental in the modern sense of the term. And since there is no evidence that John formed an eschatological community, Christian baptism had a significance which the baptism of John did not have. The developments which Bultmann attributes to the Hellenistic Church are legitimate expansions of the idea of purification from sin and initiation into the eschatological community. The denial that the Eucharist was more than a common meal is entirely without foundation. Had Bultmann been able to make use of the Qumran material, he would have seen that at Qumran the common meal was a messianic banquet; and this rite is not to be attributed to the influence of the mystery cults.[3] Reflections of the Eucharist as the messianic banquet can easily be traced in the New Testament, and these reflections can scarcely be anything but Palestinian in origin; they must therefore belong to Bultmann's "earliest Church." The messianic banquet is more than a common meal, and it has a sacramental character in at least a minimal sense. What this minimal sense may be we shall see when we discuss Bultmann's basic idea of the sacraments.

We have noticed that Bultmann places the development of the

[3] F. M. Cross, *The Ancient Library of Qumran* (Garden City, 1958), pp. 63–67, 177–179.

sacramental idea in the Hellenistic Church; and the thesis as such is antecedently probable. Bultmann's synthesis of the significance of the sacraments in the Hellenistic Church is excellent.[4] Baptism signifies purification from one's sins, the naming of the neophyte in the name of the Lord (the "sealing"), exorcism, the bestowal of the Spirit, and participation in the death and resurrection of Christ. This fourth element, Bultmann affirms, originated in the Hellenistic Church. In the earliest liturgy of the Eucharist Bultmann finds three motifs: the "really sacramental interpretation," which means the partaking in the flesh and blood of Jesus; the death of Jesus as the sacrifice of the new covenant; the death as the expiatory sacrifice. The original meaning of the act he finds to be sacramental communion with Christ, and this by participation in the glorified and risen body which was crucified.

To these elements of the Hellenistic Church Bultmann adds others which are peculiar to Paul.[5] For Paul baptism is primarily incorporation in Christ, the fourth element which we noticed above as a later addition. This formula in Paul is to be understood as an ecclesiological and eschatological formula; to acquire this new personal relation to Christ is to become a member of the Church, the eschatological congregation. A second new element in Paul is that baptism makes the salvation event present. The Eucharist in Paul is the sacrament of unity in the one body of Christ and of fellowship among Christians. The Eucharist is also a proclamation of the death of Christ; like baptism, it makes the salvation event present. In none of these features does the reader of Bultmann recognize anything exotic; they have been a part of sacramental theology and liturgy for many centuries.

But when the reader searches for some basic idea of a sacrament in Bultmann, he finds things less clear. One passage is so important as a key to Bultmann's thought that it should be quoted in full:

[4] *TNT*, I, pp. 136–137.
[5] *Ibid.*, pp. 311–314.

154

[A sacrament is] . . . an act which by natural means puts supranatural powers into effect, usually by the use of spoken words which accompany the act and release those powers by the mere utterance of their prescribed wording. Indeed, the sacramental act may confine itself completely to the speaking of a word or a formula. The concept "sacrament" rests upon the assumption that under certain conditions supranatural powers can be bound to natural objects of the world and to spoken words as their vehicles and mediators. If the conditions are fulfilled (if, for instance, the prescribed formula is correctly spoken and the material is thereby "consecrated"—i.e., laden with supranatural power), and if the act is consummated according to the prescribed rite, then the supranatural powers go into effect, and the act, which apart from these conditions would be only a purely worldly, natural one like a bath or a meal, is itself a supranatural ceremony which works a miracle. Though in the primitive stage of the history of religions sacramental action can hardly be distinguished from magic, still in the course of history the difference becomes even greater, depending upon what conditions must be fulfilled by those for whom the sacrament is to be effective and upon what supranatural powers are to be put into effect. The pre-supposed condition may be a specified state of the body, or it may be a state of spiritual preparedness. The powers may be such as only serve the enhancement of physical life, or such as promote the life of the spirit. In the latter case, it is true, the paradoxicality of the sacrament is increased. How can spiritual powers be bound to material elements as their vehicle? Finally, a sacrament can be etherealized into a symbol; then a psychological effect instead of a miraculous one.

It is clear that in earliest Christianity the sacrament was by no means a symbol, but a miracle-working rite . . .[6]

It would take some exercise in dialectics to reduce this paragraph to "an outward sign instituted by Jesus Christ productive of inward grace." Yet in the area of ritual and symbol exactness of definition may be deceptive; it may convey a clarity which the reality does not exhibit. In fact, neither the standard catechetical definition nor Bultmann's paragraph clearly says that the sacra-

[6] *Ibid.,* p. 135.

ment is a rite which effects that which it signifies. What is it that gives certain signs their sacramental power? This is the radical question of sacramental theology. Since the symbol is an arbitrary sign in any hypothesis, its effectiveness can only come from the deliberate attachment of symbol to effect, as in language. The sign is effective because someone has determined that it shall be effective. This as well as anything else distinguished the sacramental rite from the magical formula, and it is the most important of the "certain conditions" under which "supranatural powers can be bound to natural objects of the world and to spoken words as their vehicles and mediators." The sacrament is meaningful only in the context of Christian life and worship; traditional theology says that the sacrament is meaningful only as an act of the Church. But the Church has not herself attached effectiveness to the symbol, for she recognizes that she has not the power to create this attachment. The Church dispenses the sacraments; she does not institute them. She does not find them in nature, nor does she borrow them from other communities. The New Testament is quite clear that the disciples say that they baptize and celebrate the Lord's Supper in virtue of a commission given them by Jesus. That they said this is of vital importance for the Christian conception of the sacraments, and it does not make much difference for the conception of the sacraments whether the critic insists that this commission had no basis in historical reality. In the apostolic Church Jesus was recognized as the only medium by which "supranatural power" was released in the world; this view, and the conviction that they could deal with the sacramental release of supranatural power only within the terms of the commission of Jesus, is as primitive as anything in the New Testament. This is as far as the historical and literary critic can take it.

The commission of Jesus is the element which Bultmann omits when he attributes the development of the idea of sacramental efficacy to the Hellenistic Church under the influence of the mystery religions. To do Bultmann credit, he does more than induce artificial respiration into the corpse of the earlier theories about Christianity as a mystery religion. We noticed above that he treats the fourth element in the baptismal symbolism, participation in the death and resurrection of Christ, as added by the Hellenistic Church to the original symbolism. This is formed, he says, on the analogy of the initiation rites of the mystery cults in which the initiates shared in the death and resurrection of the cult deity.[7] He argues that the ritual bath is not "adapted to serve as a reproduction or dramatization of what had happened at Jesus' death and resurrection. Jesus did not die by drowning." Baptism came to be a participation in the death and resurrection because it was a Jewish initiation rite, and Hellenistic Christians knew no initiation rite other than the rites of the mysteries. But this is not a simple assimilation of baptism to the mysteries. "It cannot be denied that this whole interpretation brought along with it the danger that Christian existence might be built up entirely upon Hellenistic sacramental magic instead of being understood as eschatological existence. But, on the other side, the possibility seized by Paul was also given: to interpret it as an existence determined by Christ's death and resurrection and hence to understand the sacrament as an actualization, here and now, of the occurrence of salvation."[8] Similarly, Bultmann finds that the Lord's Supper is a sacrament in the sense of the mystery religions; it is communion with a once dead and risen deity, and it has the fate of the Kyrios as its founding cause—"the mode of thinking characteristic of the mystery religions."[9]

About this several remarks can be made. The first is that Bultmann's understanding of the mystery cults is in disagreement with much recent scholarship. Martin P. Nilsson, after a thorough study of the sources and of the modern literature on the mysteries, concludes that the differences between the mystery cults and Christianity are far more numerous and far more

[7] *Ibid.*, p. 140.
[8] *Ibid.*, p. 144.
[9] *Ibid.*, p. 148.

decisive than the resemblances.[10] In particular, he finds that just those elements on which Bultmann lays stress are not relevant. There is no real death and resurrection, and in the mysteries there is no god who really dies and rises. There is no sacred communion with the god in a ritual banquet. The initiation rite is not founded on the fate of the cult god. These are serious considerations, and they cast doubt on the statement that the Hellenistic Church developed its sacramental system under the influence of the mystery cult. They are of even more interest because Nilsson makes these points with no direct reference to Bultmann, whom he does not name. The resemblances between Christianity and the mystery cults are merely superficial; but there are resemblances, and they must be explained.

A second observation may help to explain these resemblances, which occur in terminology and in ritual actions. Both Christianity and the mystery cults developed in the world of the eastern Mediterranean. The region was not culturally homogeneous, but by the beginning of the Christian era the phenomenon called syncretism had become characteristic of the religions of the region. Syncretism means a tendency to assimilate various religions to each other in their conceptions of the divine and their cult. In any given culture certain symbols acquire a religious character, and the number of such symbols is limited. There are resemblances between different ritual systems not only because the number of possible symbolic expressions is limited, but also because the symbol which is not known as religious is meaningless to members of the cult group. Both the ritual bath and the ritual banquet were common religious symbols; no mystery cult is known in which these two symbols had the value and the meaning which they had in primitive Christianity.

The background of the cultic symbolism both of Christianity and of the mysteries is far more ancient and far more wide-

[10] M. Nilsson, *Geschichte der griechischen Religion* (Munich, 1950), II, pp. 651–672.

spread than Bultmann recognized. This background is found in the entire ancient Near East, which included Israel. In ancient Near Eastern religions—as far as a safe generalization is possible—the major cultic act was the ritual recital and reënactment of the saving event. The saving event could be mythological as in the Mesopotamian New Year festival, or it could be historical, as far as its cultic reënactment is concerned. In the recital the story of the event was formally proclaimed; to illustrate again, the story could be the creation myth of Mesopotamia or the story of the Exodus in Israel. Concerning the ritual reënactment we are much less well informed; we have no rubrics or book for the performance. But the reënactment was symbolic; and this does not mean that it was dramatic. In the developed ritual of the Passover the symbolic reënactment consisted in the Passover supper; and to this one might apply Bultmann's somewhat inept remark that the death of Jesus did not occur by drowning. Neither did the Exodus occur by eating; but we are dealing with symbolism, and symbolism is determined by choice. In baptism the saving event is symbolized and reënacted by symbolizing its effect on the individual person. In the Eucharist the saving event is symbolized and reënacted by symbolizing its effect on the community. Neither symbol is a complete portrayal or a dramatic representation; neither need be. But each is in its own way the ritual recital and reënactment of the saving event; and thus each falls into the common background of religious symbolism of the ancient Near East and the Hellenistic world. Within this background it was impossible that resemblance should not occur. Early Christian writers themselves were impressed by the resemblances, and devoted themselves to an apologetic which attributed the mysteries to a diabolical imitation of Christianity. Nilsson asks whether modern scholars have not continued this line of thought.[11]

It is within this background that the idea of sacramental efficacy in the New Testament must be sought; but before the

11 *Ibid.*, p. 657.

159

search can be undertaken it is necessary to notice Bultmann's interpretation of Paul. Bultmann does not classify Paul simply with the Hellenistic Church; and the differences which he finds in Paul's sacramental theology, if they are genuine differences, justify the separate classification. The dominant sacramental idea in Paul, according to Bultmann, is the incorporation of the Christian into Christ. "In Christ," he says, is not a mystical formula but an ecclesiological formula; and the Church is the eschatological congregation. Incorporation into Christ signifies the beginning of eschatological existence. Baptism and the Eucharist are participation in the salvation event, the death and resurrection of Christ. They make the salvation event present to the believer.[12] This seems to be a legitimate development of what Bultmann conceives to be the earliest form of the sacraments; but when he comes to the efficacy of the sacramental rites in Paul, he introduces another and a disturbing element.

Baptism, he says, is an objective event occurring to the baptized which certifies his participation in the death and resurrection. This appropriation of the event is the same as the appropriation which comes through the preached word. This efficacy is even more apparent, he says, in the Eucharist. The Eucharist does indeed in Paul have the specific effects of making the participants one body in Christ and of instituting fellowship among them. But the primary efficacy of the sacrament does not lie in the elements; it lies in the act as a proclamation of the death of Christ (1 Cor. 11:26), a proclamation which makes the death a present reality.[13] Thus the sacraments seem to be reduced to the proclamation, and the effect of the sacraments to faith. The sacraments will be in this hypothesis symbolic acts not of the sacramental type but of the type performed by Isaiah when he walked naked about the streets of Jerusalem (Is. 20:1-6), by Jeremiah when he broke the wine flask (Jer. 19:1-15), and by Ezekiel when he mimicked the siege of Jerusalem and the flight of its inhabitants (Ezek. 4-5). These

[12] *TNT*, I, pp. 311-314.
[13] *Ibid.*, pp. 313-314.

160

acts have the efficacy of the prophetic word, and this efficacy has in the Old Testament a quality which can loosely be called sacramental.[14] But they have not that efficacy which comes from the reënactment of the saving event; and perhaps no other distinction between the two can be made. In Bultmann's hypothesis there is only one real sacrament, the proclaimed word, and only one real sacramental effect, faith. In this interpretation, I believe, Bultmann has restated in a more modern form the classical view of Lutheran theology.

But this classical view, and Bultmann's restatement, are not to be dismissed as sheer distortions of New Testament belief. Certainly, the sacraments in any hypothesis presuppose the proclaimed Word and the Church which is formed by the proclamation. The proclamation does indeed have a unique efficacy, and it does make the saving event and Christ himself present to the hearer. A study of our own ritual of baptism will show that the sacrament is by no means divorced from the proclamation. The entire ritual is clearly an admission to the Church, physically symbolized by the passage from the vestibule to the baptistery. The Word is proclaimed in the recital of the Creed, to which the candidate responds by a profession of faith; for faith is what he asks of the Church of God at the beginning of the ritual. The last questions asked of the candidate are whether he believes and wishes to be baptized. The practice of infant baptism should not be taken as rendering these elements meaningless. The Church wishes that someone who is a responsible adult shall answer on behalf of the candidate. Perhaps in modern practice we have concentrated too heavily on what has been determined—by what reasoning it is difficult to say—as the essential sacramental rite, and paid less than due attention to the ritual of proclamation and profession of faith, treating them as mere "ceremonies" which can be supplied if they have been omitted in an emergency. The ritual of baptism does not

---

[14] John L. McKenzie, S.J., *Myths and Realities* (Milwaukee, 1963), pp. 44–53.

suppose a purely passive recipient; he responds, either for himself or through another.

It is not irrelevant to notice that in the ritual of the Eucharist the homily has recently been restored to its place of honor; this sacrament too should contain the element of proclamation. But even without the homily the ritual includes readings from the Scripture, which supply the element of proclamation. The profession of faith is found in the ritual here also—explicitly when the recitation of the Creed is a part of the ceremonies, and one wonders why the Creed is not found in every celebration of the Eucharist. But even without the Creed the profession is made in the responses of the congregation, and in the somewhat recent ritual of the elevation of the species for public view. Bultmann may have understated the sacraments, but he has not overstated the importance of the proclamation. Without the proclamation and the response of faith, the sacraments can easily be degraded in the popular mind into a type of spiritual supermagic.

The ritual recital is the element of proclamation in the sacramental rite. Unless the rite is interpreted and given meaning by the recital, the action, which is a reënactment, has no sacramental significance. The significance of the action must be grasped, personally or vicariously, by the person who receives the sacrament as well as by the Church which administers it. The hearing of the recital generates the communion of faith by which the candidate becomes a member of the Church; and membership means not merely that one is enumerated among the members, but that one shares in the life of the Church. This life is rooted in faith in the proclamation. Surely in any genuine liturgical renewal the ritual recital will be more emphatic than it has been in prevailing practice for quite a long time.

We are still searching for the idea of sacramental efficacy, but we may have come closer to finding the inadequacy in Bultmann's interpretation. The identification of sacrament and proclamation which he finds in Paul seems to have become his own dominant thought. That the cross (or the cross and the resurrection) becomes a present reality is stated by Bultmann in at least two other passages in his writings.[15] What is missing here is the reality which illuminates the entire New Testament, but which strangely does not illuminate the theology of Bultmann. This reality is the person of Jesus Christ. Bultmann always speaks of the saving event or the proclamation, but not of him who is the actor in the saving event or who is most frequently the object of the proclamation and faith in the New Testament. I suggest that this may be traced ultimately to his skepticism about the historical Jesus; and I ask further whether skepticism about the historical Jesus does not by some occult law of thought lead to a lack of perception of the Christ of faith. Bultmann has written: "For them [the first preachers of the Gospel] the cross was the cross of him with whom they had lived in personal intercourse. The cross was an experience of their own lives. It presented them with a question and disclosed to them its meaning. But for us this personal connection cannot be reproduced. For us the cross cannot disclose its own meaning; it is an event of the past. We can never recover it as an event in our own lives. All we know of it is derived from historical report. But the New Testament does not proclaim Jesus Christ in this way. The meaning of the cross is not disclosed from the life of Jesus as a figure of past history, a life which needs to be reproduced by historical research. On the contrary, Jesus is not proclaimed merely as the crucified; he is also risen from the dead. The cross and the resurrection form an inseparable unity."[16] Substitute "Jesus Christ" for "cross" in the first seven sentences of this quotation, and I think we have a legitimate extension of Bultmann's thought.

As he says, the New Testament does not proclaim Jesus in this way; and demythologizing was intended to issue in another form of proclamation. But whether it can succeed here is per-

[15] *NTM*, pp. 34–38; *GV*, I, pp. 288–289.
[16] *NTM*, p. 38.

haps the heart of the question. In the New Testament it was not merely the saving event but the person of Jesus Christ which was rendered present by the proclamation. The apostles and evangelists seemed to think that no different faith was demanded by those who heard the proclamation than was demanded from themselves. Those who heard the Gospel had no less a personal encounter with Jesus than the apostles had had. This is the mysterious power of the word of the Gospel, that the person of Jesus Christ is present in it. Had the apostles thought otherwise, it is difficult to see how the New Testament could use Jesus Christ and the Gospel interchangeably to designate the objects of the proclamation and of faith. To believe in the Gospel is to believe in Jesus. And so for them the Gospel could make the cross and Jesus himself an experience of the lives of the hearers; it was an event of their lives; it could present a question and disclose its meaning.

The same principle is true of the sacraments. They are encounters with the person of Christ and not merely the presentation of the saving event; although they are that too. And this conception of the sacraments does not imply pseudo-mysticism. For Paul, one encountered Christ in the Church which is his body; and the Church is a living and perceptible reality. The divine life of Christ flows to the members only through the whole body into which they are incorporated. Each sacrament attaches the believer to the Church more closely in its own proper way; there is a multiple sacramental system and a multiple symbolism because attachment to the Church is too meaningful to be expressed in a single symbol. In a sense which is not theologically inexact the radical sacrament is the Incarnate Word, the original reality in which the presence and activity of the divine becomes present in the world. The efficacy of the sacraments comes from the fact that they make Jesus Christ present; he becomes an event in the life of the believer—to adhere to Bultmann's terms. Bultmann, indeed, is not unaware of this feature in the New Testament; but he regards the Johannine conception of the Eucharist as sacramental union with the person of Jesus as a secondary expansion.[17] For Bult-mann this means that it is not a part of the original kerygma and therefore a deterioration. There is no doubt that the encounter with Christ can be misconceived as a type of pseudo-mysticism or as the encounter of two isolated and solitary realities; but when it is so conceived, it is not conceived in New Testament terms. The believer encounters Christ in and with the Church.

I said above that Bultmann seems to have made the Pauline position—as he conceives it—his own; and in the hypothesis that the Church must have sacraments, the statement will stand. I wonder, however, whether Bultmann's own position, if fol-lowed to its conclusions, would not lead him to the Johannine position—again as he conceives it.[18] Bultmann, by the judicious use of criticism, finds that the sacraments have a very small place in John. He suggests that the author "compromises with the ecclesiastical use of baptism and the Lord's Supper, but that these remain objectionable to him because of abuses, and that he therefore remains silent about them. In reality the sacraments are superfluous for him." This strikes one as a curious para-phrase of Bultmann's own position; and it is entirely in harmony with the movement of his thought towards proclaiming the Gospel in philosophical terms and of the existentialist *kerygma* as the only effective force. It is the proclamation, as we saw above, that is for him the only real sacrament.

Some have not altogether accurately pointed to traces of gnosticism in Bultmann's thought. This is inaccurate because Bultmann is extremely hard to type in any classification. But he has produced an intellectual *kerygma* addressed to the mind; and he has not met his own demand of explaining the meaning of *human* existence. The Gospel of salvation is addressed to men, not to minds; and the purpose of the Gospel is not to make life intelligible but to make it livable. Man is hopelessly a material reality, and it is as such that he expects redemption. It is also as such that he is incorporated into the body of Christ,

[17] *J,* pp. 174–177.
[18] *Ibid.,* p. 360.

the eschatological community. He is not asked for a merely intellectual acceptance of Christ; he is asked to identify himself with the visible and tangible reality of the Church. In human existence no such association is possible without the effective symbols which are as perceptible as the community with which one is identified. The heresy of the purely spiritual Church is never very far from our doors. The sacraments are a unique set of symbols not because they are symbols, but because of the encounter with Jesus Christ which they effectively signify. As such they respond to a genuine human need.

In summary, one may say that Bultmann's sacramental theology is consistent with his general theology. He has, with his characteristic genius, asked many of the right questions about the sacraments. The Church never understands her sacramental ministry as well as she might; and the danger of magic is real. Bultmann has turned our attention to the proclamation in the Church; he has at the same time turned our attention to the sacraments. We are, it seems, only at the threshold of a renewal of sacramental theology. It is somewhat overdue.

VIII. BULTMANN ON KERYGMA AND HISTORY

By Claude Geffré

For Bultmann the kerygma as a free gift of God enables the events of salvation history to become "salvific events." Precisely as salvific these events are fully accessible to faith alone and do not fall under the domain of historical research. Much has been written about the "unbridgeable" gulf thus established between the Jesus of history and the Christ of faith, but Bultmann's concept of history, which underlies this entire problematic, has not always been made clear. The following study is a reflection on the import of his distinction between *Geschichte* (existential history) and *Historie* (the empirical study of historical facts) in Bultmann's theology.[1]

Although Bultmann does not engage in lengthy reflection on this distinction (we find little more in his writings than the opposition between the two adjectives *historisch* and *geschichtlich*), it is essential for an understanding of his theology, and is closely linked to his conception of theology as a theology of existence rather than a theology of objects. The latter reflects

---

[1] *Historie* means the science of history, the empirically determinable brute facts; *Geschichte* means history, certain events, which not only happen but existentially touch others, the event together with its import for others. There are no two English words which can make this difference clear; certain circumstances and the context should make it evident which kind of history is meant. (Editors' note.)

in an objective manner on the "what," the conceptual content of saving events. It is related to Bultmann's idea of myth, to the incompatibility which he sees between God and the world. Bultmann's idea of revelation is the Word of God addressing, challenging man, a pure "that," an event which occurs in the world but which is not an event of the world. Later we shall see that the manner in which Bultmann opposes miracle (*Mirakel*) and wonder (*Wunder*) is an excellent illustration of the distinction between scientifically determined past history and existential history. All of this controls his view of faith as an absolute paradox which does not rely on historical signs.

As a study in theological dialogue the following essay will ask whether Bultmann's problematic does not invite all Christians to reflect on the originality of salvation-history in relation to the empirical world history of past events. It seems that Bultmann understands better than Oscar Cullmann that saving events cannot be reduced to any other historical event. Bultmann must be given credit for having stressed so forcefully the permanent actuality of the salvific event realized in Jesus Christ and the consequent radical newness of the time inaugurated by the coming of Christ.

We must, however, mark out the limits of our agreement with Bultmann. The distinction between two meanings of history is fruitful for highlighting the originality of salvation history. But in Bultmann's thought this distinction is tied to a philosophical conception of time which is debatable; it is also too closely linked to the radical opposition which he sees between God and the world, between the eternal and the historical. This is so true that we have the right to ask whether Bultmann does not compromise the Judeo-Christian revelation in its most decisive mystery, namely, the presence of the eternal in time, the epiphany of the invisible God under historical signs, in other words, the very mystery of the Incarnation. The inevitable question is this: can we forego speaking of the Judeo-Christian God in mythological fashion, if we understand "mythological" as Bultmann does? Or, again, where does the paradox of the

Christian faith lie? Does the Christian faith explain the mystery of a "temporalization" of God? Or is it rather that the believer adheres to the event of the Word of God without the support of any visible sign of this Word?

In the first part of this study we shall try to clarify the theological import of the distinction between historical science (*Historie*) and existential history (*Geschichte*). In the second section we will emphasize Bultmann's positive contribution to our understanding of salvation history and try to clarify the uneasiness we feel at this chasm he draws between the empirical dimension and the divine dimension of a salvific event.[2]

THE EXISTENTIAL INTERPRETATION OF HISTORY

According to Bultmann, the living God of the Bible can be encountered only in the real experience of our existence. The only thing we can say about God is what he does for us. The object of my faith is not God in himself, but the reality which determines my existence. In saying this, Bultmann wishes to

[2] The following are the principal works used: *JW, HE;* "The Problem of Hermeneutics," *EPT*, pp. 234–261; "Die Geschichtlichkeit des Daseins und der Glaube," *ZThK*, 27 (1930), pp. 329–364; Bultmann's review of O. Cullmann's *Christ and Time* (Philadelphia, 1959), "Heilsgeschichte und Geschichte," *Theologische Literaturzeitung*, 73 (1948), pp. 659–666. Studies on Bultmann's thought in this area: L. Malevez, *Le Message chrétien et le Mythe* (Paris, 1954); R. Marlé, *Bultmann et l'interprétation du Nouveau Testament* (Paris, 1956); H. Ott, *Geschichte und Heilsgeschichte in der Theologie Rudolf Bultmanns* (Tübingen, 1955). The validity of Ott's criticism has been questioned from the Protestant and Catholic viewpoints: P. Lengsfeld, *Tradition et Eglise* (Paris, 1964), pp. 245–248; A. Malet, *Mythos et Logos: La Pensée de R. Bultmann* (Geneva, 1962); G. Greshake, *Historie wird Geschichte* (Essen, 1963); G. Hasenhüttl, *Der Glaubensvollzug* (Essen, 1963), pp. 62–83; J. M. Robinson, *A New Quest of the Historical Jesus* (Naperville, 1959); O. Laffoucrière, "Bultmann et l'histoire," *Revue d'histoire et de philosophie religieuse*, 38 (1959), pp. 219–231; R. Marlé, "Histoire et historicité chez quelques theologiens protestants," *Recherches et Débats*, 1, (1956), pp. 89–102.

169

remain faithful to the Lutheran intuition of the *theologia crucis* as opposed to the *theologia gloriae* or theology of a sapiential type. Yet he puts at the service of this intuition the existential analytic of Heidegger for whom every affirmation about any reality whatsoever is always an existential affirmation about man. For Bultmann, then, every affirmation about God will of necessity be an affirmation about man.[3] He does not, however, deserve the reproach so often made against him, namely, of reducing theology to anthropology. He only wants to draw the consequences for theology of the epistemological *a priori* of the phenomenological method, that is, that every act whereby being (and therefore God) is known can be understood only through the elucidation of that being which itself raises the question of being, man. Some may be surprised at this meeting of Lutheran theology and a philosophy which maintains that it is a theology of finitude (the transcendence of *Dasein* in Heidegger is a transcendence from radical finitude).[4] But Bultmann replies that Heidegger's existential ontology is a philosophy which remains neutral. It makes no judgment as to the character of real existence of realities but studies only the conditions of possibility of real objects. "It would be an illusory maneuver if theology, in order to analyze the fundamental structures which always determine *Dasein,* were to refuse, as regards this point, to listen to philosophy which expresses, as adequately and in as 'neutral' a way as possible, the being of *Dasein*."[5] Bultmann thus incorporates without any hesitation into his theological project the Heideggerian concept of "ec-sistence" to express the historicity of *Dasein*. The "transcendence" of human existence in its openness on nothingness becomes for him at the existential level of faith openness on God.

[3] *GV,* I, pp. 26–27.

[4] On *Dasein's* transcendence as an ontological transcendence of radical finitude, see A. Chapelle, *L'ontologie phénoménologique de Heidegger* (Paris, 1962), pp. 160 ff.

[5] R. Bultmann, "Die Geschichtlichkeit des Daseins und der Glaube," *loc. cit.,* 331.

To speak of man as existence is to speak of him as an historical being.[6] Following Heidegger, Bultmann interprets temporality starting from human reality and not from the reality of the things of the cosmos, as did ancient philosophy. "Analysis of the historicity of *Dasein* tries to show that this entity is not 'temporal' because it 'stands in history,' but that, on the contrary, if it exists and can only exist historically, it is because it is temporal in the very basis of its being."[7] *Existence* signifies a potentiality-for-being, open on the future, a future as yet not realized but which is a structural element of *Dasein*. The future indeed plays a privileged part in constituting existential temporality: "authentic temporality temporalizes itself in terms of the authentic future."[8] Thus the temporality of man designates his possibility of attaining to the full authenticity of his being or of missing it, if he remains tied to past. Temporality is an ontological affirmation and designates a structure of being: it does not designate the real cycle of past-present-future.[9] The ontic realization of temporality as existentialistic will be history (*Geschichte*). Being in history as a characteristic element of the existence of man signifies that in each "now" of a decision man is responsible for the past and the future. Because man is within history, because he is essentially a potentiality-for-being, he can live in a way that is either authentic or inauthentic. As we are speaking about the ontic level of decision, that is, the concrete determination of existence (and not about the ontological level, or the general possibilities of a being which is not yet realized), man's historicity participates in the ambivalence of

[6] On man as historicity, see *ibid;* Malet, *op. cit.*, pp. 8 ff.; Greshake, *op. cit.*, pp. 19 f.

[7] *BT*, p. 428.

[8] See *ibid.*, p. 378.

[9] The three dimensions of the moment: coming-towards, present, future, are, for Heidegger, "extases"; they designate the phenomena of a coming-towards-one, a back-to-oneself, and the letting-oneself-be-encountered. See *BT*, pp. 328–329.

171

the ontic level: it can designate an existence which may be either authentic or inauthentic. At any rate, to speak of man as in history is to speak of him as free: that is, only the history of liberties deserves the name of history as *Geschichte*.

What about the existential interpretation of history as science? History raises the question of the conditions of understanding historical reality and takes into account this fundamental presupposition: its object is historical only if it has reality as some phenomenon of human existence.

Historical knowledge as existential knowledge in contrast to the objective knowledge proper to the natural sciences, always reveals to me, as I read the past, new possibilities of existence. I do not reflect about a past event to gain objective knowledge of it, as I would with a museum piece. If this event is an historic (in terms of existential history) event, that is, a possibility of human existence, it concerns me not as a what but as a that. In other words, it is a challenge. It calls me to decision so that in and through this act of historical knowledge I actualize my potentiality in a new way. "Thus it is that the historical restitution is born which makes 'the past come to us' as a witness and as a medium of the possibilities of existence eternally offered by being to man."[10] "For Bultmann, as for Heidegger, every reading of history takes its place in the universal and perpetual human quest for possibilities of existence."[11] In his little book *Jesus and the Word,* Bultmann gives perfect expression to the originality of this relation of man to history: "Our relationship to history is wholly different from our relationship to nature. Man, if he rightly understands himself, differentiates himself from nature. When he observes nature, he perceives there something objective which is not himself. When he turns his attention to history, however, he must admit himself to be a part of history; he is considering a living complex of events in which he is essentially

[10] P. Barthel, *Interprétation du langage mythique et théologie biblique* (Leiden, 1963), p. 79.
[11] *Ibid.,* p. 78.

involved. . . . In every word which he says about history, he is saying at the same time something about himself."[12]

Unless we have grasped the originality of this historical knowledge as an original mode of realizing a possibility of one's own *Dasein*, we shall totally misunderstand Bultmann's hermeneutical principle. To measure the import of this understanding, we must recall what Heidegger means by understanding.[13] "Understanding" existentially does not aim at knowledge but designates a "power-of-being," a "having-to-be." "What is existentially included in understanding, is the kind of being of *Dasein*, as potentiality-for-being."[14] Thus every existential understanding of an event, of a text, a document, is based on an existential self-understanding, an understanding of my existence which projects itself towards its authentic being. This understanding of my own projection of existence implies an understanding of being, for there can be no grasp of self towards a potentiality-for-being without an understanding of being. For Heidegger there will be no understanding of history without a new self-understanding and without a pre-understanding, that is, an openness to being which gives the historian an affinity for all the existential possibilities of a past event or of a text. To cite Gadamer: "We can talk of history only insofar as we are ourselves in history."[15] Bultmann calls this the existential encounter with history[16] in opposition to the objective knowledge of the exact sciences or of metaphysical thought which moves according to the scheme of subject and object.

On the theological level, pre-understanding becomes the

[12] *JW*, p. 3.
[13] See *BT*, pp. 182–195.
[14] *BT*, p. 182.
[15] H. G. Gadamer, *Le problème de la conscience historique* (Louvain, 1963), p. 44: "For Heidegger . . . , the fact that whenever we speak of history, we can speak only as historical beings ourselves, means that it is the historicity of the human 'being there' in its unceasing movement of waitings and forgettings, which is the very condition of being able to bring the past back to life."
[16] *HE*, p. 117.

question of man questioning himself about God, and self-understanding is given by faith which discovers in the witness of Scripture the most authentic possibility of human existence. To know how to read Scripture is to discover beyond myth the new understanding of myself offered me by God, which alone will permit me to reach the full stature of my authentic existence. To have faith is to decide to choose unceasingly my own authentic being.

Historie and Geschichte

Whereas English has only one word, "history," German has two words which are often used interchangeably in common parlance: *Historie* which comes from the Greek ἱστορειν (to seek, the desire to know); *Geschichte* which comes from Old High German *giskiht* (a chance event).[17]

In Bultmann's perspective, *Geschichte* has the meaning of the event itself, the *Geschehen,* while *Historie* designates the science of the object of events, of history.[18]

[17] " '*Historie*,' derived from the Greek ἱστορειν (to examine, become acquainted with, acquire knowledge of), has in Western linguistic tradition the primary meaning of knowledge or a science of the object of history. '*Geschichte*,' on the other hand, derived from Old High German *giskiht* (contingent events, thing), has above all the meaning of the happening itself." G. Greshake, *op. cit.,* p. 37. On the distinction between *Historie* and *Geschichte* in Heidegger, see *BT*, pp. 424–434.

[18] "Where the two concepts are contrasted one with the other or distinguished from one another, *Historie* means the science of the objective factual event, and as such something other than *Geschichte*." G. Greshake, *op. cit.,* pp. 37–38. It would be interesting to compare Bultmann's distinction between *Historie* and *Geschichte* with the distinction made in a Kantian perspective by Loisy, between "historical phenomena" and "the heart of things" or an inaccessible noumenon. Blondel, in opposition to historicism, distinguishes between *l'histoire-science* and *l'histoire-réalité,* but this is no longer the opposition between phenomena and an inaccessible noumenon. It is the opposition between the "reality which has been experienced" and the scientific representation of the real, the opposition between the concrete and the abstract. On this point see H. Gouhier, "Tradition et développement à l'époque moderniste," *Ermeneutica e Tradizione* (Rome, 1963), pp. 79–92.

To understand the import of the distinction between *Historie* and *Geschichte,* we must recall all that separates the naturalist conception of history, which was that of the Greeks and (in modern times) of authors such as Vico and Spengler, from the existentialistic conception of history in authors such as Dilthey, Croce, Jaspers, Heidegger, and Collingwood.[19]

Gadamer in his book on the historical consciousness has shown how illusory was the ideal, so dear to the nineteenth century, of historical science as an exact science. Dilthey's whole endeavor was precisely to provide the basis for the difference between the natural sciences and the humanities, namely, that historical knowledge is a mode of self-knowledge. After Dilthey, it is Heidegger who has most effectively underlined the originality of historical facts as compared to facts of nature. The objective restitution of facts from the past is an illusion of nineteenth-century historicism. The historian can understand the facts of the past only by reliving them himself. "What formerly appeared as prejudicial to the concept of science and method, as only a 'subjective' way of approaching historical knowledge, is in our day in the forefront of a fundamental inquiry."[20] In other words, there is no reading of the history of the past which does not involve a hermeneutic.[21] The historian, insofar as his existence (*Dasein*) is projected towards his future possibilities, must ask new questions of the past. That is why history always has to be rewritten. The facts of the past are past and gone inasmuch as they were localized in time and space, but their meaning is not exhausted: the past is a present, or better still a future which continually summons me.[22] For

[19] See *HE,* chapters 6, 7, 8, 9; A. Malet, *op. cit.,* pp. 65–75.

[20] H. G. Gadamer, *op. cit.,* pp. 44–45.

[21] On the hermeneutical problem in philosophy as well as in theology, see *Ermeneutica e Tradizione, ed. cit.,* also the thought-provoking remarks of P. Ricoeur on the double tradition at the origin of our modern concept of hermeneutics in his recent book, *De l'interprétation: Essai sur Freud* (Paris, 1965), pp. 29 ff.

[22] R. Bultmann, "Die Geschichtlichkeit . . . ," *art. cit.,* pp. 335 ff. "Facts of the past only become historical phenomena by having a meaning for a

175

Bultmann, this existential conception of history is of biblical origin. In the history of Israel, each event can find its meaning only in function of the end of history. The past as past holds no interest for the Old Testament writers. The fact "Abraham" is less important than its significance as related to its fulfillment. "The meaning in history lies in the divine education or in the direction to the goal. If there is an interest in knowledge, it is self-knowledge, and the historian calls his people to self-knowledge in reminding them of the deeds of God in the past, and of the conduct of the people."[23]

Even if Bultmann does not reflect explicitly on the difference between the concepts of *Historie* and *Geschichte,* he makes a clear distinction between two types of historical knowledge: improper and proper. Improper historical knowledge has as its object objective, historical facts, facts which are impersonal, not existential facts, or "the becoming of nature or of man as a being which is determined biologically, psychologically, sociologically."[24] Proper historical knowledge has as its object that which is an "event." Ultimately, this is the history of liberty and only this type of knowledge deserves the name of history in the sense of *Geschichte*. These two types of knowledge are opposed to each other as the knowledge of what something is, and that it is.

Historical knowledge ceases to be authentic, or in other words true, when it objectifies, "disposes" of something which as event is not capable of being objectified. This is exactly what

---

subject who is himself located in, and participating in, history; they have no meaning except when they say something to a subject who understands them. Not indeed that the latter assigns them a meaning according to his own personal whimsy, but because they take on a meaning for someone who is linked to them in a historical life. In a certain sense, *every historical phenomenon has its own future, for it is there first of all that it really shows what it is.*"

[23] R. Bultmann, *HE,* p. 18. This conception of biblical history may be likened to that of G. von Rad, *Old Testament Theology* (New York, 1962). (See particularly his concept of actualization [*Actualisierung*]: the fact of repeating without saying again.)

[24] See Malet, *op. cit.,* p. 7.

mythical thought does along with any theology which speaks of God or salvific events as if it could examine them. The process of objectifying thought in history does not lead simply to subjectivism. On the contrary, it is at the service of the true objectivity of the historical fact as a manifestation of human existence. The historical fact as an interrogation of my existence is not itself until it touches me. It is when I treat the fact as if it were a dead document that I betray the truth of the historical phenomenon. For Bultmann, the most subjective interpretation of history is at the same time the most objective.[25]

The only authentic knowledge which corresponds to the "that" of the events of salvation history is faith as decision. Here Bultmann is faithful to the intuition of Kierkegaard, for whom faith is not of the order of knowledge but of existence.

If *Historie* and *Geschichte* are opposed to each other as two modes of historical knowledge, for Bultmann they are two dialectical moments bearing on the same reality. There is only one human history.[26] The existential interpretation of history will involve as an essential, integrating part an objective consideration of the past. I can understand the same fact as objective fact located by historical science, and as existential if I

[25] *HE*, p. 122. Bultmann says that the most "subjective" interpretation is here the most "objective," in other words that only one who is moved by the question of his own existence can understand the demands made by the text. This notion of "existential objectivity," which is absolutely essential to an understanding of Bultmann's theological program, has been emphasized by A. Malet. It is interesting to note the relationship on this point between Kierkegaard and Bultmann (see R. Refoulé, O.P., "La vague bultmannienne," in *Revue des sciences théologiques et philosophiques,* 48 [1964], pp. 253 ff.).

[26] See G. Greshake, *op. cit.,* p. 39: "The opposition between *Historie* and *Geschichte* is thus a dialectical absolute only in the plenitude of existence (precisely like the antithesis between authenticity and unauthenticity). It is concerned with one and the same history to which, nevertheless, man is always differently related: viewing it objectively or understanding it existentially." This existential dialectic of *Historie* and *Geschichte* concerned with the same real history was not clearly understood by H. Ott, who tends to make two levels of being correspond to these two levels of history. On this subject, see the remarks of Lengsfeld, *op. cit.,* pp. 247–248, and Greshake, *op. cit.,* pp. 38–39.

receive through it a new understanding of myself (the event of the cross, for instance). There is only one history, but to the extent to which a believer passes from an inauthentic to an authentic existence, historical phenomena of the past become "saving events."[27]

In this respect, it is interesting to compare the distinction between *Historie* and *Geschichte* with the distinction which Bultmann makes between miracle as *Mirakel* and as *Wunder*. The *Mirakel* is the brute fact, historical, objective, which can be registered and which, as such, lacks interest for existence: it can be the object of a neutral, uncommitted knowledge. The *Wunder* is the historical fact as God's action for me; it is a call to a new realization of myself, which is accessible only to faith as an existential knowledge.[28]

It must be granted that Bultmann did not hypostatize existential history and scientific history as two domains of being; he recognizes that there is only one history when one is concerned with historical, human events. It seems clear, however, that his whole problem about this double concept of history is linked to an irreducible opposition between two forms of time: impersonal time, the chronological time in which the phenomena of nature and the facts of history occur, and real (existential) time, the qualitative temporal moment of human existence which is a point and purely qualitative.

We have good reason, then, to ask if Bultmann does not make too radical a cleavage between existential time and ordinary human time. We shall take up this problem later. The benefit resulting from Bultmann's reflection on history—and in this he is indebted to Heidegger—is in helping us to understand that there is no absolute beginning (nor, therefore, a beginning of human history) in the strict sense except at the level of liberty. Nature is transformed, is subject to becoming, but it has no history. Man is "in history." Because of his liberty, it can

27 See Bultmann, *KM*, I, p. 37.
28 On the distinction between *Mirakel* and *Wunder*, see Malet, *op. cit.*, ch. 7; Greshake, *op. cit.*, p. 41.

never be said that his future is contained in germ in his present, and his present in his past. Man is always openness, projection. Human time as existential must not be disjoined from human time as duration measuring the natural becoming of man. Otherwise, history would be dissolved.

Kerygma as Actualization of the Historic Salvation Event

Let us see now how Bultmann applies his distinction between histories to biblical revelation. In order to do that we must say a word about his concept of revelation.[29] Revelation is not the communication of intellectual truths; it is the salvific event of God summoning man to an authentic decision. Revelation is a "that" and not a "what." Revelation as salvation history, as an eschatological event which addresses my faith is summed up in the Christ-event. Considered as a salvific event evoking my existential commitment in faith, Christ is not historical, yet nevertheless he is related to the historical fact of Jesus of Nazareth.

Revelation is the *eschatological* event realized in Jesus Christ. It is clear that this event is not accessible to historical science. But on the other hand, revelation is linked to a historical fact which can become the object of historical investigation. The question then is to know how faith as an existential eschatological act can be dependent on an objective, historical fact. How can an historical event in the past become present in the existential sense? In a word, how does *Historie* become *Geschichte*?

According to Bultmann, it is the kerygma which effects the passage from one to the other, forging the link between the Jesus

[29] We shall quote this characteristic text from Bultmann: "*Gottes Offenbarung ist primär ein Geschehen, nicht eine Wissensvermittlung. Aber sie begründet ein Wissen und eine Lehre, sofern sie ein Sich-verstehen ermöglicht.*" "God's revelation is first and foremost an event, not a transmission of knowledge. But it is the foundation of knowledge and of a teaching in as much as it makes a new self-understanding possible." *GV,* I, p. 178.

of history and the Christ of faith. Kerygma is the present act which makes the historical person of Jesus and the historical events of his life present. It does not make them present as historical events (as such, they are not salvific events). Kerygma makes them present as an interrogation addressed to my existence.[30]

It is kerygma which unveils the historical and eschatological meaning of an objective, past fact. In the act of the Word of God, Christ is present. But I cannot know him fully with an objective knowledge. I can only encounter him in an existential knowledge, in the act of faith by which I pass from an unauthentic existence to an authentic one.

In other words, thanks to kerygma as a free gift of God, the events of the history of salvation become salvific events, or more precisely still, eschatological events. That is why, according to Bultmann, Jesus Christ as the eschatological event is not (as for Cullmann) the center of history: he is the end of history. There is nothing more to be awaited; inasmuch as Christ is the end of history already accomplished, every event takes on a new dimension. Faith, as man's response, is itself an eschatological event outside of time. The believer participates in the historicity proper to the divine event of salvation: he touches the last realities. He has already passed from death to life. But faith as the new creation is not a phenomenon which can be located, an event of empirical history, any more than it is the salvific event itself. Bultmann goes so far as to show an extreme reserve in regard to the term "salvation history," and he reproaches Cullmann with understanding the expression as meaning history in the vulgar, empirical sense.[31] "He is much more

[30] See Greshake, op. cit., p. 63: "Each salvific event present in the kerygma is thus nothing other than the envisaging of the historic person of Jesus in the historical happenings of our redemption, which, however, precisely as historic are not existentially present and thereby are also not salvific happenings, unless they become present to my existence as a summons mediated by the proclamation of the kerygma."

[31] "The problem begins when it is asked what is the meaning of the concept 'history' in the compound 'salvation history'—whether one is

concerned about finding a concept of history which would be a full concept, that of a history in the dynamic reality of which man can understand himself as interrogated by a past which concerns him and in the perspectives of his future (in opposition to the abstract viewpoint of the historian)."[32]

The Resurrection as Preaching of the Cross

The way to understand how the historical events of Jesus' life through the kerygma become eschatological events is to see the link established by preaching between the cross and the Resurrection.

Bultmann realizes that the cross is an event with a date in universal history. This event like other facts can be known by objective, historical research. But it is the kerygma which will bring to the fore the existential meaning of the cross as the eschatological event bringing salvation to us in a definitive way. Now the profound meaning of the cross as a saving event is the Resurrection: "Faith in the Resurrection is really the same thing as faith in the saving efficacy of the cross. The saving efficacy of the cross is not derived from the fact that it is the cross of Christ: it is the cross of Christ because it has this saving efficacy. Without that efficacy it is the tragic end of a great man."[33]

The fact of the cross like any other historical fact has no interest in itself. What matters is its existential reality, its bearing for me. The cross as Word of God as "that" is: "If I die believing with Christ, then I live with him" (see Rom. 6:4). It is in the event of preaching that the historical event of the cross becomes the eschatological event of God's action, inseparable from the Resurrection which expresses its meaning and significance. The Resurrection unlike the cross is *not* an event which

---

asking from the viewpoint of modern historical science or that of faith."
Bultmann, "Heilsgeschichte und Geschichte," *art. cit.,* p. 663.
[32] Lengsfeld, *Tradition, Ecriture et Eglise, ed. cit.,* p. 248.
[33] *KM,* I, p. 41.

can be historically verified;[34] it is accessible to faith alone. But in faith it constitutes an indissoluble unity with the historical event of the cross which becomes by that very fact the eschatological event of the salvific action of God which is irreducible to the empirical phenomena registered by historical science.

The primitive community objectified the Resurrection as an eschatological event into an historical event, into a miracle of the return to life of a dead man. The community wished to make out of a divine, unobjectifiable act, an object of faith, an object which could be verified, an event of the world. That is precisely the essence of myth. Bultmann believes that the accounts of the appearances and of the empty tomb are of late formation. They are the fall-out of the early paschal faith. To treat them as proofs which support faith in the Resurrection as an eschatological event is to make faith into a pseudo-faith, a human work, whereas it is a gift of the Spirit. The same must be said of the other Gospel legends: the virgin birth, the temptation in the wilderness, the Ascension.[35] What matters is their eschatological bearing, their intention to show that Jesus is the Completely Other, the saving event of God. Contrary to the belief of certain critics, demythologizing does not have only a negative tone: it clarifies the meaning of the myth, its eschatological bearing.

In conclusion we can see the correspondence between *Historie* and objective knowledge, and between *Geschichte* and faith. It is in the gratuitous preached summons of the kerygma that knowledge as objective knowing becomes the decision of faith, and that past fact becomes existential history for me in my faith.[36] Jesus of Nazareth becomes the Christ of faith, the saving of God in favor of humanity. This helps us to understand the paradoxical affirmation of Bultmann which has caused such

[34] *KM,* I, pp. 38 ff.
[35] See Bultmann, *HST,* pp. 209–321. In this regard, see the comments of A. Malet, *op. cit.,* pp. 151 ff.
[36] See Greshake, *op. cit.,* p. 90.

scandal: "The historical problem is not of interest to Christian belief in the Resurrection."[37]

DIALOGUE WITH BULTMANN

The merit of Bultmann's reflection on the double concept of history lay both in its reflection on the originality of salvation history in relation to profane history and in strongly underlining the theological character of faith as a reply to the Word of God. It is well known that Cullmann and Bultmann have mutually reproached each other with being ignorant of history. "For Bultmann," Cullmann writes, "the historical element which characterizes the doctrine of the early Christians is not essential but is the mythical means of expressing an a-historical, a-temporal truth, which would form its real substance."[38] Catholics, in general, have been in agreement with Cullmann and have appreciated the manner in which he has shown the originality of biblical time as compared to the cyclical time of the Greeks. Yet Cullmann's conception of salvation history is not entirely above reproach. Bultmann's reservations on this subject should be heard. Bultmann's distinction between *historisch* and *geschichtlich* is somewhat too systematic and we shall have to ask later whether he does not reduce history (in the ordinary sense) to historicity. But at any rate he shows how a salvific event is irreducible to any other historical event, precisely because God himself is involved in such an event.

In his review of Cullmann's *Christ and Time,* Bultmann admits that he cannot see how history in the expression "salvation history" means anything other than it does in the expression "world history." How does salvation history in the Old Testament fundamentally differ from the history of the people of

[37] *KM,* I, p. 42.
[38] For an over-all refutation of the positions of the Bultmann school on salvation history, see the recent book of Cullmann, *Salvation as History* (New York, 1966).

Israel as a historian could write it?[39] In other words, Cullmann seems to remain at the level of empirical history in which the salvific events occur in a linear succession. He retains the Jewish conception of time, that of the apocalypse, with this difference: that Christ, instead of being situated in the future, is situated in the past, at the center of history, separating it into two halves: the time before Christ and the time after Christ.

According to Bultmann, Cullmann misunderstood the specific character of the salvific event because he makes it into an objectifiable event which can be represented. But in virtue of its dimension as a divine and eschatological event, it cannot be objectified and can be met only in the existential act of faith. Cullmann's conception of salvation history suffers from two serious lacunae: (1) Christ as the divine salvific event is not considered as the eschatological and definitive event actually present at every instant of salvation history. This latter is not reducible to universal history. (2) On the other hand, because he does not take man's historicity into account, he does not show how Jesus Christ as salvific event is accessible only in faith, as an existential and eschatological act, and is thus himself inobjectifiable.

Bultmann's double concept of history helps us to respect the divine dimension of the salvific events in relation to ordinary historical events. As a divine event, Christ is not a phenomenon of this world. And as eschatological, salvific event, he can be reached only by faith and not by simple historical experience. Malevez speaks of the *événementiel divin* to express this fundamental dimension of salvation history which Bultmann describes.[40]

---

[39] "I cannot see that for him, 'history' in the compound expression 'salvation history' has a meaning different from that in the compound, 'world history,' or that the Old Testament salvation history is fundamentally distinguished from the history of the people of Israel which is also perceivable by the historian." Bultmann, "Heilsgeschichte und Geschichte," *art. cit.,* p. 662.

[40] L. Malevez, S.J., "Les dimensions de l'histoire du salut," *Nouvelle revue théologique,* 96 (1964), p. 572: "To sum up, the divine event is not simply a phenomenon of this world, and it is as it presents itself in this way (through its phenomenal expression) not to experience but to

It is true that in the man Christ Jesus, God becomes visible, God enters time—and we shall have to ask whether Bultmann gives enough weight to this real Incarnation. But it is equally true that his dimension of a divine event does not fall under the scope of an historical enquiry. There is a transcendence about the divine event which is accessible only to faith. Purely historical knowledge can know in Jesus only a man like other men. "The paradox of faith lies in the fact that it understands an event which can be verified in its natural and historical context as being nonetheless an action of God."[41] Similarly, the risen Christ as the glorified Lord was never seen by human eyes. The apostles could be eye-witnesses of his apparitions, but it was only through faith that they could adhere to the trans-phenomenal reality of the risen Christ. The Resurrection, as an action of God, is something entirely different from the miracle of the return to life of a corpse. There must be stress on the divine component of the events of salvation history. Precisely as acts of God, the historical events are irreducible to the natural phenomena of universal history and they are accessible only to faith as an existential decision.

The second merit of Bultmann's existential theology is his insistence on the theological character of faith. He stresses that faith as an existential act has no other specific motive than the Word of God revealing himself in the event "Jesus Christ" and that faith participates in the historicity proper to this event; it is an eschatological act, which makes us new creatures and installs us even now in the last times.

Critical Questions

1. The Realism of the Incarnation. Through his distinction Bultmann has thrown into greater relief one essential component of salvation history: the events of salvation as acts of

---

faith, that it is formally salvific. . . . The divine event-life [*événementiel*] remains transcendent to the body which it assumes."
[41] *KuM,* II, p. 198.

God in history are irreducible to the events of empirical history. The event as Word of God cannot be objectified as a phenomenon of the world: it is pure paradox which demands a response of pure faith. Salvation as an act of God in Christ is a real event, but it cannot be objectified at the level of representative thought.

In spite of this consistency which is acknowledged to belong to salvation history, the Bultmannian conception of God's interventions in history seem shaky. We should recall that because he uses the phenomenological method, there are certain questions raised by an older, ontological theology which he cannot answer. The question of the relationship of eternity and time is one of these. Similarly, he can say nothing about the nature of God; thirdly, he believes that the vestiges of God in history will elude all objective knowledge. With man's historicity, the problem is not that of the presence of the eternal in time, but of the future for the present.

It is not, however, only his philosophical presuppositions which prevent Bultmann from answering certain questions which are essential to an understanding of Christianity. It is his conception of myth and his radical opposition between the world of God and the created world which prevent him from envisaging any real relation between the eternal and time. It is precisely the encounter of the eternal event of God with past history which makes the latter become existential history. But, if *Historie* becomes *Geschichte,* it is not because the transcendent God became present in the world in the decisive event that is Jesus Christ; it is through the kerygma, the Word of God actually present. Jesus of Nazareth, a man like others, becomes the event, the act of God who demands the obedience of faith.

To the extent that Bultmann radically rejects the mode of objectifying thought as mythological, he refuses to objectify the unique event that is Christ Jesus at the level of the divine and human natures. The encounter of the divine with the human, of the eternal with time, will not take place in the person of Jesus Christ, but in his Word, in preaching. For Bultmann, the

186

Jesus of history is the decisive place and moment of man's salvation. Cullmann is exaggerating when he refuses to concede that much to Bultmann. "The redemption of which we have spoken is not a miraculous supernatural event, but an historical event wrought out in time and space."[42] But, as eschatological event, Christ's role is merely that of notifying man of his salvation.[43] Bultmann is not interested in the real relation of Christ as man to God. This then gives us the right to ask questions about the realism of the Incarnation. As Henri Bouillard puts it: "It now remains to be seen whether the work that God accomplishes in Jesus Christ consists solely in transforming *our existence* by faith in the word as preached by the church, in the new relation we thereby contract with God, but would it not consist initially of a unique relation of the *man Jesus* with God, a relation that would afterwards become, in our Christian faith, a mediating agent of our new relation with God?"[44]

Bultmann shows that a history where God intervenes is a history of an absolutely unique type, but it is hard to see how God really intervenes in history. To objectify such an intervention is to succumb to mythical thought, to suppress the paradox of faith. Did God really, objectively, come into the history of the world in the central mystery of Jesus Christ, a stumbling block for modern man as it was for the Jew and the Greek? Any objectifying of God's action in nature or in history has its foundation in a mythical mode of thought and is incompatible with modern man's picture of the world. The New Testament often uses this mode of thinking. We must, therefore, demythologize the New Testament, submit it to an existentialistic interpretation for the man of today.

Bultmann's systematic opposition between the non-worldly

---

[42] *KM,* I, p. 43.

[43] Malevez writes: "This same Christ has no other part to play than that of proclaiming salvation by his message and the Word of God; that is all; his person lacks mystery, and has no particular relation to the God who sends him; his Resurrection or his survival are not important for our salvation" (*Le message chrétien et le mythe, ed. cit.,* p. 117).

[44] *The Logic of Faith* (New York, 1968), p. 133.

and the worldly, the divine and the human myth and meaning, above and below, makes us uneasy. Bultmann saw clearly that God's vestiges in history cannot be pinpointed, represented. Jesus Christ as saving event is accessible to faith alone. And it is true that the unique relationship which unites the human nature of Jesus to the Word is not a phenomenon. The union of the divine and the human in Christ is realized, for Bultmann, only on the level of the Word as eschatological act. He is not concerned about the real unity of the incarnate Word with God made man. Certainly, he has the right to avoid a Christology on the level of natures; this road would be closed to him by his philosophical starting point. But, if we cannot (without falling into myth) state in a theological discussion that God objectively and really became in Christ Jesus a man of the world, then we have to say that myth is an essential datum of revelation itself. The myth par excellence, it is said, is the idea of a preëxisting God become man and redeeming us by his death and resurrection. Is that a myth or is it rather the paradox of the Christian faith?

A contemporary eye-witness of Jesus' human life would not see God; he could only believe. But his faith bears precisely on the fact that God himself became man, that it was God who was born, who lives, suffers, and dies. Does even traditional theology go far enough with the reality of the Incarnation when it affirms, in the name of divine immutability, that "becoming" only affects the created term of the hypostatic union, human nature?[45] It would have to be shown how God, without ceasing to be the immutable God, can really "become" in the Incarnation. As Karl Rahner says: "God can become something, he who is unchangeable in himself can *himself* become subject to change *in something else*."[46] The fact of the Incarnation

[45] On this point, see the important remarks of Malevez, "Les dimensions de l'histoire du salut," *art. cit.,* p. 520.

[46] "On the Theology of the Incarnation," *Theological Investigations,* IV (Baltimore, 1966), p. 113. Rahner writes elsewhere: ". . . the assertion of God's immutability, of the lack of any real relation between God and the world, is in a true sense a dialectical statement. One may and

is an indication for us that divine immutability should not be understood as a static rigidity. All that is meant by it is that God is not changeable as a creature is; the divine mode of his immutability escapes us. Aquinas's theologoumenon on the non-reciprocity of relations between God and the creature is in itself unattackable: its function is to show that God does not depend on his creature. It does not, however, exhaust the relationships between God and his creature, particularly in the supernatural order. How can one simultaneously affirm the reality of God's love for man and deny the reality of the relation of God to his creature? Moreover, the mystery of the Holy Trinity shows us that there are in God real relations which do not, as such, imply any imperfection or dependence.[47]

So, Bultmann is not denying that Jesus Christ is an historical event, an event which can be dated and which takes its place in temporal duration in the chronological sense. But using the pretext that one can never objectify God's transcendent action

---

indeed must say this, without for that reason being a Hegelian. For it is true, come what may, and a dogma, that the *Logos* himself has become man: thus that he himself has become something that he had not always been *(formaliter);* and therefore that what has so become is, as just itself and of itself, God's reality. Now if this is a truth of faith, ontology must allow itself to be guided by it (and in analogous instances in the doctrine of the Trinity), must seek enlightenment from it, and grant that while God remains immutable 'in himself,' he can come to be 'in the other' and that *both* assertions must really and truly be made of the same God as God" (*Theological Investigations,* I [Baltimore, 1961], p. 181).

[47] "The affirmation . . . that God is not dependent on the world or on history which must be expressed by the thesis that there does exist a *real* relation of man to God, but that on God's side there exists only a *'relatio rationis,'* a non-real relation to men, is, to say the least, extremely equivocal. All that St. Thomas, for instance, means by this thesis is a refusal to accept that God is really dependent on his creature. This thesis is unexceptionable, yet with it all has not been said. For no statement dare lead to a denial of the reality of God's relation to man; otherwise the danger remains that we, more Hellenic than Christian, will fail to understand the reality of the love of God as a reality in God himself" (E. Schillebeeckx, O.P., "Die Heiligung des Namens Gottes durch die Menschenliebe Jesu des Christus," *Gott in Welt* [Freiburg, 1964], II, p. 45).

in a reality which is of this world, he fails to show how on the level of the person of the Incarnate Word there is a real insertion of the eternal in time. In virtue of the radical abyss between the transcendent world of God and the world of experience, one cannot see how the Resurrection is anything other or more than the signification of the cross, namely, the real, ontological glorification of the man Jesus who had been laid in the tomb, and through that the beginning of something radically new, a new world in the old creation. The inadequacy of our conceptual representations of God's action in the world does not make it illegitimate to talk about the relations of God and the world from the point of view of its goal.

We know that revelation is concerned essentially with the person of Jesus, Son of God, who died and rose, yet Bultmann forces us into a choice between false alternatives: the "what" or the "that" of revelation. Beyond both there is the "who" irreducible to a pure point-like event, or to an objective truth. Does not an existential encounter between the Word of God and faith not always presuppose an acceptance that God worked in Christ? Why should the action of God in Christ be more mythical than the transformation of our existence by the kerygma?[48] Bultmann has kept only the first two of the three essential elements of the primitive kerygma: the call to repentance; the promise of God's pardon and of the gift of the Holy Spirit; the witnessing to Christ's death *pro nobis* and his Resurrection (a statement which implies faith in his Lordship).

2. The Temporality of Christ. Bultmann practically reduces the human temporality of Christ to existential time, to the pure moment of free decision. How legitimate is this? One gets the impression that the human duration of Christ is reduced to a succession of acts which are purely point-like without ever making a true temporal continuum. Similarly, it seems as if the history of the Christian community is reduced to a succession of

[48] See Bouillard, *op. cit.*

190

eschatological "nows" which are the members' decisions in faith.

It is clear that the history of a free being is something other than the history which measures the becoming of natural phenomena. But when we speak of human time, we never have the right to make a radical split between existential history, and time in the ordinary sense as a measure of duration.[49] Is it not a sign of a radical anthropocentrism if I give meaning and value to history in general only when it becomes my history?[50]

At the level of Christ's human temporality, we cannot dissociate his spiritual temporality in the sense of historicity and his bodily temporality in the sense that all of his actions are measured by the world of time in the ordinary sense. The point at issue is again the reality of the Incarnation.

For Bultmann, the depth of Jesus like any other event of his life is simply a news item without any intrinsic interest. Insofar as the existential decision of Christ is also the eternal action of God, that is, precisely as it is Word of God, the death of Christ concerns me and is a challenge to me. Bultmann always juxtaposes God's eternal action and the pure unobjectifiable instant of Christ's existential decision without there being any real entrance of the eternal into time. The very mystery of Christ is the emergence of the eternal in time. All of Christ's actions are measured simultaneously by eternity and human

---

[49] J. Mouroux, *The Mystery of Time* (New York, 1964), pp. 131 ff.

[50] "Although it is true that the 'historicity' of the human being is a necessary condition for speaking about history, yet this condition is not the only one, and it is hard to see what can authorize this confusing reduction of what is generally called 'history' to the 'historicity' of personal existence. . . . To speak in this way of history while meaning historicity is bound to cause much confusion and obscurity. . . . Even Ebeling himself says we must distinguish the historicity of human existence from history properly so-called, and that the one does not always suffice to explain the other. History, he explains, always refers to these supra-individual contexts which always precede concrete existence, determine the concrete, historical locus of this existence and thus provide, in a certain way, 'the stuff of personal decisions' " (R. Marlé, "Histoire et historicité chez quelques théologiens protestants," *art. cit.,* pp. 100–101).

temporality. Bultmann would reply that, using the phenomenological method, he cannot speak of the relations of eternity and time. He only raises the question of the relation between the future and the present moment of existential decision. But this depreciates the real history of the man-God Jesus Christ by inaugurating a radically new contemporaneity of God and history to the unique advantage of the existential history of the individual believer.

Mouroux has said: "Christ, *in time,* is the Being who *transcends* time, but who *expresses himself really* through and by means of time."[51] Just as his humanity is an epiphany of his divinity, so his temporality is an epiphany of the eternal God. In Jesus Christ the eternal God really becomes the contemporary of all the "nows" of the human history which continues to run its course. Bultmann safeguards this contemporaneity at the level of the Word as an ever actual event of God. But we see the foundation of this contemporaneity at the level of the very being of Jesus Christ, God made man.

3. The Devaluation of Historical Signs. According to Bultmann, it is impossible to prove objectively that the kerygma is an historical summons from God. "There can be nothing which justifies the Word of God; it is its own justification."[52] There is no criterion of credibility, because the kerygma in its formal structure has nothing objective. If the kerygma is objectified, I am not hearing the call of God but its objective expression.

Bultmann replies to his critics that faith is in no way a blind fideism. "To the extent that the object of faith is unknowable apart from faith, faith itself is a type of knowledge, because God's revelation to which faith adheres is truth."[53] The only criterion of the truth of faith is that man, summoned by the kerygma, is capable of understanding himself as someone loved by God. In other words, the real-life experience of obedience in

[51] Mouroux, *loc. cit.*
[52] *GV,* I, p. 142.
[53] *J.* p. 333.

faith is the only guarantee of faith. Bultmann would apply to the believer Kierkegaard's statement: "The only true explanation of what truth is, is in the truth itself." We can, nevertheless, ask whether the accusation of fideism is not justified. The reasonableness granted to it by Bultmann is in fact concomitant with the act of faith itself. He rejects any condition of reasonableness or motive of credibility prior to faith.

To put it briefly, because he sees a radical opposition between past fact and existential history, Bultmann accords no value to the historical signs through which revelation is mediated. The very notion of sign is mythical, that is to say, unthinkable; it would presuppose that God's action can be objectified, made visible at the level of a phenomenon of empirical history. The formal motive of faith is the uncreated witness of God himself, but we should not conclude from this that there are no signs of credibility which support the reasonable character of my faith. The humanity of Jesus, his teaching, his miracles, the sublimity of his moral life, do not exhaust the transcendence of revelation as Word of God but they are signs which might lead to confessing his divinity.

This disregarding of signs seems to us to run directly counter to God's own pedagogy in revelation as an incarnation of the Word of God in human words and in the events of human history. As is clearly shown by his understanding of the apparitions of the risen Christ, Bultmann cannot reconcile the authenticity of signs and the transcendent character of faith as paradox. He forgets that signs are not demonstrative proofs; they surrender their ultimate meaning only to those who understand them with the eyes of faith. In spite of this fact they still remain true signs. The invisible God made himself present through these privileged historical signs of his revelation. What we have to do is to decipher in the sign the divine meaning which it simultaneously hides and reveals. Because of the radical opposition which he sees between the world of God and the world of experience, Bultmann retains only the "veiling" aspect of the sign. The paradox of faith consists in the fact that

193

an historical event accessible to our experience can still be an action of God.[54] Under pretext of safeguarding the paradox of faith as a real-life encounter with the eschatological event of the Word of God, Bultmann compromises the living dialectic of kerygma and history, which is the very law of a Christian knowledge of Jesus Christ. "The apostolic kerygma accepted in faith refers back to the prepaschal event from which it springs, and in its turn, the event, when it has been recognized, leads to the kerygma which alone can give it its full meaning."[55] I think we must reject the preferred alternative: the Christ of faith or the Jesus of history. To the extent that Bultmann fails to recognize this mutual interplay of history and mystery, he undermines the very originality of the Judeo-Christian revelation.[56] What must finally be criticized in Bultmann's thought is his starting point, his conception of the Word of God as pure "that," as event which cannot be objectified. Granted, revelation is not a "what" in the sense of a doctrine of the past; it is the ever present event of the Word of God. But this Word of God translates, expresses himself through a group of historical, visible signs, all of which point to a unique event, Jesus Christ, the Word made flesh. Faith is a real-life encounter with the Word of God but it is

[54] The paradox of faith lies in the fact "that it comprises an event which can be verified both in its natural and historical context and also as being a divine action" (*KuM*, II, p. 198).

[55] X. Léon-Dufour, *Les évangiles et l'histoire de Jésus* (Paris, 1963), p. 489.

[56] "The life of Jesus of Nazareth can be read only in the light of the mystery of Christ as it was witnessed to by the apostles after the paschal event. On the other hand, the mystery of Christ as a mystery of faith is always rooted in, and founded upon, the events of the life of Jesus narrated for us by the evangelists. This living dialectic between history and mystery is the foundation of the double movement in our Christian knowledge of Jesus Christ. Walking in the footsteps of the apostles, we can retrace the path which led them from the historical Jesus to the mystery of Christ. But, like them, we too must always return to the events of Jesus' life, discovering a new depth in them in the decisive light of the risen Christ" (Geffré, "Histoire et mystère dans la connaissance du Christ," *La Vie spirituelle* [1964], p. 630).

194

always based on an encounter with Jesus Christ as an historical event.

Bultmann's enterprise is remarkable in its emphasis on the divine component of the salvific events: the presence or absence of God is not a verifiable phenomenon open to historical investigation. But to safeguard this position, he remains prisoner of an absolute dialetical theology where God is defined as being not of the world, and the world is defined as not being of God. Pushing the Lutheran doctrine of justification to extremes, Bultmann tries to avoid degrading faith into a human work. This is why he removes all human support from it. But by a strange paradox, while Bultmann wishes to take a position opposed to liberalism, it can be asked whether his theology does not result in a reduction of Christian faith to a philosophical faith, whether the whole sphere of the religious is not dissolved into the sphere of the ethical, whether the paradox of faith as adhesion to the objective mystery of God's entry into the world is not reduced to the dramatic decision by which I pass from an unauthentic to an authentic life.

The scandal for twentieth-century man, as for the Jew and the Greek, is that God really became man in Christ Jesus.

IX. BULTMANN AND HEIDEGGER

By Helmut Peukert

In a certain sense it belongs to the greatness of a significant work that it be many-sided, capable of various interpretations, especially when the interpretations have had their own development. Their historical effect rests to a great extent on the very complexity of the work. This is true of Bultmann's work, and even more so of Heidegger's. The relationship of the two can and will be more precisely defined, but we must expect from the beginning that this relationship contain various tonalities. Can we find a point of reference which brings into view the totality of both men's work along with their relationship to each other?

We could consider Bultmann's theology as theological anthropology with a reduction of all statements to the dialectical structure of eschatological existence in its presuppositions and its actualization, and then compare this with Heidegger's analysis of existence in *Being and Time*.[1] In many ways, however, another problematic seems to precede even this one: the

[1] An introductory bibliography: G. Kuhlmann, "Zum theologischen Problem der Existenz, Fragen an Rudolf Bultmann," *ZThK*, 37 (1929), pp. 28–57; J. Macquarrie, *An Existentialist Theology* (New York, 1956); H. Haug, "Offenbarungstheologie und philosophische Daseinsanalyse bei R. Bultmann," *ZThK*, 55 (1958), pp. 201–253; O. Schnübbe, *Der Existenzbegriff in der Theologie R. Bultmanns* (Göttingen, 1959); G. Noller, *Sein und Existenz: Die Überwindung des Subjekt-Objekt-Schemas in der Theologie der Entmythologisierung* (Munich, 1961).

question of *theological hermeneutic*. Like a prism it includes every point of departure for the following study. Hermeneutic seems to correspond to the central interests of all of Bultmann's theological work. In his dialogue with Karl Jaspers he emphasized: "The real problem is the hermeneutic one, that is, the problem of interpreting the Bible and the teachings of the Church in such a way that they may become understandable as a summons to man."[2]

Heidegger's thought, too, in an encompassing way right up to and including his recent writings, can be seen as ἑρμηνεύειν, hermeneutic.[3] At the same time it is precisely the hermeneutical act which is the place where philosophy and theology meet. In his reflection on this act Bultmann determines the relationship of his theology to Heidegger's thought.

With the work of Schleiermacher and Dilthey in broadening the meaning of the concept hermeneutic to include the methodical question of historical understanding, this problem (further developed by Bultmann) has become a central question of "theology according to Bultmann." And when we take this as the basic point, questions arise which are equally unavoidable for Catholic theology, ones rooted in the entire problematic. These questions did not first come to light in our century. Their relationship to philosophy delineates the history of Christian theology. With the Enlightenment a new sharpness enters, finding its pinnacle in the thought of German Idealism (whose problems are far from solved). Bultmann himself notes this.[4] On the other hand, Western philosophy is unthinkable without its relationship to theology.

The results for theology of Bultmann's personal contacts with Heidegger during their years together at the University of

---

[2] *KM*, II, p. 184.
[3] Heidegger, *Unterwegs zur Sprache* (Pfullingen, 1959), pp. 121 ff.
[4] Bultmann recognizes that with Heidegger's thought the authentic motifs of German Idealism attain their majority. Bultmann, "Heidegger," *RGG* (1928), 2nd edition, II, p. 1688.

Marburg[5] can be understood only within a broader horizon. This framework of their mutual relationship is limited to certain fundamental characteristics; they can best be presented through the following four steps. To begin, we will briefly describe the theological situation of the time when Bultmann found help for theology in Heidegger's thought. Bultmann's use of Heidegger rests mainly on the early period of Heideggerian thought, almost exclusively on *Being and Time*. Next we can see exactly how Bultmann's theology employed Heidegger's thought, and, finally, determine the full relationship and limits of both to each other.

THE HERMENEUTICAL SITUATION OF THE EXEGETE

Bultmann is within that great tradition of exegetes who through criticism without conditions have studied the New Testament above all as a historical source.

The history of the historical-critical study of the New Testament has shown that these exegetes were led by the goal of discovering through radical criticism the true, authentic picture of Jesus behind the portrait of dogmatic orthodoxy, even behind the New Testament itself. From this result faith would either find support, or find every support removed (as Reimarus, who gave the first impetus to the entire work, remarked). The various pictures of the "historical Jesus" discovered in this undertaking showed by their very contradictions that in general there could be little clarity over the nature of the method being used; much more the picture discovered very often

[5] From 1922 until 1928 Heidegger was in Marburg; he then accepted a position in Freiburg im Breisgau. From 1921 until 1951 Bultmann was Professor for New Testament Exegesis at Marburg. The first volume of *Glauben und Verstehen* (Bultmann's collected essays) is (1933) and "remains [second edition, 1954] dedicated to Martin Heidegger in thankful recollection of the time in Marburg."

showed clear characteristics of the researcher himself who was supposed to be "free from presuppositions."

One of the most dramatic developments of the history of theology was the recognition that the conscious method and the complexity of the reality under study must first be clarified. The New Testament itself became the strongest impulse towards finding out what the historical-critical method should accomplish, and what idea of historicity should be presupposed. Only too obvious was the fact that the evangelists did not wish to compose a biography of Jesus, but that their primary intention was (instead of historical-rational-critical-factual report) to witness to the believing experience as a call empowering to faith. The "kerygma" was discovered in the New Testament, the contemporary grace-filled call and claim which was the horizon of meaning for all other statements. What is attainable as factual knowledge about the "historical" Jesus can be grasped only in methodical separation, in critical destruction of the total witness based on "history." The expression "historical (*historisch*) Jesus" (in contrast to the "biblical," or the "historic" [*geschichtlich*] Jesus, or the "kerymatic Christ") became the title for a problem of method within theology itself. And this is how the hermeneutical problematic developed; this is the problem Bultmann saw challenging him at the beginning of his theological work.

Three tasks present themselves to the exegete as historian. (1) He must try through a critical test of the value of character and source in the text of the New Testament to extract whatever knowledge can be attained about Jesus of Nazareth. This Bultmann attempted in his book *Jesus* (1926) on the basis of his earlier study in form-criticism, *The History of the Synoptic Tradition* (1921). (2) Next he must historically delineate the kerygma of the New Testament in its motives, structures, and its own horizon of expression. As such, it is the witness of the faith of the early church. This is how Bultmann sees his *Theology of the New Testament* (1955). (3) Historical research must also study the relationship between

199

the claim of Jesus in his preaching and the statement of New Testament preaching, determining the dominant form of continuity or explication.[6]

But even after this historical research one question remains completely unclarified: how can the claim of Jesus, or the claim of the kerygma in the New Testament, be such a decisive message over and for me that I accomplish (or forfeit) my salvation through my acceptance in belief (or rejection in disbelief) of this kerygma? This biblical question can also be expressed more abstractly: In which horizon of historicity must the believer's existence and the event which unconditionally yet historically encounters him be conceived? How should these things, from which he experiences in history his salvation, be understood? In and towards what do we interpret the kerygma of the New Testament? Bultmann, the historical-critical exegete with his strict appreciation of method, saw this as the decisive hermeneutical question.

What we have just mentioned can be illustrated in two areas of New Testament study to which Bultmann devoted significant works. Bultmann, one of the founders of form-criticism, is interested in presenting as fundamental the history of the primitive Christian tradition, that is, the process of interpretation and explication in the New Testament and prior to it. As early as 1921 Bultmann saw the decisive tendency of the Gospel according to Mark to be the interpretation of the tradition about Jesus with the help of Hellenistic myth.[7] In the study of comparative religion Bultmann and his disciples pursued further how certain views, for example the use of gnosis, were employed in the formulation of the kerygma. The result of this work is *Primitive Christianity in its Contemporary Setting* (1949). So, the exegete views himself as the interested counterpart to a process of interpretation within the New Testament which is not at all unified; he himself has to interpret

[6] See Bultmann, *Das Verhältnis der urchristlichen Christusbotschaft zum historischen Jesus* (Heidelberg, 1960).
[7] *HST*, p. 372.

in order to reach the reality behind the text. In his review of the second edition of Karl Barth's *Römerbrief* in 1922,[8] Bultmann demanded that the Scriptural text be understood in light of the reality; this implied criticism—a program which received in 1941 the name "demythologizing." The question is, however, which critical, methodically tested criteria does the exegete have at his disposal in order to bring the reality out from under its various interpretations and into the light? Which hermeneutical principles does an interpretation demand—an interpretation of a further historical but conditioned (through the many influences summed up as comparative religion) interpretation of a prior event?

For Bultmann the hermeneutical question was radicalized in the movement called dialectical theology. Inasmuch as—against liberal theology—it held fast to the absolute summons and claim, the transcendence of the Word of God, Bultmann and Barth agreed. But Bultmann immediately added: "God's being other, his transcendence means the striking through of the total man and his entire history."[9] For Bultmann, revelation cannot simply eliminate its addressee, if it really wants to speak to him. It must, rather, in some way place him in question, in such a way that he will clearly know and acknowledge this—yet also be able to turn away from it. A new possibility of the same man must be opened. To avoid the dilemma of an absolute dialectical theology (a theology which threatens "to change into pure transcendental philosophy"),[10] we must see how man can grasp the Word of revelation which has grasped him. How are we to understand the hearing and the hearer of a revelation taking place in history? What does it mean to be a "hearer of the Word"?

For Bultmann, the structure of dialectical theology flows, too, into the question of a hearing which understands the historical Word of revelation. This problem reaches its climax

---

[8] Bultmann, "Barths *Römerbrief*," *Christliche Welt,* 36 (1922), p. 360.
[9] *GV,* I, p. 13.
[10] Bultmann, "Barths *Römerbrief*," *art. cit.,* p. 360.

in the conditions for the hearer of this Word himself. In 1927 Bultmann wrote an essay, "The Significance of 'Dialectical Theology' for the Scientific Study of the New Testament."[11] Bultmann saw the essence of dialectical theology in the insight that man's existence is an insight into the historicity of man's existence. In 1927, Heidegger's *Being and Time* appeared. Meanwhile Bultmann had met Heidegger and had gained through him means towards clarifying this theological situation of the exegete.

Let us turn first to Heidegger's position in *Being and Time,* its background and its thought. Then we can understand something more of how Heidegger's thought could appear to Bultmann as needed, decisive help.

HISTORICITY AND HERMENEUTIC IN HEIDEGGER'S *BEING AND TIME*

The same objection could be raised against a considerable number of the studies on Bultmann's theology and its relationship to Heidegger: that they lose themselves in the analysis (although some consideration is necessary) of individual concepts and terms such as "existence," "world," "authenticity," "fallen-ness," and so forth. This method inevitably loses the full connection, the tendency of the thought as a whole. Only in a larger picture can the individual ideas really be understood. At the same time, it is easily overlooked that Heidegger himself is partially motivated by theology on the path towards his ontological and existential analyses.

Like all philosophers since German Idealism, Heidegger thinks in the horizon of a deep consciousness of the history of European metaphysics. Little by little he arrived at the decisive insight that metaphysics since Plato conceived of thought as a seeing, being as something constantly standing before our eyes, as the constantly present. Even in modern metaphysics this

[11] *GV,* I, pp. 114–133.

character of Being remains unthought, even if metaphysics goes beyond everything given into the subjectivity of the subject. This is also valid for the phenomenology of Husserl, who tries to understand everything in the light of the constitutive performance of the transcendental ego. Similarly, Dilthey, who became conscious of his task as a historian through a fundamental methodological question allied to Hegel and who sought to be a historian through a hermeneutic of history, cannot solve (for Heidegger) the ontological problems at the bottom of all this.

In the lectures Heidegger held after the First World War he developed a new point of departure. At its center was the actualization of real life, factual day-to-day living. If the question about Being is to be properly asked, its actualization, that is, in its temporality, must be considered. This led to the development of *Being and Time*. "Still, Heidegger's early lectures show that the primitive Christian faith has guided his thought to his decisive questions."[12] Two of these lectures are quite important for us.[13] In the winter semester of 1920–1921 Heidegger presented an "Introduction to the Phenomenology of Religion" where he made reference to the "actual experience of life" which comes to expression in the letters of Paul. In 1 Thessalonians 4:13 ff., Paul rejects any determination of the second coming of Christ and asks Christians to lead a life before the open and threatening but non-objectifiable clouds of the future. In 2 Corinthians 12:1–10, Heidegger sees a direction of Paul not to flee to myths, story, apochryphal or apocalyptic reports, but to stay put, to accept the weakness of the actuality of life.[14] In a lecture entitled "Augustine and

[12] O. Pöggeler, *Der Denkweg Martin Heideggers* (Pfullingen, 1963), pp. 35; 36–45. Pöggeler is the first to develop extensively this relationship.
[13] See the list of Heidegger's lectures and seminars (expanded by Heidegger himself) in W. J. Richardson, *Heidegger: Through Phenomenology to Thought* (The Hague, 1963), pp. 663–671.
[14] See Pöggeler, *op. cit.*, p. 37.

Neo-Platonism" (summer, 1921), Heidegger made reference to the danger in Augustine of falsifying this factual life threatened from restlessness, suffering and cross, and through neo-Platonism, changing it into a timeless, non-historical *fruitio Dei*. Luther experienced and expressed in its original character this real, actual reality of life (an actuality which, by the way, does not come from *Angst* and the reference to individual death).[15] Usually, a thought tuned to image-producing thinks Being as a being-at-hand, an object, missing its temporal-historical actualization in time's own self-realization. Therefore, it cannot accurately present the question of Being.

This is the decisive step on the way to *Being and Time*. The work is to show "that the central problematic of all ontology is rooted in the phenomenon of time, if rightly seen and rightly explained, and we must show how this is the case."[16] "In the exposition of the problematic of Temporality the question of the meaning of Being will first be concretely answered."[17] At the same time these analyses will serve to highlight the nature of a hermeneutic of history as the method for the humanities, and thereby accomplish what Dilthey wanted.[18] Heidegger's point of departure reflectively included the proper area of theology and prepared for a new theology in the sense of Luther.[19]

The question of the meaning of Being for Heidegger can therefore be accurately asked and answered only on the basis of the agitation of the actual human-being in terms of *Dasein,* human existence. This reality manifests itself phenomenologically. Among other examples Heidegger's most well-known is the phenomenon of *Angst*.[20]

---

[15] *Ibid.*, pp. 40, 43.   [16] *BT,* p. 40.

[17] *Ibid.*   [18] *Ibid.*, p. 62.

[19] See H. H. Schrey's report on Heidegger's lecture in 1927 ("Phänomenologie und Theologie") in "Die Bedeutung der Philosophie Martin Heideggers für die Theologie," *Martin Heideggers Einfluss auf die Wissenschaften* (Bern, 1949), pp. 9–12; See *BT,* pp. 30 f.

[20] See *BT,* 40; see also Heidegger, *Existence and Being* (Chicago, 1949).

In *Angst* man is not afraid of individual beings. A being can at most be the immediate occasion for a basic *Angst* to rise. With *Angst* a man is afraid of (before) "nothing." "The clear night of the nothingness of *Angst*" dominates.[21] It is exactly *Angst* which shows that human existence cannot flee itself, but that it must be itself ultimately, that it is directed back to itself and to the totality of beings. It manifests itself as finite transcendence.[22] This transcendence means the transcending movement of human existence in which it goes beyond itself and beings, but discloses itself precisely in its finite facticity and in its reference to beings. Transcendence makes possible and forces relationship to self and to beings. For this structure of finite human existence (transcending itself necessarily in its relationship to self) Heidegger selected (drawing on Kierkegaard) the term "existence." "The 'essence' of *Dasein* lies in its existence."[23] Heidegger calls the formal description of this structure *existential* analysis, as distinguished from the vital, individual *existentiell* act of individual existence being lived in the concrete.[24] Naturally, the first form of analysis, existential-ontological analysis, is possible only on the basis of the actualization of concrete individual existence. But it presupposes no contentual objective determination, only *Dasein* related to itself and simply transcending this actualization. The significance of this point of view can only be fully understood in light of the history of modern philosophy.[25] It includes at least two implications which were quite important for Bultmann.

[21] Heidegger, *Existence and Being,* p. 369.
[22] *Ibid.,* p. 370.
[23] *BT,* p. 67.
[24] The German *"existential"* implies an analysis based on Heidegger's fundamental ontology, the ontological structures of existence; *"existentiell"* means the concrete, personal events of existence. The latter is translated by "existential," the former by "existential-ontological" or a similar phrase. – Tr.
[25] See W. Schulz, "Über den philosophiegeschichtlichen Ort Martin Heideggers," *Philosophische Rundschau,* 1 (1953/54), pp. 65–93, 211–232.

The interpretation of transcendence in its unity of going-beyond and concrete existence means for Heidegger the successful transcending of the subject-object problematic of philosophy since Kant. For Kant, a knowledge which goes beyond the realm of empirical objects is impossible. A transcendental can go beyond the empirical only on the basis of its prior categories, given conditions for the possibility of knowledge present in the subject. Leading the process back to one of the poles means an even sharper tension between subject and object. The Being of transcendental subjectivity and the Being of the *Ding an sich* remain ontologically (in the Heideggerian sense) without clarification. So, the problem arises—how can we go beyond subjectivity and objectivity to the ground of their own possibility? This step cannot lead to a being; rather, the realm of beings, the realm of subjects and objects as such, must be passed beyond.

This happens in the transcending actualization of human existence in view of the non-objective, "nothingness." "Only on the basis of the original manifestness of Nothing can our human *Da-sein* advance towards and enter into what is. . . . Were *Da-sein* not, in its essential basis, transcendent, that is to say, were it not projected from the start into Nothing, it could never relate to what is, hence could have no self-relationship."[26] This ontological problematic (which, naturally, has nothing to do with Nihilism) is more closely unfolded in terms of the temporality and historicity of human existence. They will illuminate just how subjectivity and objectivity find their roots in a more radical event.

A view of the transcendental concept of *world* in Kant's philosophy can clarify what Heidegger means. In his work *Vom Wesen des Grundes* Heidegger says that transcendence is aimed at world because in transcendence itself being as a totality is opened to human existence. "We call that towards which *Dasein* as such transcends the world, and we precise transcendence as Being-in-the-world. World defines the unified

[26] Heidegger, *Existence and Being*, pp. 369 f.

206

structure of transcendence; as belonging to this structure the world-concept is called a transcendental."[27]

For Kant, the idea of world, a described unity and totality of the world, can never adequately be objectified in an empirical *Anschauung*; this idea has only "transcendental" validity.[28] The idea of world is for Kant the "radical concept of all appearances"[29] or the absolute totality in the synthesis of appearances.[30] Similarly, for Heidegger, world becomes the "title of finite knowledge in its totality."[31] The decisive (and in Kant hazy) question of "the transcendental validity" of totality is explained by Heidegger from transcending, that which unfolds the totality of beings. Existence can be understood from this totality; existence interprets itself in its light. World-understanding and self-understanding are, therefore, indissolubly bound; a change in one means a change in the other. Since existence exists ultimately in history, the world is also always a historical thing. The manner of how the self is related to history determines the relationship of the world and vice versa—a determination which is closer to the biblical κόσμος than to the ancient spatial concept of world.

If we want to compare Heidegger's thought with Thomistic epistemology, we must note that Heidegger's concept of existence has basically nothing in common with *existentia*. For Aquinas, the structure of finite knowledge lies in the unity of the *excessus* of the agent intellect, the conversion of the intellect to the imagined images, and the return of self (*reditio in seipsum*). Contemporary students of both forms of epistemology such as Karl Rahner, Bernhard Welte, and others have tried to interpret Aquinas's structure through a consequently transcendental questioning, developing both Aquinas's and Heideg-

---

[27] Heidegger, *Vom Wesen des Grundes* (Frankfurt, 1955), p. 19.

[28] Kant, *Critique of Pure Reason,* tr. N. K. Smith (New York, 1929), B 384, p. 319.

[29] *Ibid.*, B 391, p. 323.

[30] *Ibid.*, B 434, p. 385.

[31] Heidegger, *Vom Wesen des Grundes,* p. 31.

ger's position further.[32] This has shown as a by-product that Heidegger is concerned not with a primitive existentialism, but with basic problems of ontology.

Being and Time unfolded the basic event of human existence in more detail. Heidegger's analysis took place in two sections. In the first, "Preparatory Fundamental Analysis of *Dasein*," the structural elements of existence are provisionally set up. "State-of-Mind" (*Befindlichkeit*) is an existential-ontological determination of *Dasein,* insofar as human existence always finds itself in a determined situation and mood. "Understanding" (*Verstehen*) means the activity of human existence forecasting and transcending the various horizons of meaning. What understanding opens up is not only objectified, conceptualized contents of things, but directions of activity, possibilities of existence itself. Inasmuch as existence is open to itself, it can express itself in "discourse" (*Rede*) and bring to speech the basic event of transcendence. At the same time, Heidegger shows that this unified structure is modifiable, that existence as concrete being-in-the-world can pause at open objectivity, can thereby interpret itself in "falling" (*Verfallen*), that it can lose its own authentic self-being.

The second section of *Being and Time* studies the "meaning" of this structure of existence. Meaning means horizon in and towards which (*woraufhin*) a being is to be understood. Since it is a question of an understanding of existence itself, meaning now means the horizon within which existence can understand itself and beings, not unauthentically—from and through objects —but in its totality and in the authentic, radically transcending activity of self-being. Temporality manifests itself as such a horizon. Temporality is not something outside human existence, but rather the way in which this existence *is*. Temporality actualizes itself in time temporarily (*zeitigt sich*) in the being of *Dasein;* temporality is the meaning-structure of the event of existence. Therefore, it is only a radical interpretation of the event of transcendence.

[32] See K. Rahner, *Spirit in the World* (New York, 1968).

Existence actualizes itself in such a way that in understanding the open possibility of existing, the future of existence itself is opened up. But in the development towards the future, existence is turned back to its mortal, finite facticity. In its future, *Dasein* comes to itself and finds itself as There-being *(Da-sein)*, as having already been. Only in this activity can existence be present to itself, present in the act of existing in time. "This phenomenon has the unity of a future which makes present in the process of having been: we designate it as 'temporality.' "[33] Only from this original temporality can we determine what time—whether in physical scientific expiration or in common understanding—means.[34]

For Heidegger, existence's relationship to history can be seen only through the structure of the more basic temporality. If human existence exists in time, then in its basis existence is historical.[35] For inasmuch as existence finds itself in the present as already having been (and finds this by drawing on its future), the possibility of history consists in the possibilities of its own existence. "Only an entity which, as futural, is equiprimordially in the process of *having-been,* can, by handing down to itself the possibility it has inherited, take over its own thrownness and be *in the moment of vision* for 'its time.' "[36]

The *moment* of authentic temporality is the origin of the relationship to history. In this moment, existence is summed up with all of its possibilities; it courses before death as the ultimate possibility of its Being and receives its mortal finite-

---

[33] *BT,* p. 374.

[34] It is possible to see Heidegger's analysis of temporality as his own discovery, even if it is unthinkable without the previous contributions of Kant, Hegel, Schelling, Kierkegaard, and Husserl. Its significance is best seen in its reference to Aristotle and Augustine. For Heidegger, temporality remains in the differentiation of its finitude and does not withdraw in the mediation of its self. This could be shown through the formal-dialectical determination which is a contrast to Hegel: "Temporality is the primordial 'outside-of-itself' in and for itself" (*BT,* p. 377).

[35] *BT,* p. 428.

[36] *Ibid.,* p. 437.

209

ness as its own. In this serious act, existence also receives history as its own; it does not flee into freedom from obligation (non-obligatoriness). It recognizes that it is qualified here and now through past and history, and it can only be really touched in history. But then, there are two relationships to history, the authentic and the inauthentic, for existence can be formed towards either way. Inauthentic relationship to history sees it as the simple succession of events along the endless line of flowing time. In this "objective" view of history human existence is basically untouchable by history. Authentic relationship in and to the historical comes—comes historically—out of the ground of authentic, finite, and temporal existing.

With this analysis of authentic historicity Heidegger wants to show how Dilthey's view has been fulfilled, for in a methodology of history we are concerned with "the cultivation of the hermeneutical situation which—once the historically existent *Dasein* has made its resolution—opens itself to the repetitive disclosure of what has-been-there."[37] "Hermeneutics is the way this understanding enlightens itself; it is also the methodology of historiology, though only in a derivative form."[38] But also, this is the very point which Bultmann found intriguing and which he tried to employ successfully in his own theological work. Before we turn to Bultmann's theology, we should at least ask whether Heidegger himself reaches his goal. The explication of authentic temporality, he said, would explain the question about the meaning of Being. But the third section of the first part of *Being and Time,* which was to be titled "Time and Being,"[39] never appeared. The last sentences from *Being and Time* are: "How is this mode of the temporalizing of temporality to be interpreted? Is there a way which leads from primordial *time* to the meaning of *Being*? Does *time* itself manifest itself as the horizon of

[37] *Ibid.,* p. 449.
[38] *Ibid.,* p. 450.
[39] *Ibid.,* pp. 63 f.; see also pp. 202 f.

Being?"[40] These questions have never been answered—although Heidegger's later thought has tried to give some answer. We have to agree with Otto Pöggeler when he writes: *"Being and Time* remains a fragment; the study which was set in motion never arrived in this work at its goal."[41] But it was exactly these unpublished sections from *Being and Time* to which Bultmann referred in his hermeneutical reflections. What consequences this had for his theology remains to be seen.

THEOLOGICAL HERMENEUTIC AS EXISTENTIAL INTERPRETATION

If Bultmann employed Heidegger's analysis theologically, then it was because of his interest in the process of understanding. Certainly, he emphasized again and again that individual concepts of Heidegger can be used to unravel what the Scriptures say because they are somehow the impregnated result of theology. According to Bultmann, Heidegger "never made any secret that he had been especially influenced by the New Testament (Paul in particular), and by Augustine and in a special way by Luther. . . . If anyone wants to understand Heidegger's influence on my theology, then he must keep this in view."[42] Bultmann in his theology of the New Testament interpreted biblical ideas (above all, Pauline anthropology) with Heidegger's existential insights.[43] And it can hardly be denied that an existential explication of New Testament concepts such as κόσμος, σῶμα, φῶς, and σκοτία offer a certain amount of clarity and insight, despite the controversial nature of many of the

[40] *Ibid.,* p. 488.
[41] Pöggeler, *op. cit.,* p. 64.
[42] A letter by Bultmann dated May 13, 1955, cited in G. Ittel, "Der Einfluss der Philosophie Martin Heideggers auf die Theologie Rudolf Bultmanns," *Kerygma und Dogma,* 2 (1956), p. 92.
[43] See J. Macquarrie, *An Existentialist Theology* (New York, 1956).

details.[44] More important than this historically explicable relationship between biblical and existential ideas is the basic theological-hermeneutical question: how is historical revelation to be understood inasmuch as it concerns me, decides about me, makes my salvation possible, and how can I as a theologian or preacher responsibly and intelligibly speak of this? Again and again, especially in his essay on hermeneutic,[45] Bultmann has underlined that Heidegger through his analysis of understanding and interpretation has brought this problem to an appreciably new clarity.[46]

Bultmann begins with an analysis of the hermeneutical circle, which dominates every interpretation. Schleiermacher and Dilthey before Heidegger saw the structure of this circle. At the root of their thought themes from German Idealism are at work. Every understanding and interpretation of a reality is, according to Bultmann, only possible if the interpreter has a definite *preliminary understanding* of the reality (*Vorverständnis*), in whose dimensions (*woraufhin*) he can interpret.[47] This thesis has often been misunderstood. Bultmann does not always speak too clearly, but his concept of preliminary understanding ultimately means an existential structure, "the existential *fore-structure* of *Dasein* itself."[48] *Dasein* in its Being as understanding is already planned as a "preliminary way" (*vor-weg*) towards understanding. The formal structure of existence is this: it is able to adapt unto itself some reality in the transcending dimensions in express "interpretation" ($\dot{\epsilon}\rho\mu\eta\nu\epsilon\dot{\iota}\alpha$).[49]

Theological hermeneutic must study the structure of this circle. Any theology which is intellectually responsible must understand clearly the dimensions and implications of its own preliminary understanding, or otherwise fall victim to un-

[44] On individual aspects of Bultmann's theology see G. Hasenhüttl, *Der Glaubensvollzug* (Essen, 1963), pp. 31–63.

[45] *EPT*, pp. 234–261.

[46] *Ibid.*, pp. 251 f.

[47] *Ibid.*, p. 240 f.; See *GV*, III, p. 147.

[48] *BT*, p. 195.

[49] *Ibid.*, p. 201.

reflected prejudices.[50] Every discipline has an area where it studies its own object, its own plan of procedure, its own horizon of questioning: these are the limits of its intelligible discourse. For theology this horizon, the leading direction (*woraufhin*) of its study and discourse,[51] can only be the *question of God* by which every man is moved.[52] But a question can be articulated with more or less accuracy. The problem is to ask with the greatest possible degree of accuracy: how is the question of God structured? In the following summation and interpretation of Bultmann's thought we can discern these fundamental aspects: (1) First, a preliminary understanding seen strictly as the *question* of God is not to be understood as prior possessed knowledge. A question which is *really* a question is asked in the open horizon of the entire movement of questioning and expects that it will first be limited through the answer.

(2) The question of God is a movement of existence itself, not just a question about understanding something. Because understanding is always a motion of transcending existing, the questioning about God is existence itself in its questioning activity towards God.

(3) The most extreme question possible for man is therefore not understanding asking about a causal relationship to the first causes of all beings. The most extreme possibility and furthest horizon of transcending existing (therefore, all questioning) is the possibility of this existing in its radicalness as finite transcendence. The searching quest looks for, as its ultimate, the making possible of the finite mortal existing. The question of God as the creator is thereby the same as the question of the possibility of individual existence. Inasmuch as existence is temporal and historical, this questioning itself is only possible in the horizon of historicity.[53]

[50] *GV*, III, p. 143.
[51] *EPT*, p. 241.
[52] *KuM*, II, p. 192.
[53] See Bultmann's interpretation of Jn. 1:14, in *J*, pp. 39 f.

(4) The question asks, therefore, not simply about how we can highlight existence, about the right analysis of existence, but about the *communication of existence,* about the original event which makes existing possible, which "bestows existence."[54]

(5) Existential-ontological analysis, as the illumination of existence, can give a plan for the direction of the question, its structural analysis and possible answer; it cannot mediate the event of individual and authentic existence itself. According to this understanding, we can never speak of God in theology as a pure, "objective" *An-sich* but only as the one to whom questioning existence develops itself, of the one who frees existence for authentic existence. The ultimate horizon of possible discourse is the event of the liberating encounter itself. God can be discussed only inasmuch as human existence is being discussed at the same time.[55] Philosophical existential analysis, even if it does not speak of God, has its right and role in the development of a formal preliminary-plan of authentic existence without deciding about the concrete events in this existence and without confusing the illumination of existence with its transmission. We still have to ask whether this theological interpretation of Heidegger's thought is justified or possible.

The believing understanding of this historical event of salvation which makes my own salvation possible—how does this take place? The horizon of this particular understanding cannot be an objective treatment of history. This would only present a series of historical facts. Even if someone asserts that this or that fact concerns me, still the way in which it concerns me, the kind of claim it has on me remains obscure. I can be reached, struck through history only when I in my relation to history risk myself, am radically challenged, and when my own life is made possible in this encounter with history. My own possibility of being, my own future, has to be opened, and this opening to the future must free me from the burden of the

---

[54]*KuM,* II, p. 191.
[55] See *GV,* I, pp. 26–37.

past (which always obstructs my future); I am freed unto my freedom. This demands a gathering together of my fleeing life into the present in this liberating encounter with history. The horizon of this encounter is authentic temporality, taking place in the *moment* of decision.[56] This moment of decision is not disparate from the temporality of my human existence, but rather its enabling source.[57] In the moment of decision, I decide about my past and future life.

This liberation of myself for myself cannot come through myself. I can only become what I, qualified by my past, am.[58] My freedom and my future are given only in the encounter with the liberating act of God. This act of God encounters me in the kerygma of Jesus Christ as the act of the liberating love of God.[59]

That God's love entered history and human life with Jesus Christ is not simply a fact discernible in historical-critical study, but an event which calls me in the kerygma to its sphere of influence, to its *kairos,* revealing for me the moment of my own real self-development.[60] God's saving act in Jesus of Nazareth is "eschatological" in that it calls me now, in the "now" of its event, the event which is the ultimate possibility of history, the "fullness of time" (Gal. 4:4). It calls me in my faith, giving me freedom to be myself. The eschatological event of God's revelation, then, takes place in the horizon of authentic—bestowed through God's act—temporality.

Theological hermeneutic must then have the job of highlighting theology within the horizon of this event. Hermeneutical theology, as Bultmann sees it, differs from a purely *existential* experience and expression of faith. Because theology best grows in dialogue with the structure of authentic, believing existence,

---

[56] See Hasenhüttl, *op. cit.,* pp. 228 ff.

[57] See R. Berlinger, *Das Werk der Freiheit* (Frankfurt, 1959), pp. 24 ff.

[58] *NTM,* pp. 27 f.

[59] *Ibid.,* pp. 32 ff.

[60] See *J,* pp. 39 ff.

215

it is existential in the sense of an *existential-ontological* interpretation. To speak of God's activity does not go beyond theology as existential interpretation since it is strictly referred to the event of authentic existence in time. God is seen as the liberator of the horizon of theological discourse. When Bultmann describes any discourse about God's activity as "analogical discourse,"[61] this means that the nature of analogy is strictly determined within this event itself. This also shows what Christology is. Bultmann refers to Melanchthon's sentence, *"Christum cognoscere est beneficia ejus cognoscere,"* and this means that Christology can only be seen as soteriology, and vice versa. Christology is possible only within the scope of the eschatological event of salvation and its "soteriological," "existential" interpretation. Any dogma about Christ must be interpreted in this light.

Now in the framework of this existential-ontological interpretation Bultmann's demythologizing finds its realization. The statements of the New Testament can find validity only within the event of salvation understood existentially. A presentation must "interpret the theological thoughts as the unfolding of the self-understanding awakened by the kerygma."[62] The difference for today's understanding comes, for Bultmann, from the different picture of the world given by the New Testament. He places a second criterion beside the principle of existential interpretation: the "modern, scientific view of the world."[63] Any evaluation and criticism of this aspect of Bultmann's thought must be able to discern what is based on existential interpretation and what on a particular world-view. Neither Bultmann nor Heidegger (who is quite critical of this modern concept of *Weltbild* and accepts myth as a basic form of human discourse)[64] rejects the basic historical right of mythical

---

[61] *KuM,* II, p. 197.

[62] *TNT,* II, p. 240.

[63] Heidegger, "Die Zeit des Weltbildes," *Holzwege* (Frankfurt, 1950), pp. 69–104.

[64] See Heidegger, *An Introduction to Metaphysics* (New Haven, 1959).

presentation; they do demand, however, that interpretation here and now must make it intelligible.

THE RELATIONSHIP OF BULTMANN AND HEIDEGGER—A THEOLOGICAL QUESTION

Heidegger's existential-ontological analysis became relevant for Bultmann through a particular thesis; Heidegger had adequately worked out the question of authentic self-existence.[65] Philosophy cannot answer the question of where God is concretely encountered. Its achievement is a "formal" and "neutral" analysis of the possibility of authentic understanding and existing, the development of this formally and existentially without saying what is the direction (or goal) towards which human existence concretely (that is, existentially, personally) is opened. "So, the believing comprehension of the sensitivity of human existence is not misdirected by analyzing this existence as leading to the question towards God, but rather is explained."[66]

Bultmann can find support in the fact that for Heidegger existential-ontological analysis includes no existential prior decision. "Existential interpretation will never seek to take over any authoritarian pronouncement as to those things which, from an *existentiell* point of view, are possible or binding."[67] "In the existential analysis we cannot, in principle, discuss what *Dasein factically* resolves in any particular case."[68] "The resoluteness in which *Dasein* comes back to itself, discloses current factical possibilities of authentic existing, and discloses them *in terms of the heritage* which that resoluteness, as thrown, *takes* over."[69]

The decisive question is, however, whether existence can be

[65] See *KuM*, II, p. 192.   [66] *Ibid.*, p. 194.
[67] *BT*, p. 360.   [68] *Ibid.*, p. 434.
[69] *Ibid.*, p. 435.

217

encountered by revelation. Bultmann, at any rate, develops an analysis of existence which seems to imply it could indicate authentic self-being made possible through existence itself, radical self-assertion of man which in itself is despair.[70] It can interpret itself only in a questioning openness. It is clear that here we have the decision on how existential analysis is open to theology, and how theology is determined through this philosophy.[71]

We have already noted that *Being and Time* remains a fragment, and its question is still there in the concluding pages —how the manifestation of time temporally (*Zeitigung der Zeit*) should be conceived. In general we must concede that the analyses in *Being and Time* are ambiguous. Existence becomes itself transparent in the feeble power of its finite, thrown being-to, which finds its enablement in the finite event of itself for which it is not competent. This self-illumination (not fully determined) introduces two modifications: *Dasein* can grasp itself in its power-less power, and can assert itself in the overpoweringness of beings only by having decided for itself. In his later writings Heidegger interprets this self-understanding as metaphysics, which in its inner nature is nihilism. *Dasein* can also (and this is the possibility which is newly explicated in the so-called "reversal" [*Kehre*]) understand itself in reference to Being, out of the truth of Being which is a "mittence" to finite *Dasein*. Temporality remains the ontological basic event; Being itself illumines itself in the temporally ec-static, open differentiation of *Dasein*. Existence is ec-sistence as and for an openness to Being related already to *Da-sein* as There-Being. Temporality comes to pass as time in the event of the uniting of Being and *Dasein*. A "converted" thinking thinks *Dasein* out of the mystery of Being disclosing itself, as event. It brings this event as such to speech recalling for us that language and interpretation—hermeneutic—is only possible

[70] *NTM,* p. 29.
[71] See J. B. Metz, "Christliche Philosophie," *LThK,* II, pp. 1141–1147.

out of this event, and that this event is, hermeneutically, the more original.[72]

We have now overlapped into *Being and Time*'s point of departure, seeing that the analyses developed there must be considered out of a prior happening. This prior event guards and confirms them, rather than simply denying them. Temporality and historicity remain the horizon of all human existence now considered more deeply in its origins.

This is not the place to discuss in detail the question of God in Heidegger's thought.[73] Basically, it is a question of whether historically finite existence can be absolutely encountered in its ground through revelation, whether existence not only illumines but can be communicated (that is, bestowed), *or* whether the horizon of existential concrete possibility is limited to what existence on the basis of its facticity can be drawing on itself. While Karl Jaspers not only rejected any concretizing of historical revelation, but also conceived transcendence in a thoroughly undialectical, monological way (as what simply appears in the free actualization of existence),[74] Heidegger, at least in his later interpretation of *Being and Time,* has thought out the Being of man in an ultimately dialogical way as open to absolute encounter. When theology and philosophy meet, it is exactly here at this openness. We can reverse the question, and ask whether many basically theological expressions in Heidegger's thought have not been philosophically "naturalized." The question, in whose occurring *kairos* (transcending every authentic historicity) God himself en-

---

[72] Schulz, *op. cit.,* p. 221.

[73] See J. Moller, *Existentialphilosophie und katholische Theologie* (Paderborn, 1952); H. Ott, *Denken und Sein* (Zollikon, 1959); J. M. Robinson, J. B. Cobb, Jr., eds. *The Later Heidegger and Theology* (New York, 1963); B. Welte, "Die Gottesfrage im Denken Heideggers," *Auf der Spur des Ewigen* (Freiburg, 1965), pp. 262–276.

[74] See H. Fahrenbach, "Philosophische Existenzerhellung and theologische Existenzmitteilung: Zur Auseinandersetzung zwischen Karl Jaspers und Rudolf Bultmann," *Theologische Rundschau* (NF), 24 (1957/58), pp. 77–99; 105–135.

counters us, is no longer a question for philosophy, but for man being grasped by faith.

Bultmann's adoption of the analyses in *Being and Time* through his own interpretation cannot simply be qualified as unjustified as much as individual points may be questioned. Some ambiguousness in *Being and Time* enables Bultmann to present his specifically dialectical-theological interpretation of the paradoxical identity between the event of salvation and the historical event, the Word in preaching and the Word of God, authentic moment and the eschatological moment, the ultimately dialogical paradox of the affected, free encountering event of revelation.

Heidegger's and Bultmann's points of departure have a historical rightness about them. Still, should theological hermeneutic as existential interpretation exclude other aspects? *Being and Time* did not successfully develop the authentic temporality of discourse.[75] The incompleteness in Bultmann's theology of language and his too sharp separation between the *historisch* and the *geschichtlich* might be considered as effects of this. In the New Testament the Word belongs (this is shown by the purely literary character of the gospels with their relation to tradition and traditions) to the very constitution of the saving event. The structure of the eschatological event of our salvation is fundamentally manifest in a unity of event and interpreting Word. The way in which the event reaches the Word, opening itself in this Word of address and witness, is ultimately not thought out in Bultmann's theology. Ernst Fuchs and Gerhard Ebeling have developed this area of hermeneutic.

Moreover, Bultmann apparently has not correctly seen the hermeneutic function of death in Heidegger's analysis. The unity of the preaching, of the life and death of Jesus, Jesus' resurrection as fulfilling completion, escapes his interpretation. An "implicit Christology" in all of this is not developed.[76]

[75] See *BT*, pp. 400 f.
[76] Bultmann, *Das Verhältnis der urchristlichen Christusbotschaft zum historischen Jesus, op. cit.*, pp. 15–17.

220

A well-known absence in *Being and Time* is the lack of seeing "Being-with" (*Mitsein*) within an analysis of intersubjectivity and social existence. Following upon this is a similar absence in Bultmann's thought of questions about intersubjective existence and social communication, the social dimension of the kerygma, and the eschaton as the unfolding of the future of a being who is with others.

It is beyond the purpose of this essay to indicate how Heidegger is active within Catholic theology, active within an existential and existential-ontological hermeneutic in the widest sense of developing Christology, the Trinity, grace, and eschatology.[77] Karl Rahner and Bernhard Welte have made beginnings here.

If we speak today of a Bultmannian theology, then this means too that theologians and pastors can no longer return to a position before him. Many of the problems which he developed, stimulated by Heidegger's thought, still remain stimulative and crucial on the philosophical and theological levels. To have seen these directions clearly is not the least of Bultmann's important contributions.

[77] An example might be Karl Rahner, S.J., "The Hermeneutics of Eschatological Assertions," *Theological Investigations,* IV (Baltimore, 1966), pp. 323–46.

X. BULTMANN AND TOMORROW'S THEOLOGY

By Thomas F. O'Meara

Bultmann's work during the first half of the twentieth century has raised or focused most of the questions polarizing and expanding today's theology. The Christian churches in the last four decades of this century are faced with the challenges raised by the social, political, and intellectual revolutions of the preceding years. But now, the questions, the problems, the issues before the churches are awaiting answers.

In contrast to the content of Karl Barth's dogmatics, Bultmann's work appears as an outline for theology, for *theology challenged to rethink its mission radically*. We are struck by today's questions in his writings, but few accept or clearly perceive there the full answer.

To understand today's revolution and tomorrow's theology, we must distinguish three levels in Bultmann's work. First, there is the level of historical-critical exegesis, of scholarly studies on the religious world at the time of the composition of the New Testament; secondly, there is the view of the New Testament writings as different theologies, responses by Greek, gnostic, Aramaic, Jewish minds to revelation; finally, there is Bultmann's practical, pastoral theology for today—demythologizing. Once we have distinguished these horizons with their principles and goals, it is equally important to realize their interplay. Even Bultmann's critical exegesis is based on implicit hermeneutical

222

principles, principles which are presupposed and which become explicit in demythologizing. On the other hand, the theology of demythologizing draws upon the view of the New Testament developed by critical exegesis. For instance, the affirmation that all revelation is verbally bound in a theology, the need for demythologizing, the rejection of the miraculous in John, the identification of the "coming" of a divine person in John or Luke with gnostic myths[1]—these stem from a radical setting aside of any self-disclosing presence of God beyond yet in history. And so, although it is important to distinguish his important commentary on John from his pastoral program of demythologizing, it is legitimate to say that the basic hermeneutical principles for each level of his thought are the same.

There is a corresponding, general criticism for all three levels. It flows from the word-centered nature of Bultmann's thought and is being corrected by theologies of process (Ogden), of history (Pannenberg), of the future (Metz, Moltmann), of society (Cox). Word, idea, meaning in Bultmann's thought have a terminal quality. Human wrestling with a unique revelation is categorized as myth or theology; the dialogue between God and man is realized in the preached word of God's acceptance, in human faith and existential meaning. Form-criticism is not really so much a key to the narrated person, event, life, or situation (*Sitz im Leben*), but a guide to theology-making verbalized by the community. Theology itself, human language, and conceptualization cannot, ultimately, speak of God either from the point of view of Bultmann's affirmation that to speak

---

[1] For instance, Bultmann designates the passage Lk. 12:49, "I have come to cast fire upon the earth," as gnostic (*The History of the Synoptic Tradition* [New York, 1963], pp. 154 ff., 162 ff.). Yet in the Coptic, gnostic *Gospel of Thomas* (logion 10), we have a real gnostic version of this passage. Does gnosticism extend *ad infinitum?* This questions anew the transference of similarities in form from the complex religious milieu of the first century not only to the form but to the meaning of the New Testament. What we might call the middle principles of Bultmann's work, the expansion, for instance, of the form-criticism method or his general insights into Hellenism and Paul to the all-embracing positions working against the tradition and letter of the text, become one-sided, based on presuppositions either unexpressed or simply asserted.

of God is to speak of man, or from demythologizing's ultimate conclusion—the one act of God accepting us. It is neither the universe, the New Testament, nor God who demands demythologizing, but the mental framework of "modern man." Bultmann in a sense did return to the "material," the real concerns of theology; he went beyond historicism, psychologism, and Hegel. But for him understanding is in the material itself. Existential interpretation makes the word to be God's Word for me. The prior hermeneutic for me is not just an interpretation (for then it could be a pure falsification of the text) but is intrinsic to what is said.

Theology has been concerned in the past few years with what Husserl took as his motto and unrealized goal—*zu den Sachen selbst:* to the realities, the things, the happenings, the people themselves. It is not enough to discern the role of New Testament theology and community. It must disclose the things and persons their words express.[2] Going beyond the limitations of word to the realities of life and history and existential interpretation can have a liberating effect. Bultmann's limitation of God's action to existential meaning and of transcendence to existence is narrow enough to be a return to mythologization in an opposite direction.

To return to Bultmann and theology tomorrow. Why is Bultmann's influence so extensive? Why has he suggested so many problematics? Not because of the conclusions of his theology but because of his response to the needs of the kerygma-world dialogue. Within book and essay we find the demand that Christian preaching and theology be existentially

---

[2] "The act of the believer's faith terminates not in a mental proposition but in a reality" (Thomas Aquinas, *Summa theologiae*, II–II, q. 1, a. 2, ad 2). The recognition of Pauline and Johannine theologies is to agree basically with Bultmann. The problem is to reconcile individual and communal believing reaction (more than interpretation) to Jesus the Christ with the preserving role of the Spirit and the Scripture for coming generations. And, then, we set out this believing reflection, this varied intensity of interpretation of the existential phenomena of Jesus' life in the Christ-event (which can be called a theology yet a privileged one distinct from that of Augustine, Aquinas, or Luther). See K. Rahner, "Theology in the New Testament," *Theological Investigations,* V (Baltimore, 1966), pp. 23–41.

and meaningfully encountered by man today. Is not this entire endeavor grounded in Bultmann's early realization that the world had become radically secular? Catholic theology, especially, is going through a decade of "destruction" (in Heidegger's understanding), forging new horizons of Christian understanding. The future emerging from today's confusing situation (this future will not be less confusing for mentalities formed as ours have been), tomorrow's reflection on being Christ-in-the-world will not be a continuous evolution, but a retrieve of the past Person and on-going Spirit of Jesus Christ.

To try to approach this future, let us look at some key issues in the present Roman Catholic theological revolution, issues definitely related to the thought of Rudolf Bultmann: (a) hermeneutic and analogy—the problem of God-talk; (b) the event of Jesus Christ as personal anthropology; (c) theology as Christian anthropology. Then we will go on to their roles in tomorrow's theology. To discuss Bultmann as a stimulus to Roman Catholic theology is not to imply that Catholic theology is fully separate from Protestant theology. There can be a basic Christian theology for Christians inasmuch as they share fundamental realities of revelation. Here the present needs, revolution, self-understanding, tradition of Roman Catholicism question Bultmann in a dialogue with trends. This is more a motion towards enlightenment than a critique.

BULTMANN AND THE CONTEMPORARY ROMAN CATHOLIC THEOLOGICAL REVOLUTION

Hermeneutic and Analogy: The Problem of God-Talk

Bultmann's pastoral demand to demythologize the New Testament record of God's revelation in Jesus Christ is in his own words, "a hermeneutic method."[3] "The real problem, in other

___
[3] *KM,* I, p. 191.

words, is the hermeneutic one, that is, the problem of interpreting the Bible and the teachings of the church in such a way
that they can become understandable as a summons to man."[4]
Karl Rahner traces the entire debate over demythologizing to
the problem of "the meaning of eschatological statements in
general,"[5] that is, the interpretation of transcendent statements
and their relationship to Scripture, experience, and faith. For
Bultmann, the reason for demythologizing and the center of
revelatory Word-events is man; human existence is the
hermeneutic of the Word and event of God in Jesus; meaning-
fulness for human daily life is the interpreter of God's one
action of acceptance of us in the cross. Out of this Heideggerian
insight grew the new hermeneutic's approach to Bible and
Christianity, which is one of the dimensions of the world-wide
encounter between language, communication, and theology.[6]

Aristotelian philosophy and the medieval theology of the
analogy of being are related to this. But, it should not be thought
that challenging developments and new points of view are pre-
contained in Aquinas's thought on analogy. Apart from Rahner's
efforts (and Maréchal's and de Petter's lesser known but important epistemological contributions) on biblical theology, the
evolution of dogma, Catholic theology has been at a standstill
in the area of religious language for decades.[7] Analogy (the
entire problematic of man talking about God) is as difficult as

---

[4] *Myth and Christianity* (New York, 1958), p. 60.

[5] "The Hermeneutics of Eschatological Assertions," *Theological Investigations,* IV (Baltimore, 1966), pp. 323–330, 334.

[6] For a survey of the state of the question and the roles of Heidegger
and Bultmann, see John Macquarrie, *God-talk* (New York, 1967).

[7] "The Development of Dogma," *Theological Investigations,* I (Baltimore, 1961), pp. 39–78; "Considerations on the Development of
Dogma," *Theological Investigations,* IV (Baltimore, 1967), pp. 3–35;
"Überlegungen zur Dogmententwicklung," *Mysterium Salutis,* I (Einsiedeln, 1965). On de Petter and Maréchal, see E. Schillebeeckx, "The
Concept of Truth and Related Problems," *Ecumenism and the Roman
Catholic Church* (Westminster, 1966), pp. 142–186. Paul Tillich once
thought that his symbolic theology was the same as Aquinas's analogy;
recent Catholic study on analogy has spent itself on the role of Cajetan
as interpreter of Aquinas.

it is crucial. When the insight of Pseudo-Denis and Aquinas have been exhausted, the precise way in which terms and realities are referable to the totally-other God (as known by us in a way where concepts and words have twofold orientation without "containing" both realities) is far from satisfying.[8] The tenuousness presented in Aquinas's teaching of proportions and proportionalities has not been sufficiently emphasized nor is the possibility of real affirmation of the non-empirical (epistemological contact between the divine and created analogues) through proportion clear.

Analogy is taught in theology but is theology taught analogously? The extent of analogy in all of theology and the multiple problem of religious language is rarely shown in the New Testament theologies, in the sacraments, in community and ministry. How often do we recall that analogy is a form of non-knowledge, a form of equivocation? Basically, we do not know God. Bultmann rightly rejects any theology which makes God an object of an intellectual discipline without qualification, which allows man through his mind with or without faith to pull God into a universe science tells us is empirically closed.[9] He rejects the theology which disclaims the existential impact in the individual's acceptance of Christ. There are ways in which the subject-object structure could be overcome, not eliminated but described by dialogue between subject and object, an interplay and exchange in the pre-analytic stage.[10] God is both the object

---

[8] Schillebeeckx, *art. cit.*, pp. 156 ff.

[9] See T. O'Meara, "Rudolf Bultmann's Theology of God," *Irish Theological Quarterly,* 34 (1967), pp. 37–60.

[10] "Heidegger has given himself the task to overcome, to go beyond the subject-object scheme. This does not mean he suffers from the illusion that this frame of reference can simply be done away with. He realizes too well that this subject-object scheme remains basically unchangeable. . . . Heidegger offers in contrast to the ontology of non-existentially related things (*Ontologie der Vorhandenheit*), in which the subject-object scheme is founded, another ontology (that of *Dasein*)" (G. Noller, *Sein und Existenz* [Munich, 1962], p. 46). See Bultmann, *Myth and Christianity,* p. 58. Schmittals adds: "This distance between subject and object does not correspond to the original understanding of man, world, and God. If 'encounter' meant for modern thought grasping an

and mysterious formality of religious affirmation. Faith grounds the horizon from which Christian reflection and life can be lived; this faith is the gift of God, the presence of God's grace for personal dialogue in us. Faith does not build a supranaturalistic world upon the real world, but allows the horizon, the dimensions, the dynamic of life to be through, and to go further towards, Christ. God is not only the object of our faith but the initiator and cause of it. By justification and faith God is present in us. We need to know, then, more about the epistemology of faith before we can be too sure about the epistemology of theology. The ground of both never lies at our disposal nor is it their mission to speak to us of God himself. Revelation is for us; yet its past, happened dimension remains, and must become, necessarily, meaningful for us today, the only hearers of the Word.[11] Christian truth coming from faith is beginning salvation, disturbance and hope, truth and promise; it is not a pedagogical analysis for me. Revelation through the Word made flesh and blood is not knowledge of God but the realities of how God is for all of us.

For any participation in the dialogue of grace,[12] the point of departure and horizon will be the human hearer and knower. The problem of hermeneutic and analogy is man. The experi-

---

object *through me,* 'encounter' meant originally that the encounter offers something for me. For example it is not possible to see in the Bible man as an isolated object contrasted to God and world. . . . Bultmann likes to clarify this problem with the phenomenon of love, friendship or trust. Can I, as subject, picture love as an object, "objectify" it so that it is only the object of my thought, discourse and judgment?" (W. Schmittals, *Die Theologie Rudolf Bultmanns* [Tübingen, 1966] pp. 30–31).

[11] Thomas Aquinas, *Summa Theologiae,* I, q. 1, a. 1; G. Ebeling, "The Hermeneutical Locus of the Doctrine of God in Peter Lombard and Thomas Aquinas," *Journal for Theology and the Church,* 3 (1967), pp. 70–111.

[12] "Revealed religion is essentially a dialogue, an encounter of man with the living God; it is a *theologal,* personal relationship to God thanks to grace or thanks to the personal summons of God" (E. Schillebeeckx, "Die Heiligung des Namens Gottes. . . . ," *Gott in Welt,* II, [Freiburg, 1964], p. 43).

ence of reality precedes and determines all religious and transcendent references, even the New Testament Word and faith.
Bultmann may subjectivize the biblical letter and the expressed
reality and so move his hermeneutic of demythologizing to
man's existence. This cannot escape the fact that all religious
words, even "God," "existence," and "meaning," are analogous
and mysterious surrounded by the horizons and problems of
language and grace. Analogy looks to the proportionate, derived,
related and relative, negative content of the terms we use. Until
now the permission for a double-directed, analogous affirmation
of both "God" and man "existing" was derived from creation
as a caused project of God. This tenuous relationship of cosmic
dependence grounded what was referred to God by virtue of
either Christian revelation or God's creative activity. God's
being-in-act is unknown, but something about him might be
hesitantly affirmed under these multiple conditions. This is,
naturally, not to answer the problem of God-talk but to mention some ontological conditions, equally as necessary as
epistemological ones.[13]

A new approach lies in Heidegger's analysis of the lighting-
process, the presence of Being and truth before man's existence.
W. J. Richardson writes of Being and man's knowing in
Heidegger:

> In this new phase (the "later Heidegger"), what is to be said of
> Being? It reveals itself as *alētheia* in beings and as being, but be-
> cause of itself Being is not a being, it hides itself in beings too. As
> a result, every manifestation of Being is finite, i.e., is constricted
> within the finite beings that it lets appear. Every revealment, then,
> is at once a concealment of the rich plenitude of Being, and this
> phenomenon of simultaneous revealment-concealment Heidegger
> calls mystery. . . . Now what characterizes any given epoch of
> history is precisely the way Being reveals itself in beings at a given
> time.[14]

---

[13] Schillebeeckx, *art. cit.*
[14] W. J. Richardson, "Heidegger and Theology," *Theological Studies,*
26 (1965), pp. 94–95.

These few remarks indicate another approach to the problem of religious language. Instead of man abstracting concepts from the created world and applying them to the Creator, instead of concentrating on the dynamism or illuminism of the human intellect, Heidegger's thought suggests both dimensions: man the knower before whom Being discloses and simultaneously hides itself in beings, and the transcendent character of Being. How this can be developed so that Being discloses and hides directions towards God, so that Being becomes neither a super concept nor a super reality, and so that this ontological disclosure does not become a revelation in nature parallel to Christocentric grace and faith (nor a Barthian verification of our concepts and words), remains to be seen. At least such thinking opens up new possibilities.

Roman Catholic theologians owe much to Bultmann for their mounting realization that we cannot speak to the problem of religious language only in terms of *analogia entis*. Actually, both the world and all religious problems occur in a dual dimension of the secular and the religious, the existential and the Christian, therefore in nature and grace. Men rarely approach God outside of faith-moments, and in all men life is the horizon of offered or rejected Christian grace, the supernatural existential. The bare affirmation of a true secular humanist can disclose an "anonymous Christian," a man whose authentic human dimensions implicitly are Christian on both the epistemological and ontological-theological levels. To affirm man truly is to affirm Christ.[15]

---

[15] "A man who lets go and jumps, falls into the abyss that is there, not only as far as he has plumbed it. To accept and assume one's human condition without reserve (and just who does so remains obscure) is to accept the Son of man, because in him God has accepted and assumed man. If Scripture declares that he who loves his neighbor has fulfilled the law, this is the ultimate truth for the reason that God himself has become this neighbor, so that whenever we accept and love our neighbor we are at the same time accepting and loving the one Neighbor who is nearest of all to us and farthest of all from us" (K. Rahner, "Jesus Christ," *Theological Dictionary* [New York, 1965], pp. 241–242).

Bultmann supposes that, if it were possible for Christian thinking to rid itself of the mythological imagery, faith in God and Jesus Christ would be attractive for contemporary man. The difficulty is deeper. Whatever the image, it is only an expression of the fundamental, problematical analogy (of reality and of idea) between man, and God "beyond" this world of our experience. This problem is illumined by Bultmann, but it is not answered, even initially, for he himself retreats to an undeveloped "analogy."[16]

Christology

There is a paradox in Bultmann's theology. Although God becomes alive through Christian faith in Jesus' cross and our accepted existence, there seems to be little specifically Christian about this faith or about the means by which God acts for man. The "content" of Christianity is limited to a man who dies on the cross, and the paradox of faith is that there is no reason to accept this particular man as the definitive saving event. Jesus Christ's being becomes God's action for man, but Christ has no significant role here other than inspirational. Bultmann writes: "That God has acted in Jesus Christ is, however, not a fact of past history open to historical verification. . . . Since it is faith in the crucified and risen Christ, this self-understanding is not an autonomous movement of the human world but the response to the Word of God, which proclaims the manifestation of the grace of God in Jesus Christ."[17]

Bultmann's Christianity raises the question as to whether it

16 *KM,* I, pp. 196 ff.

17 *KM,* I, pp. 207–209; Günther Bornkamm writes that throughout Bultmann's theology "Jesus Christ has become a mere saving fact. Everything which goes beyond this brutum factum, one might almost say this periodic 'thatness' of the saving fact, is for Bultmann either past history or mythology" (Demythologizing in the New Testament," *Kerygma and History,* eds. C. E. Braaten and R. A. Harrisville [Nashville, 1962], p. 186).

fulfills the religious demands of man, or whether it is another form of liberalism, a too secular faith planning the secular city rather than bringing light to it. This negative role in Bultmann's theology raises the Christological question: can Jesus Christ remain central in a faith where "myth" includes everything beyond our experience?

Is there not a connection between Bultmann's centering Christianity in God-man actions and his minimalization of the Incarnation? The constant longing for incarnation in man begins again; the ancient theological problem of immanence and transcendence, the union of the divine with the human, is radically unsolved. Without a real, important, and permanent presence of God in Jesus of Nazareth, Bultmann's theology as a perspective may seem to be post-Christian . . . or pre-Christian. Actually, in Bultmann's theology of God, God takes the place of Christ. God's encounters with man are all of the same cloth, taking place within man's existence. Bultmann's description of our encounter with God in our neighbor drawn from Matthew's Gospel overlooks exactly this point.[18] The Christian who fed the hungry man, visited the sick and imprisoned, did indeed encounter the divine, the presence of the ultimate judgment, but he did so not in encountering God himself, but in Jesus Christ. Jesus Christ makes the situation (it is not merely a parable) fully meaningful because he is both man and God, both the sufferer on earth and the transcendent. The purpose of this pericope is Christological; man encounters now the "eschatological," not in God but in Jesus Christ. Bultmann says that Paul solved the philosophical problem of how God could contact the world by making use of Gentile formulas about a mediator, a Son of God who is both God and man.[19] Nevertheless, their basis could be a definitive entrance of God in history presented in Paul's theology of this extra-theological. The event is fully comprehensible only by faith focused on history.

[18] Bultmann, "The Idea of God and Modern Man," *Journal for Theology and the Church,* 2 (1966), pp. 83–95.
[19] Bultmann, "Jesus and Paul," *EF,* pp. 183 ff.

A theology of God and man without sufficient reference to Christ as person, teaching, and event for the knowledge and action of God is also a fault of Catholic theology. Bultmann has shown that a theology of God must be anthropocentric. But it must also be Christocentric. The appeal of Teilhard de Chardin's theology of the Christic divine milieu of our evolving cosmos includes both dimensions. Faith must be our faith, but faith in God and Christ is a risk, a risk to trust them, not ourselves.

Zu den Sachen selbst, to the things themselves! Bultmann rightly describes Jesus Christ on the cross as an event, yet he does not go far enough. The only anchoring place among the different (but not necessarily opposed) Christologies of the New Testament is to see them as biblical, interpretive, Spirit-guided reflections and reactions to the fullness which was the man Jesus Christ. He is neither an undistinguished man nor a Chalcedonian structure, but an event which can never be fathomed or totally expressed by any one culture or theology. Biblical Christologies are privileged interpretations, true and partial, born of faith yet formed in a limited perspective. The event of Jesus is both personal (ontological) and active, both Christic and salvific.

Bultmann remains within the Chalcedonian framework inasmuch as his human monophysitism is at one end of the spectrum. Jesus Christ is not proclaimed, does not fulfill his human transcendence with a personal-ontological continuity with the Father. Faith rather than grasping Christ by these interpretations fabricates them. The problem for theology after Bultmann, especially in dialogue with more history-oriented theologians such as the Pannenberg circle, is to show how faith and history, the transcendent and the empirical, meet in Jesus Christ. This emphasizes the person and happenings narrated rather than a past communal religious experience or a contemporary theological hermeneutic.

The entire panoply of Roman Catholic theological enterprise, from curriculum and catechetics to graduate studies, is entering the disquieting era of recognizing the human factors in the New

Testament witness and message. The increased interest and consequent confusion is not surprising since most Christians come to the complex world of the New Testament with one of two old and insufficient Christological mentalities: the first is that of Chalcedon; the second is the nineteenth-century Protestant biographies of Jesus as the good man and ethical teacher. For centuries there has been no real, full encounter between the biblical witness to Jesus and our contemporary human life. From the Chalcedonian perspective (which can be both true and inadequate), Christ is said to have two natures and one divine person. Yet today nature implies the expanse of verdure, and person indicates the human psychological dimension. The conclusion was that whereas Jesus "has" a humanity he "is" God. Just the opposite is true: he is a man and this man-ness has some mysterious ontological grounding in the reality we call God. A contemporary Christology will be man-centered; it will see the reality of Christ, the person-event of Jesus of Nazareth becoming the Christ in social, historical, dynamic, and personal terms corresponding to the dimensions prominent in the New Testament. This Christ will speak to confused anguish and to hopeful future, to emerging and to automated nation, to the poor, the defeated, the discriminated, the questioning. Its revolutionary nature will stand over against churches and nations who refuse to renew to serve men, and over against totalitarian systems which prefer revolution to individuals. Jesus will refuse to identify himself with the establishment—political, ecclesiastical, or philosophical-theological; he will offer life, answer, truth, and hope, but these will not be only of this world. In short, Jesus' being-a-man in the *Logos,* his being-in-the-world, his life-towards-death-and-resurrection, will center in Jesus the man and will thereby be God's affirmation with reservation of the transcendence of humanity. Since Christ is the beginning and end of Christianity, Christian theology takes a more man-centered point of view, a view which is Christocentric and theocentric (with God acting for man and remaining mysterious).

234

Theology as Christian Anthropology

In 1933 Bultmann dedicated the first volume of his collected essays on exegetical and theological topics to Martin Heidegger, "in thankful remembrance for the time together in Marburg." That Heidegger influenced Bultmann's theology—even prior to his essay on demythologizing (which was not a new direction but consistent with his previous work)—is clear. But in 1941 with his program for interpreting rather than eliminating the mythical content of the New Testament, an interpretation which would be according to Heideggerian existentialism, Bultmann became linked to Heidegger.[20] Heidegger's interpretation of man's existence in the world was not to be a substitute for the New Testament message; it was a profane analysis of human existence (*Dasein*) remarkably similar to the New Testament, to some extent based on Christian theology. Nor was it correct to say that Christianity was not needed, for the existential analysis of man could not bring its own fulfillment as the Christ-event and faith could.[21] Heidegger seems to agree that Bultmann had understood his analysis of man correctly.[22]

What was crucial in this area, however, was that only one aspect of Heidegger's thought had been employed—his analysis of man (*Dasein*).[23] An impression of the full extent of Heidegger's fundamental ontology cannot be gotten from Bultmann.

[20] *KM,* I, pp. 15, 16, 24 ff.

[21] "Here, then, is the crucial distinction between the New Testament and existentialism, between the Christian faith and the natural understanding of Being. The New Testament speaks and faith knows of an act of God through which man becomes capable of self-commitment, capable of faith and love, of his authentic life" (*KM,* I, p. 33).

[22] G. W. Ittel substantiates this with letters from Bultmann and Heidegger; see "Der Einfluss der Philosophie Martin Heideggers auf die Theologie Rudolf Bultmanns," *Kerygma und Dogma,* 2 (1956), pp. 90–108.

[23] On the reaction of Bultmann and his pupils to the charge that they did not fully understand Heidegger, see *The Later Heidegger and Theology* (New York, 1963), pp. 63 ff.

Heinrich Ott, by establishing a dialogue between Barth and Heidegger, suggested new possibilities; theology could find a fullness of new perspectives.[24] Heidegger is concerned with existential ontology and hermeneutic. Heidegger's "retrieve" of ontology opens new perspectives for theology which is personal, existential, and ontological in dynamic categories. An anthropocentric-existential perspective sets the scene. Furthermore, the forgetfulness of Being in metaphysics for Heidegger is a neglect of analogy, while the discovery of the mystery and fullness of Being in beings takes place in the dimensions of time, history, language, and ontological truth. Beyond Being is the holy and only then can the word "God" be introduced. Reality discloses itself before man, lighting up his finitude, concerns, secularity, inter-personal nature, historicity.

The healthy upheaval within Roman Catholicism since John XXIII is a shift from the theocentric to the anthropocentric. Rahner, Schillebeeckx, Metz, join with their younger American counterparts in calling for a theology which can be described as a Christian anthropology, a Christian humanism.[25] The man in these terms is the man who lives in the secular city, or the third world. The task of theology is to realize how profoundly the individual man affects the faith and worship he creates and needs. It no longer ignores the transcendental structure of knowledge, the form of the subconscious, the eventual as well as symbolic role of language, the pressure of economic system and social forms. Only men alive today exist; all others past and future are not concerns of the Christian mission. Proclaimed Scripture, meaningful religious education, correlated theology, valid Church structures and sacramental worship leading to community *diakonia,* find their practical realization in men today. Just as the New Testament is for men (as Jesus Christ died and rose for men), so Christian preaching and reflection (theology)

---

[24] *Geschichte und Heilsgeschichte* (Tübingen, 1955); *Denken und Sein* (Zurich, 1959); *The Later Heidegger and Theology.*
[25] See the various essays in *The Word in History* (New York, 1966).

can and must be centered in man. Bultmann has helped form this fundamental shift and its nuances.

BULTMANN AND TOMORROW'S THEOLOGY

Partially, tomorrow's theology will be the extension and variations not just of dialogue with Bultmann but of his own achievement. Three areas have already attained prominence in a post-Bultmannian way: (a) the Jesus of history and the Christ of faith; (b) the new hermeneutic; (c) secularization. Each of these, paradoxically, implies a return to the reality beyond the word (this is true even of the new hermeneutic where the word is the reality interpreted by man).[26]

The New Quest for the Historical Jesus

Along with the other dialectical theologians Bultmann shared the views that Christianity depends on faith, not philosophy, that God is totally different from man, that Christianity and faith do have a reference to the historical cross. As is well known, Barth, Tillich, and Bultmann went their separate ways.[27] Although the latter two were skeptical about knowing Jesus in history, both (Tillich states he followed Bultmann here) did go beyond the barrier which Albert Schweitzer had erected before the historical Jesus. Bultmann raised anew the question of the

[26] The theologians of the New Hermeneutic, and post-Bultmannians in general, have not been able to participate in this growing theological movement back to the realities themselves. H. G. Gadamer, the most important philosopher of these hermeneutical directions after Heidegger, has spoken of an "ontological turn in hermeneutic." This is not surprising if we recall that for Heidegger neither phenomenology, fundamental-ontology, the horizon of *Dasein,* nor language is ever set aside or rendered passé. See *Wahrheit und Methode* (Tübingen, 1960) p. 77, 261–465.

[27] See J. D. Smart, *The Divided Mind of Modern Theology* (Philadelphia, 1967).

relationship of our faith to the man Jesus by affirming the central role of Jesus on the cross.

Students and colleagues of Bultmann have reopened various possibilities for determining what the New Testament can and does tell us about Jesus in history. Günther Bornkamm and Erich Dinkler (Heidelberg), Herbert Braun (Mainz), Hans Conzelmann (Göttingen), Gerhard Ebeling and Ernst Käsemann (Tübingen), Ernst Fuchs (Marburg), and James M. Robinson (U.S.)—each has his own development of Bultmann's stimulus of a "new quest for the historical Jesus."[28] For political and theological reasons these post-Bultmannians dominate the German Protestant theological faculties, and their work has great influence in the United States. Vis-à-vis the Protestant churches, who have misgivings about the influence of Bultmannism,[29] Käsemann gave ecumenical voice to today's liberal theology at the Faith and Order Conference at Montreal in 1963. The post-Bultmannians are concerned with Jesus' personal history and how it grounds the rest of the New Testament writings which are the witness and product of faith, theologies, interpretations.

What the new quest claims to have established is that Jesus confronted his hearers with the God who is near when he proclaimed God's reign being near. Jesus intended an historical encounter with himself to be an eschatological encounter with God. Jesus' human existence raised the paradox that he was the bringer of eschatological salvation. While this new quest has opened critical Protestant exegesis to the action of Jesus in history, it has not offered any convincing or verifiable guidelines by either ecclesial faith or by historical method for when the New Testament writings are unfolding history or when

[28] For a detailed description of this movement and these exegetes, see James M. Robinson, *The New Quest of the Historical Jesus* (London and New York, 1959).

[29] The movement within the German Evangelical (Lutheran) Church called "No Other Gospel" now numbers tens of thousands who are concerned about the preaching of a demythologized Gospel in the parish pulpit.

238

they are commenting theologically upon it. Each of the post-Bultmannians has his own standards, his own hermeneutics of history. We must agree with Bultmann that each discipline does have a hermeneutic or method and prior suppositions. But, if these are not to be prejudices or closed opinions, they must in some way be measured by the message, hence the life and history of the man they are trying to convey. Human existence may be one hermeneutic for the revelation of God in Jesus Christ, but it is one-sided, coming subsequent (because the New Testament is "good news") to Jesus himself, to his person and history.

The New Hermeneutic

Language is moving to the center of culture and Christian theology: the mass media, the electronic oneness of world-history, dialogue between continents, religious education, symbol (Jung and Tillich), myth (Bultmann), critical exegesis, hermeneutics in language-event (Gerhard Ebeling) or word-happening (Ernst Fuchs).[30] Paul Ricoeur in a contribution to this central problem develops the insight that for Freud dreams are a hermeneutic of human existence[31]; Wittgenstein has focused on linguistic analysis, while the American experience brings forth the languages of the computer and McLuhanese.

The "new hermeneutic" is not only a dominant theology of language, but for many it is theology itself (this is also true for some British theologians of linguistic analysis applied to theology). For Ebeling, theology is hermeneutic, the interpretation of God's Word to the world today, since the Word is prior

[30] For a survey of the New Hermeneutic, especially Ebeling and Fuchs, see *The New Hermeneutic,* eds. J. M. Robinson and John B. Cobb (New York, 1964).

[31] Paul Ricoeur, *De l'interprétation* (Paris, 1966); see Pierre Barthel, "L'interprétation *symbolique* des représentations d'origine et de structure mythiques par Paul Ricoeur," *Interprétation du language mythique et théologie biblique* (Leiden, 1967), pp. 287–382.

to grace. "The relation between faith and word in the process of understanding and interpretation is not a relation that moves from the subject to the word, but rather from the word to the understanding subject. Faith adds nothing new to the word, but is the becoming effective of the word as that which it claims to be—as God's Word."[32] With the new hermeneutic, the word must be effective, while the content and message has been demythologized to a positive affirmation of human existence and acceptance. What is handed on, the *traditum,* exists only as it is transmitted. The question of hermeneutic forms the focal point of theological problems today, Ebeling says. He goes on to show how this is true of all branches of theology from the Old Testament to missiology. Why? Because hermeneutics is translating the Bible's word so that it can be heard today. Tillich had already developed the correlation method for theology, but Ebeling's accent is on interpretation as the meaningful reading of the text by a subject, not on relating questioning man to a responding revelatory message. Ebeling can be freer with the remainder of the biblical kerygma and interpret it in what appears a more subjective way since actually both poles of his "correlation" are human interpretation.

Hermeneutic implies two closely related things: first, the Bultmannian personal, existential prior understanding which the believing reader brings to the text. The text will speak to him, interpret his existence in light of God's positive Word. Secondly, language is not an objectification of concepts which it reproduces computer-like, but, following Heidegger, a letting speak of man and some aspect of reality. Man is not reproducing reality in language but expressing himself; even more important, both man and being come to expression as language itself speaks. Language-events are words themselves in their original meaning born out of profound experience with reality and in their meaning in existential encounter. "The basic thing about a text is not what the author wants to express in words by developing his point of view. What is basic is what wills

[32] Ebeling, *Evangelische Evangelienauslegung* (1963), p. 382.

fundamentally to show itself and have its say prior to or apart from any subjective intent."[33]

The new hermeneutic goes beyond Bultmann in employing and applying Heidegger. For Ernst Fuchs our prior understanding is not so important. Reading the text interprets me now; the end, not the beginning of religious hermeneutic is self-interpretation; its means are encounters between contemporary man and the Word today. Hermeneutic is faith's doctrine of language, and language has become prior (as medium and as happening) to the preached and scriptural word, prior to human existence. Language, according to Heidegger and Fuchs, is a letting be; faith allows the word to show us how man should be, especially in relationship to God. "The fundamental question of theology is letting God be God."[34] This has both a positive and a negative side: letting God be before us in the Word, and letting God be truly godly, transcendent, ineffable. Fuchs agrees with Bultmann that language is directed to man and being is related to existence. But also, both being and man are directed to language, and through it to God. The Reformation was right that man does not have faith at his disposal. But the reason for this does not reside in the presence of sin, but prior to that, in the total dependence of faith on word, on God's Word.[35]

Gerhard Ebeling is interested in a new hermeneutic to preserve the basic role of hermeneutics, of word-event in the Reformation. In his excellent study of Luther he refers to the Reformer himself as a "language-event," and points out how the word, language, and the printed text were at the heart of the Reformation. The hermeneutic of the Reformation was *sola Scriptura*. Subsequent times have undermined this in the tension between dogma (past interpretation) and the word

---

[33] H. Franz, "Das Wesen des Textes," *Zeitschrift für Theologie und Kirche*, 59 (1962), p. 204; see M. Heidegger, *Unterwegs zur Sprache* (Pfullingen, 1954).

[34] E. Fuchs, *Hermeneutik* (Tübingen, 1958), p. 154.

[35] See E. Fuchs, *Studies of the Historical Jesus* (London, 1964).

itself. Can a fundamental *sola Scriptura* be preserved in the light of a hermeneutical demand to demythologize, or must hermeneutic discover that all is interpretation and nothing is word? Ebeling insists that the word itself is the ultimate hermeneutic, interpreting what Scripture will say to us. Scripture is not an object to understand but rather a stimulus to our religious understanding. Hermeneutic allows the word to speak to man today freed from the limitations of an historical text and removes, when necessary, obstacles which divide the word-event from communication. Reality is mediated to human personal understanding and existential encounter through word-events, happening now as we read the Scripture.

The real problem of theology, the problem which hermeneutics tries to solve, is the "connection between exposition of the text as proclamation that has taken place and the execution of the text in proclamation in the present."[36] Existential interpretation is for Ebeling the initial direction; it means an interpretation of the text by man before the word-event. Ebeling concludes that the word has primacy and hermeneutic is a faithful interpretation of it. As we saw, hermeneutic is theology itself. Before the mythical, hermeneutic can only demythologize. The word is not a word about God, making him a thing within or over against the world, but about man. Does God become a medium, an aspiration which helps man discover himself? "For God's Word is not various things, but one single thing—the word that makes man human by making him a believer, that is, a man who confesses to God as his future and therefore does not fail his fellow men in the one absolute and salutary thing, viz., the true word."[37] The purpose of the text is to be realized in preaching effectively to man. The content itself seems to be subservient to its destined impact. The hermeneutical principle is not form-criticism, not church authority, but man as conscience.[38]

[36] Ebeling, "The Word of God and Hermeneutic," *The New Hermeneutic*, p. 105.
[37] *Ibid.*, p. 97.
[38] *Ibid.*, p. 110.

242

Among the many post-Bultmannians, Heinrich Ott, professor of systematic theology at Basel, is unique. As a doctoral student he was a messenger of dialogue between his master, Karl Barth, and Bultmann, the director and subject of his doctoral dissertation. As we noted, Ott's initial works showed that Bultmann had utilized only a few early insights of Heidegger. Ott's theology is concerned with hermeneutic but also with the implications of existential-ontology; it is in knowledgeable dialogue with Bultmann and his students but retains the perspective of traditional Christian affirmation. A quite different, more ecumenical dialogue (in terms of appealing to the more traditional dimensions of Protestantism, and to Roman Catholicism) could be developed—as is now happening in a new upsurge of interest in Heidegger. His unique bridge position allows him to speak meaningfully to Catholics and Protestants, to be welcome as a co-worker by Rahner and Ebeling. Ott describes the new hermeneutical concern in these terms:

Rudolf Bultmann's outstanding contribution is to have confronted us with the problem of understanding so clearly and insistently that it has become perhaps the most important question in contemporary theology, the so-called "problem of hermeneutics." Bultmann's great and lasting achievement lies rather in his having taught us to see the problem as such. The decisive issue that divides the theologians is whether or not one has grasped the hermeneutical problem *as such*, whether one has been sufficiently impressed by its inevitability.

It is no accident that in our day it is precisely in theology that the problem of hermeneutic has appeared with particular urgency. For properly speaking, theology in its very essence is hermeneutics. . . . This understanding proceeds in a twofold direction: on the one hand, the correct understanding of the sources of the church's preaching, the biblical texts; on the other hand, the intelligibility of the sermon issuing out of these sources, both in itself and for its contemporary hearers. In both cases, however, what matters is the understanding of the kerygma. It is this which binds both aspects

243

closely together, so that, when seen in terms of the subject matter itself, they come in the final analysis to be one.[39]

Ott, remaining truer to Heidegger and Gadamer, introduces as important "the dimension of the object." Ott goes beyond the word-existence dichotomy of the other new hermeneuticians, and emphasizes the third point of the hermeneutical triangle, the reality expressed. "By means of the text we perceive the object which addresses the text as well as ourselves, and only in so doing do we genuinely come to understand the text as such. . . . If we wish to *understand* at all, then our concern must rather be with the relation of that past thinker to the object confronting him, an object which must be capable of becoming ours as well."[40] Following Ott's well-expressed insight, we can say that the biblical (and ecclesial) text does speak to us concretely but it speaks of a revelatory happening or word; its language speaks out of the milieu of a writer and a culture. While the word and language itself speaks, the word speaks a message not only to us but for us, and this message is both gleaned and encountered out of the horizon of history and language.

The Secular Future and God's Revealing Past

Bultmann, like Barth, remains a theologian of the word. Recently, theologians influenced by the weakness of words in our medium-overfilled culture and conscious of social perspectives have emphasized history, the future, the Western secular city.

Wolfhart Pannenberg describes how Bultmann's theological method of word and meaning and hermeneutic cannot really do justice to the hermeneutical problematic. Word and interpretation exist only with universal and personal history; hermeneutic

[39] H. Ott, "Language and Understanding," *Union Seminary Quarterly Review*, 21 (1966), pp. 275–76.
[40] *Ibid.*, p. 291.

does not interpret itself but that which is prior to understanding and interpretation.[41] He writes:

> Is this significance of Jesus's history recognizable from within itself? And is such a recognition already a knowledge of the revelation of God in him? Or is some supplementary explanation necessary, an explanation emerging out of faith in Jesus and not derivable from the bare facts of his story? . . . Most radically of all, Rudolf Bultmann carries out this distinction by relegating the early Christian Easter message totally to the significance side, describing it as the interpretation of Jesus' cross. . . . Such a splitting up of historical consciousness into a detection of facts and an evaluation of them (or into history as known and history as experienced) is intolerable to Christian faith, not only because the message of Jesus and of God's revelation in him necessarily becomes merely subjective interpretation, but also because it is the reflection of an outmoded and questionable historical method. . . . The reason for this is that the historical continuum within which an event has meaning also includes the present. But one may not arbitrarily attach whatever meaning one will to a given fact. Only when the original unity of event and meaning is grasped may the question of the historicity of Jesus' resurrection be properly raised again. For the event here in question can only be expressed in language of apocalyptic expectation, by the metaphorical phrase, resurrection from the dead, but nevertheless it was experienced as a concrete occurrence from without, not simply as a subjective experience.[42]

Both Barth and Bultmann viewed eschatology and history in terms of the presence of the transcendent and future in the present. Jürgen Moltmann sees God present only in his promises, only in hope. This allows Moltmann to affirm the realities of Christianity without objectifying or supranaturalizing

---

[41] W. Pannenberg, "Hermeneutic and Universal History," *Journal for Theology and Church*, 4 (1967).

[42] "The Revelation of God in Jesus," *Theology as History*, eds. J. M. Robinson and John B. Cobb (New York, 1967), pp. 127–28.

them, for we know God and Jesus Christ only in their future for us, in their coming to us. The God of Scripture cannot be possessed by us, yet he can be present to us in his promises and in his past and present action preparing faithfully his future.

Moltmann in his *Theology of Hope* raises two critical questions for Bultmann. First, Bultmann by making the questionableness of human existence and its authentic interpretation into the "governing question of revelation and salvation" sets limits on revelation and God. Self-understanding is not some special category which is prior to all conceptualization and religion, nor is it separate from a world-view, a religious content, which Bultmann says Christianity does not bring. Self-understanding is stimulated by content and is the other side of *Weltanschauung*. "Only in his outgoing towards the world does man experience himself. Without objectification no experience of oneself is possible."[43] Secondly, if revelation and faith and God's action for man are to be present only when man comes "to himself" in faith, then faith itself is the practical end of history and the believer is already perfected. Nothing more awaits him. Moltmann points out clearly Bultmann's overemphasis on realized eschatology, on subjective dialogue between man and God, on the limitations placed by considering salvation history, saving event, man in terms of human hermeneutic.[44] Moltmann observes that the message of the New Testament is radically different. If something does happen to man in faith and love, it is in terms of what has happened and will happen in Jesus Christ; he is the Messiah who has come and the Son of man who will come again.

[43] J. Moltmann, *The Theology of Hope* (New York, 1967), pp. 67–68.

[44] Heidegger cannot be blamed for stimulating an isolated word-theology. For him, man is the hermeneutic of Being; language functions hermeneutically in both. There is a difference between Bultmann's omnipresent existential hermeneutical function (which judges all things human and divine), and Heidegger's *Dasein* which is concrete existential life where reality and language reveal truth. Human reflection in terms of human existence is not the same as existential understanding cut loose from history.

J. B. Metz agrees with Bultmann that ideas such as heaven and the "next life" have little influence on the kind of man emerging in today's world. Man no longer discovers the vestiges of the Creator but the potentialities of men. "What moves the men of our time most deeply is not the encounter with the super-worldly but the encounter with the future. This future calls loudly and meaningfully to this man who seems so much the demythologizer, so a-religious. . . . The primacy of the future is unmistakable."[45] Like Moltmann, Metz points out that the Bible is an "encyclopedia" of the future. The Old and New Israels are characterized by their hope. Nor does Christ bring an end to hope; rather, he announces a new era which he has begun by his life, death, and Resurrection. But this era is still between the times, already and not yet. It will end with Christ coming again. Metz says strikingly: "Christian theology is above all a *theologia negativa* of the future."[46]

With this intersection of theologies of the future and of secularism we attain the point of view which allows us to see correctly Bultmann's influence. There are two kinds of "secular theology" (abstracting from other divisions such as radical and orthodox, Roman Catholic and Protestant). There is a theology which approaches the process of secularization and contemporary man from the point of view of the individual and his existence (in the Heideggerian sense); this is the theology of Bultmann, Tillich, Van Buren, Ogden, and the Post-Bultmannians, and can be legitimately called European (or even German). Is it capable now, in the light of the emergence of social revolution, of really going beyond Bultmann? The other, subsequent approach leads through society, through contemporary social, political, economic, and mental (e.g. communications) systems and thought-forms; it finds its pioneer in Harvey Cox, is American, and builds upon its recent and incipient foundations to become the theological wave of the future.[47] These two, existential and the social,

[45] J. B. Metz, "Experientia Spei," *Diakonia,* 1 (1966), 186–189.
[46] *Ibid.*
[47] A. H. Richardson, *Towards an American Theology* (New York, 1967).

do meet in Moltmann and Metz. The theological perspective of eschatology and future liberates them from the past frameworks of word and existence, but it still does not fully introduce the revolution and vitality of contemporary society as experienced and engaged right now, especially in the United States. As much as they call for a "political theology," this seems to be very difficult for them to develop, while the coming of age of American theologies tends repeatedly in this direction.

It is clear that Bultmann's work has little social or ecclesial dimension. Yet the deepest questioning for most Christian churches and groups is the renewal of the institutions of the church. Do the churches have in their sources the creativity for a new pluralism of effective structures? This renewal questions the present expression of church authority and mission in theology and structure. It recognizes the church as ecumenical, as pluralistic in structures and theologies (but not in faith), as servant and Christian rather than authoritarian and political. Those who resist the Spirit's call to renewal—a call echoed by the Spirit's paradoxical agent, the world—will ossify and die bringing their church down with them. The theologians mentioned above and others in whom an American, social, and progress-oriented mentality is imbedded have an enormous task ahead of them. Now it is not enough for their theology and church to reflect the culture. They must be environment-creative, and yet transcend the establishment, the core of every society. Like its master, whose mystical body it is, the church is faced with the agony of truly reflecting his paradoxical being, to be both Suffering Servant in the world and to be Word for the world under the Spirit and God the Father.

The words "Bultmannian" and "post-Bultmannian" obscure the task of theology. They imply too much and too little. As we enter the last third of this century we see that Bultmann more than Barth is the prophet, but much less than Barth is he the theologian. In the last analysis *who* is Bultmannian, what school or church or faculty agrees totally with his major conclusions? Rudolf Bultmann is the prophet of encounter between the New Testament and the secular precisely as existential and anthropocentric. In this sense he is as Kantian as he is Lutheran. He influences theology for the same reasons that Kant, Kierkegaard, and Heidegger do, because theology has not taken seriously (which is different from radically) the anthropocentric revolutions of Luther, Kant, Freud and Jung. Bultmann now joined by many others demands that Christian theology not be philosophy, that God not be man, and yet that theology be immersed in the blessed complexity of man and in the fruitful mutability of history.

Man is learning that he and his history realize their power only when they strain forward, freely yet obediently in the tide of cosmic, anthropocentric, Christocentric evolution. When man realizes believing, hopeful, and suffering transcendence precisely through his humanity, he becomes a man. That is why there is a definitive messenger of God's grace for him, why the universe groans for it, why man becomes man by allowing God in Christ to make him more than man. Man is within the world; he is not just a mind; he needs not only the word but history. This is why Paul's preaching was and still is real history, and why two decades after Jesus' life Paul could write seriously, distinguishing the employed myths from the words of hope:

> For we would not have you ignorant, brothers, concerning those who are asleep, that you may not grieve as others do who have no hope. For since we believe that Jesus died and rose again, even so, through Jesus, God will bring with him those who have fallen asleep. For this we declare to you by the word of the Lord . . . (1 Thes. 4:13–15).

INDEX

251

253

Qumran, 151 ff.

Rahner, K., 25 f., 48, 188, 221, 224, 230, 236
Reformation, Protestant, 41, 241
Resurrection, 57, 60 f., 65, 123 f., 132, 181–183, 220
Revelation, 45, 108, 120, 127 ff., 179 ff., 190, 228, 246
Richardson, H., 248
Richardson, W. J., 229
Ricoeur, P., 239
Riesenfeld, H., 62
Robinson, James M., 238
Robinson, John A. T., 22

Sacraments, 97 ff., 151–166
Schweitzer, A., 237
Secularization, 24, 245 ff.
Schillebeeckx, E., 226–228, 236
Schleiermacher, F., 197
Schlier, H., 20, 23
Schürmann, H., 62
Sin, 129

Theodore of Mopsuestia, 17, 52
Theology, 23 ff., 29, 33 ff., 72 ff.
American, 24 ff., 29, 247 ff.

dialectical, 19 f., 223 f., 237
French, contemporary, 24
Lutheran, 41, 114, 125, 162, 195, 248
pastoral, 25 f.
Protestant liberalism, 17 f.
word, 223 f., 239 ff., 244
Thérèse of Lisieux, 143
Thurneysen, E., 19
Tillich, P., 16, 19 f., 25, 237
Trinity, 189, 221

Urs von Balthasar, H., 42

Vatican Council II, 15, 16, 26
Virgin birth, 182

Welte, B., 207, 221
Weil, S., 147
Weiss, J., 16
Word of God, 82 ff., 119, 130 ff., 161, 186–188, 193 ff., 221, 239
Words of Jesus, 60, 62 ff., 75 f.
World, 142, 187
the Church in dialogue with, 25 f., 222, 236, 247 (see Secularization)

Xenophanes, 51